W9-BZB-654

Incursion

ALSO BY J. D. COLEMAN

Pleiku: The Dawn of Helicopter Warfare in Vietnam

Incursion

From America's Chokehold on
the NVA Lifelines to the Sacking of
the Cambodian Sanctuaries

J. D. COLEMAN

St. Martin's Press

New York

INCURSION. Copyright © 1991 by J. D. Coleman. All rights reserved. Printed in the United States of America. No part of this book may be used or reproduced in any manner whatsoever without written permission except in the case of brief quotations embodied in critical articles or reviews. For information, address St. Martin's Press, 175 Fifth Avenue, New York, N.Y. 10010.

Editor: Jared Kieling
Production Editor: Mark H. Berkowitz
Copyeditor: Dan Otis
Proofreader: Bruce Kamiat
Design by Susan Hood
© Maps by John D. Talbott and Associates

Library of Congress Cataloging-in-Publication Data

Coleman, J. D.
Incursion : from America's chokehold on the NVA lifelines to the sacking of
the Cambodian sanctuaries.
p.   cm.
ISBN 0-312-05877-2
1. Vietnamese Conflict, 1961–1975—Campaigns—Cambodia.
I. Title.
DS557.8.C3C65   1991   959.704′33596—dc20   90-27505

First Edition: August 1991
1   3   5   7   9   10   8   6   4   2

With Love
to
MADELINE
Kathleen
Darrell
Roger
Michelle
Joseph

CONTENTS

viii   *Contents*

MAPS

FOREWORD

General John R. Galvin
Supreme Allied Commander, Europe

The Vietnam War lives on in contemporary literature. It has become a kaleidoscope, constantly turning, producing new patterns, illuminations, and perceptions depending on how the pieces fall together for the writer.

Because of the elusive nature of the conflict, writers' points of view can differ greatly and can change as time passes. It was a different war at different times and places. No two periods of the conflict were alike. Veterans of the same unit who served at separate times could have completely dissimilar experiences, depending on where they operated and what missions they undertook during their terms of service. Frequently, those who returned after an absence to the fighting in Vietnam found themselves surprised by completely new situations. It is no wonder that the literature on the war is so varied, so multifaceted.

In this book, J. D. Coleman comes closer to a clear perspective on the nature of the American military involvement in Vietnam than I have seen before. He offers an accurate view of one segment of the war by focusing on a specific unit at a particular place and time—the U.S. 1st Cavalry Division in central Vietnam and Cambodia from late 1968 to 1970. By recounting the decisions made by the highest levels of American civilian and military leadership and exploring the consequences of those decisions on the tactics pursued in Vietnam, Coleman traces the events that molded the actions of American soldiers in a unit they proudly referred to as "the First Team."

We meet the commanders, the troops, and the enemy. We see how public opinion in the United States affects the political direction of the war in Southeast Asia. We see how military leaders alter their tactics—for better or worse; how perceptions of the combatants change as they learn of the decisions to gradually disengage U.S. forces and "Vietnamize" the war; how the North Vietnamese and the Viet Cong redesign their methods of operation to capitalize on American vulnerabilities—tactical, political, and psychological—while remaining vulnerable themselves to devastating U.S. firepower. We meet the generals, their subordinate commanders, and their staffs as they think and fight their way through battle after battle. And most importantly, we meet the American soldier who—though buffeted by the rigors of a harsh environment, exposed repeatedly to determined enemy fire, vilified by many of his countrymen, and faced by the merciless reality that only incapacitation or a seemingly ever-distant calendar date can free him from his jungle ordeal—does his duty unstintingly.

In the aftermath of the bloody Tet offensive and operations in relief of Khe Sanh, the 1st Cav moves south into the area where the North Vietnamese and Viet Cong have staged a rapid buildup. In the wild country of the Cambodian frontier northwest of Saigon, along an arc 150 kilometers wide and 45 kilometers deep, the Sky Soldiers are inserted to interdict infiltration routes from Cambodia to the Viet Cong base areas around the capital. At home public support for the war has waned; in the field, the fighting remains bitter.

Coleman gives an authoritative, accurate account of the events and men who defined these times. What emerges is a compelling story. In the classic tradition of unit histories well told, the author brings us to the realization that from the soldier's perspective this was a war much like any other Americans have fought.

Harsh and unrelenting, the war took American soldiers into the misery of combat. Young men fought because their country asked them to. They believed in their cause—but most of all they believed in each other. Their leaders—some good, some bad—applied their trade as best they knew how, adapting tactics and doctrine to the conditions of the day.

In the end, the units and their soldiers moved on—not all of the latter on their feet. In the mud and jungle of Southeast Asia they did their best; they gave it all they had. In so doing, they take their rightful place beside their forebears—honored sons, husbands, and fathers. Their country and its citizens are forever in their debt.

Coleman knows Vietnam combat from firsthand experience and writes in a graphic, arresting style. Some of his passages are so true to the battlefields of those days that many a veteran, reading them, will feel again those emotions that fade but never disappear. He has done us good service in preserving the realities of a war that those of us who fought in are still trying to understand.

PREFACE

Throughout this narrative of the interdiction campaign in III Corps that culminates with the incursion into Cambodia in May 1970, accounts of the movements and activities of the North Vietnamese Army (NVA) are interspersed with reports on concurrent actions by the American forces. Since the end of the war, several former NVA and Viet Cong military commanders have produced memoirs, but these generally tend to be self-serving documents of little value to a battlefield historian. On the other hand, intelligence gathering had reached a fairly high level of sophistication by late 1968. By using field intelligence reports, I have been able to track the movements and even the people involved in the action.

In the case of information regarding American units, the National Archives in Washington fairly bulge with documents about the units involved in the war, and I tracked down and interviewed many of the participants.

I was privileged to have served in the 1st Air Cavalry Division from April 12, 1969, until April 15, 1970. Although only a major in rank, my position of information officer permitted me to move freely throughout the Cav's area of operations and interact with most of the principals. I frequently flew with the general officers of the division and learned their impressions of the campaign. I obtained many of the quotations that appear in this book firsthand during and immediately after the battles. Other quotes are from interviews conducted over the past two-and-a-half years. I also relied heavily on the published accounts of the battles that appeared in the Cav's weekly newspaper.

The text has not been footnoted, and deliberately so, because footnotes interrupt the narrative flow. Quotations from books and publications are carefully credited as such. In no case in this book have accounts been fictionalized to improve the story line. What you read is what happened, and I have portrayed it with as much historical accuracy as is humanly possible. Historians who wish to examine facts or events in greater detail can contact the author at P.O. 1592, Kalispell, MT 59903.

Opinions about policy, strategy, and tactics, unless attributed, are of course solely those of the author.

ACKNOWLEDGMENTS

No book that requires extensive research and interviewing can take shape without the assistance of countless individuals who share their experiences, memories, and memorabilia. For this book, it would take pages and pages just to name them, so to them collectively, I express my sincere thanks. There are, however, some people whose contribution was critical and who should be mentioned individually.

A very special note of gratitude at the outset goes to General John R. Galvin for taking time to read the manuscript and write the Foreword. This is an extremely critical period for our republic as well as the NATO alliance. That General Galvin could spare some moments from his responsibilities as Supreme Allied Commander, Europe, to pen this Foreword is both gratifying and humbling.

Maps are essential tools for a military historian, and when a map of a Vietnam battle area is still marked with the precise locations of fire support bases, its worth is incalculable. My thanks to Dick Wood, former commander of the 2nd Battalion, 8th Cavalry, and division G-3, for the loan of the map and some other great research material.

During the interview process, I kept hearing about a superb monograph written by Captain John Hottell about the battle of Binh Long, but I could never locate a copy until an old friend, Colonel Jimmie Leach, came riding to the rescue in proper tanker fashion. Chapters Nine and Ten would not have been written without his help.

Matt Brennan, who probably knows as much as anybody about the 1st Squadron, 9th Cavalry, the 1st Air Cav Division's reconnaissance unit, graciously shared with me many of the stories that eventually became his third book on the 9th.

A double note of thanks to John Talbott, a lieutenant with the 1st Battalion, 7th Cavalry, in 1969 and early 1970. The maps in this book are his handiwork, and they took hours of his leisure time. He also had a shoebox full of photographs that beautifully filled some pictorial gaps. On the subject of pictures, thanks also to a former 1st Cav grunt and photographer, Dean Sharp, for digging out some old negatives and printing me several dozen pictures from which to choose.

I relied heavily on a monograph entitled *The Shield and the Hammer* written by the 14th Military History Detachment of the 1st Air Cav Division. Great reliance, too, was placed on the stories written by Cav reporters that appeared in the division's weekly newspaper, the *Cavalair*, or the quarterly magazine, *The First Team*. The team of Information Office folks who put the division's big history book together also gets a pat on the back.

Midway through the research and writing of this book I became ill. I missed the deadline for the manuscript by a substantial margin. I deeply appreciate the patience and forebearance of Jared Kieling, senior editor at St. Martin's, during this trying period. A special note of gratitude goes to my agent, Ethan Ellenberg, who took the time to read some chapters written during my recuperation period and reassured me that the illness had not appreciably eroded my writing skills. Thanks also to copyeditor Dan Otis and proofreader Bruce Kamiat, whose sharp pencils markedly improved the final product.

Finally, I must acknowledge the contributions of my wife, Madeline. Far too many leisure-time activities were missed because a husband had to devote all his available spare time to "the book." And then she doubled as a sounding board, critic, and editor as the manuscript took shape.

J. D. Coleman
Atlanta, Georgia
December 16, 1990

PROLOGUE

May 1, 1970, dawned gray and soggy after an all-night rain along the Vietnam-Cambodia border. Wisps of jungle mist rose from the tangles of underbrush, up through the canopy of trees, to disperse in the still morning air. Then, without warning, the quiet was shattered by the thunderous roar of B-52 strikes; the awesome blasts violently ripping asunder the jungle and its inhabitants. The echoes of the explosions had hardly died when massive artillery preparatory fire churned the ground. These barrages were followed by tactical air strikes and then by the rockets and miniguns of helicopter gunships.

If it had been 1967, such events could have been the start of another massive multibattalion search-and-destroy mission. But this was 1970, and the armored and infantry force under the command of Task Force Shoemaker that soon clanked across an international boundary became, officially, the first Americans to operate offensively in Cambodia. And later in the morning, when Specialist Fourth Class Terry Hayes of Charlie Company, 2nd Battalion, 7th Cavalry, of the American 1st Air Cavalry Division, jumped off the skids of the lead assault helicopter, he became officially the first American to combat-assault into the previously sacrosanct NVA base areas in Cambodia.

Thus began the most controversial military operation of the Vietnam War. Few who participated in the campaign, whether general or grunt, doubted that the decision to cross the border

1

into Cambodia was both wise and just. The American soldiers who had withstood repeated blows from North Vietnamese regular army soldiers and then watched helplessly as they disappeared, wraithlike, into the sanctuaries of Cambodia had few reservations about the morality of the invasion. Even today, twenty years after the fact, former soldiers interviewed for this book were unequivocal when asked whether they would do it again. The answer, invariably, was "Hell, yes."

But at the time, particularly in the United States, the issue was less clear, and within hours of President Richard Nixon's rather apocalyptic announcement of the operation, demonstrations had begun on college campuses. In less than six days the protest against the administration, the war in general, and the Cambodian incursion in particular had shut down many of the nation's colleges. The most notorious event took place on May 4, when four students died in a fusillade of National Guard gunfire on the Kent State campus. Within weeks, the antiwar movement, virtually moribund throughout early 1970, rallied and became a force for the administration to reckon with in the years ahead—a force, it must be added, whose influence was out of proportion to the numbers it could muster. As we shall see, it was a force that was increasingly exploited by Hanoi.

The tactical, strategic, and political trails leading to Cambodia were nearly as long as the war itself. Hanoi's use of Cambodia as a sanctuary had been a problem for American forces as early as November 1965, when the 1st Air Cavalry had defeated a North Vietnamese division in the valley of the Ia Drang and then watched in frustration as the survivors headed for their Cambodian base camps for untroubled rest and refit. In those days, so-called Cambodian neutrality was protected as zealously by American politicians and diplomats as it was by Prince Norodom Sihanouk, the head of the Cambodian state. In 1966, Major General Stanley "Swede" Larsen, commander of American forces in the Central Highlands, after observing to reporters that the enemy had fled to Cambodia to escape annihilation, had had his knuckles rapped by the White House, the State Department, and the Pentagon. He had to experience the humiliation of standing in front of network film crews and declaring, "I stand corrected. The enemy did not escape into Cambodia."

In the early days of the war, the communists controlled so much territory in South Vietnam, they had no need to develop extensive base areas in Cambodia. For example, in South Vietnam's Military Region III, the eleven-province area surrounding Saigon's Capital Military District, the Viet Cong and NVA had extensive base areas within fifteen miles of Saigon. There were, to be sure, some developed sanctuaries in Cambodia and a series of way stations at the terminus of the Ho Chi Minh Trail, but the significant storehouses were concealed in the jungles surrounding Saigon. Early in the war, the major headquarters for the communists who operated in the lower half of South Vietnam (Military Regions III and IV) was known to Hanoi as the B-3 Front as well as the Central Office for South Vietnam (COSVN) and was situated somewhere in the vastness of War Zone C, east of Tay Ninh.

This situation began to change with the introduction of American troops, who started cleaning out the caches and redoubts around the South Vietnamese capital. Then, in early 1967, the United States Military Assistance Command, Vietnam (MACV), mounted several major, multibattalion operations in the provinces north of Saigon. In January, Operation Cedar Falls was aimed against a Viet Cong stronghold just twenty-five miles north of Saigon known as the Iron Triangle. From February 22 until May 14, Operation Junction City, a twenty-six-battalion drive into War Zone C in Tay Ninh Province, uncovered numerous caches and inflicted 2,728 casualties. Even though allied forces did not physically occupy territory in War Zone C, U.S. forces' potential to repeatedly make incursions into War Zones C and D convinced COSVN that some of the previously inviolate base areas might be a good deal more secure in Cambodia. This was particularly so for tactical and political headquarters. And so COSVN moved from War Zone C to the vicinity of the "Fishhook" area of Cambodia.

The Cambodian sanctuaries played a crucial role in the communists' staging of the 1968 Tet Offensive, considered by most historians to be the turning point of the Vietnam War. Despite the notoriety of Tet, inaccuracies in accounts about it are almost as numerous as its casualties. Because the news media badly misreported the Tet Offensive in the early hours and then refused to correct their mistakes, in the months following Tet most Americans believed that the communists staged a single go-for-broke offensive aimed at South Vietnam's cities and, while Hanoi didn't achieve all of its combat objectives, it was compensated by an enormous psychological victory in the United States. Contrary to these lugubrious pronouncements by the media, the communists had their clocks cleaned during the February 28 to March 5 phase of their offensive, the first of four planned phases. Moreover, there is not a shred of evidence that the North Vietnamese Politburo had the psychological climate of the United States in mind when it laid down the basic parameters for what it called *Tong Cong Kich, Tong Khai Nghai* (TCK-TKN) (General Offensive, General Uprising).

Although many of the elite Viet Cong military units, which had spearheaded the assaults into the cities, had been decimated, the communist forces in South Vietnam had enough punch to execute Phase Two of their offensive, the so-called Mini-Tet of May 1968. This time, because of the large number of senior Viet Cong officers who had defected to the government of Vietnam, the allies knew when and where the blows would strike. And, once again, the Viet Cong units, the southerners, suffered terrible losses.

Even though the communist force structure had been weakened, having lost 170,000 casualties and 40,000 weapons of all types during the first two phases of the offensive, COSVN and Hanoi were determined to press on with the third phase of TCK-TKN. COSVN issued Resolution No. 7, which called for another countrywide offensive in August. Again, the allies were not surprised; attempts to penetrate into Saigon failed utterly, and the pure Viet Cong forces took another beating.

In July 1968, General William Westmoreland turned over command of MACV to General Creighton Abrams, who had been serving as Westy's deputy commander for the previous year. With Abrams came an immediate shift in American field operations strategy.

At the time the command transition was taking place, the Ho Chi Minh Trail, despite unrelenting bombing by the U.S. Air Force of the trial complex in Laos, was still spewing out men and materiel at an alarming rate. Additionally, an enormous amount of arms and ammunition was pouring into the VC and NVA base areas from the port of Sihanoukville in Cambodia. By September 1968, Hanoi was well into in the process of replenishing with northerners the Viet Cong main-force units lost during the first three phases of the TCK-TKN offensive. The master plan for TCK-TKN called for a fourth phase to be conducted as soon as the units were prepared.

Thus, in the "Parrot's Beak" area of Cambodia just west of Saigon, the 9th Viet Cong Division had been transformed almost totally into a North Vietnamese Regular Army division. The VC 5th Division, now also manned by the soldiers who came down from North Vietnam, was operating in and around War Zone D northeast of Saigon, while the NVA 7th Division was working out of base areas in southern War Zone C. These three presented a formidable threat to the U.S. bases in MR III and to Saigon itself. Even though much of the VC infrastructure had been destroyed during Tet, and despite the intensified pacification efforts that followed, large chunks of the countryside still belonged to the communists. Much of this area was being used by the NVA to "prepare the battlefield"; the careful pre-stocking of weapons, ammunition and food caches, medical aid stations, and the like.

This process was what General Creighton Abrams termed pushing the enemy's logistical nose out in front of his combat force. Abrams's concept was to cut off this nose, orienting on the enemy's systems rather than simply his combat units. This concept represented a fundamental change in American strategy. In an issue of *Time* magazine, a reporter wrote about this change: "Where Westmoreland was a search-and-destroy and count-the-bodies man, Abrams proved to be an interdict and weigh-the-rice man."

Although the first real test of Abrams's interdiction strategy came in the provinces around Saigon, the northernmost provinces of Vietnam—the area known as I Corps—was not overlooked. Marine Major General Raymond A. Davis, a Medal of Honor winner in Korea, who had taken over the Marine 3rd Division, was an avid advocate of the interdiction strategy. He previously had put in a stint as deputy to Lieutenant General William B. Rosson, the commander of the multiservice Provisional Corps that had been created by Westmoreland to counter the NVA threat in I Corps. Abrams, Rosson, and Davis, who had worked together during the Tet Offensive, were totally in synch about digging out the enemy's entrenched systems. The Marines' Operation Dewey Canyon in January 1969 was fundamentally an interdiction campaign.

In late summer 1968, MACV intelligence had confirmed that North Vietnam had moved one of its regular army divisions, the 1st NVA, down from the northern battlefields and had positioned it in the Fishhook area of Cambodia. The addition of this division to the communist order of battle in MR III alarmed MACV and convinced General Abrams that the communists had elected to make Military Region III their primary theater of operations. He recognized that the propaganda value of another thrust into Saigon, combined with the capture of a province headquarters city close to the South Vietnamese capital, would be substantially greater than NVA successes in or around the Demilitarized Zone (DMZ).

Abrams already had quietly closed down the Khe Sanh combat base and directed the Marines to abandon the little "beau geste" forts along the Demilitarized Zone, which tied up enormous assets in a futile attempt to block NVA egress into northern I Corps. General Davis happily complied and began a mobile defense of the DMZ, a more effective operation in terms of resources.

But the presence of the 1st NVA Division in MR III provided the urgency for the transfer of the 1st Air Cavalry Division from Quang Tri, the northernmost province in South Vietnam, to the provinces north of Saigon in MR III. The Cav began battling North Vietnamese in early November, 1968, initially fighting to keep the NVA from attacking Saigon. After the threat subsided, the Cav began a methodical campaign of interdiction, cutting the supply routes from the Cambodia bases while driving the NVA units out of Vietnam. Meanwhile, as the interdiction battles along Vietnam's borders raged, the intensified pacification program in the populated areas was accelerating with a combined force of American and Vietnamese units. The Vietnamese force modernization program, initiated by Defense Secretary Clark Clifford in late 1968 and continued under the title of "Vietnamization" by Clifford's sucessor, Melvin Laird, had been embraced by General Abrams, and was progressing with mixed results.

Sir Robert Thompson, in his *No Exit from Vietnam*, had drawn a blueprint of the correct way to fight and win the war. Abrams's strategy in late 1968 and later appears to have been a very close approximation of the Thompson blueprint, and for the twenty months covered by this book, in MR III at least, everyone was doing it right and the enemy was losing.

The gains were impressive, but few outside the American command recognized it. Certainly few knew it in the news media, which long since had abandoned reporting what units and soldiers accomplished in Vietnam in favor of trying to determine what the soldiers were thinking. Reporters swarmed over Vietnam seeking the soldiers' reaction to a laundry list of issues ranging from the Paris peace talks—including the shape of the negotiating table—through every conceivable aspect of the antiwar movement in the United States, to the viability of the Nixon Doctrine. Media reports, followed by the instant histories that proliferated during the latter stages of the war, fostered many myths that over twenty years have been elevated to the level of great truths. Among the myths that will be examined in this book are that Viet Cong and North Vietnamese soldiers and tactics were superior to those of the Americans and that this superiority led to a military defeat for the United States. Most serious historians, while they usually are critical of the overall political and strategic direction of the war, generally agree that the American armed forces fought extremely well. Those who were most intimately acquainted with the shot and shell of the war—the men who fought the battles—know who won the shooting war. They have far more respect for the tough young soldiers they faced on the battlefield than for the bureaucrats who bungled the political and diplomatic war.

Today, nearly every history of the Vietnam War, regardless of the author's orientation, slides through the twenty-eight months between Tet-68 and the Cambodian incursion in May 1970 as though that period was a relatively insignificant interlude. The year 1969, in particular, seems to have disappeared as if it were of little consequence. As far as Vietnam is concerned, 1969 is chiefly remembered for the Paris peace talks, the Nixon/Kissinger diplomatic initiatives, Hamburger Hill, Nixon's decision to unilaterally withdraw American combat forces, the increased visibility of the radical left and antiwar movement, the My Lai revelations, and Ho Chi Minh's death.

Few people are aware that General Creighton Abrams's strategy of interdiction, in combination with William Colby's pacification program, was as successful as it was. A strong case could be made that had Abrams been in command in 1967 and instituted his campaign of interdiction and pacification early in that year, the communists would never have gotten the Tet Offensive off the ground. How General Abrams's strategy of interdiction was executed and how it led inexorably to the Cambodian sanctuaries is the great untold story of the Vietnam War.

This book attempts to fill that historical gap. In the 1st Air Cavalry Division, whose role in the interdiction campaign in MR III is the centerpiece of this book, its young soldiers (and they were really just boys) beat the NVA like a drum. By March 1970, the Cav had clamped a stranglehold on every one of the VC and NVA infiltration routes, including some that stretched from Cambodia to the suburbs of Saigon. The 1st Air Cavalry Division, with the 11th Armored Cavalry Regiment and the ARVN Airborne Division, had driven the main-force NVA units back across the border and flat-out owned the jungle. From Tay Ninh on the west to Bu Gia Map on the east there was a belt 150 kilometers wide and 50 kilometers deep where NVA and VC soldiers ventured only at great risk.

The vast enemy storehouses in War Zones C and D had been rooted out, the caches picked clean, and the flow of materiel and food backed up into the Cambodian base areas like floodwaters behind a great dam. Without the Cav's interdiction campaign in 1969 and early 1970, there would have been no big Cambodian base areas, and the raison d'être for the May 1970 Cambodian incursion would not have existed.

For the 1st Air Cavalry, the road to the Cambodian sanctuaries began in late October 1968.

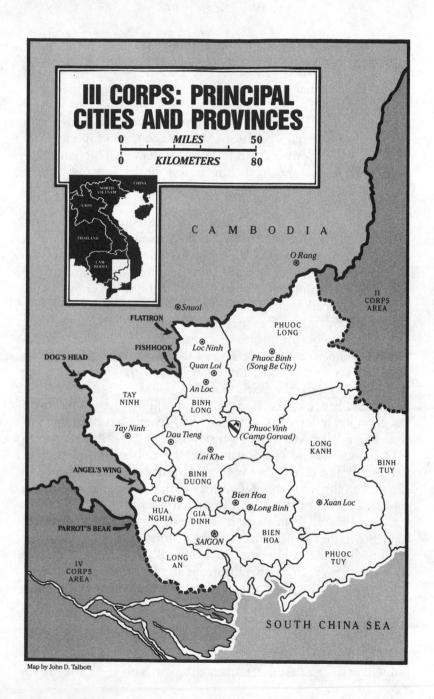

III CORPS: PRINCIPAL CITIES AND PROVINCES

MILES 0 — 50

KILOMETERS 0 — 80

CHINA

NORTH VIETNAM

LAOS

THAILAND

CAM-BODIA

CAMBODIA

O Rang

II CORPS AREA

Snuol

FLATIRON

FISHHOOK

Loc Ninh

PHUOC LONG

DOG'S HEAD

Quan Loi

Phuoc Binh (Song Be City)

An Loc

TAY NINH

BINH LONG

Tay Ninh

Dau Tieng

Phuoc Vinh (Camp Gorvad)

LONG KANH

Lai Khe

BINH TUY

ANGEL'S WING

BINH DUONG

Cu Chi

Bien Hoa

Long Binh

Xuan Loc

HUA NGHIA

GIA DINH

PARROT'S BEAK

SAIGON

BIEN HOA

IV CORPS AREA

LONG AN

PHUOC TUY

SOUTH CHINA SEA

Map by John D. Talbott

9

GEOGRAPHIC SKETCH

The III Corps Tactical Zone, also known as Military Region (MR) III, consisted of eleven provinces surrounding Saigon, and was roughly the size of the combined square mileage of New Hampshire and Vermont. The region was uniquely suited as a test area for General Creighton Abrams's concept of interdiction warfare. Coincidentally, the terrain and demographic composition of III Corps also made the region ideal as an operational area for the communists, the southern insurgents as well as the invading northerners.

Saigon, of course, was the capital of the Republic of Vietnam, which made it a choice target for the armed forces of the Viet Cong and North Vietnamese. The provinces immediately surrounding Saigon were heavily populated and thus provided an excellent recruiting and support base for the insurgency. Three of the provincial capitals, Tay Ninh City (Tay Ninh Province), An Loc (Binh Long Province), and Song Be City, sometimes known as Phuoc Binh (Phuoc Long Province), were easily accessible from Cambodia or any of the major base areas within MR III, yet were located far enough from the Saigon defense forces to preclude easy reinforcement.

With only a few exceptions the terrain in MR III was flat, with an elevation differential of perhaps fifty-five meters from the Saigon River deltas to the river's headwaters in the Fishhook region of Cambodia. The exceptions were the rolling hill country in eastern Phuoc Long Province and northeastern Long Khanh Province, the southern terminus of the Annamite mountain chain; a ten-kilometer ridge line called the Razorback just north of the Michelin Plantation in northern Binh Duong Province; and two rather spectacular terrain features—Nui Ba Den and Nui Ba Ra. Nui Ba Den was the fabled "Black Virgin" Mountain that spread over ten square kilometers and soared some 986 meters off the jungle floor just a few kilometers northeast of Tay Ninh City. Slightly smaller but still imposing, Nui Ba Ra was a 723-meter mountain just outside Song Be City in Phuoc Long Province.

The major waterways in the region were the Saigon River, which flows south from Cambodia past Saigon to the South

China Sea, and the Dong Nai River, which flows from the east through Long Khanh and Bien Hoa provinces and joins the Saigon on its trip to the sea just south of the capital city. Another river that influenced how the war was fought in the region was the Vam Co Dong, with headwaters in Cambodia west of Tay Ninh City, which flowed southeast through Hau Nghia and Long An provinces. These major rivers were fed by hundreds of small streams that wound through the region. Almost all were navigable year-round to the sampans and shallow-draft boats that the communists used to infiltrate supplies.

The roadways in the region radiated out of Saigon like spokes in a wheel. The principal highways involved in the campaign depicted in this book were National Highway (QL) 1, QL 13, QL 14, and QL 22. There were, in addition, numerous provincial roads, but many were dirt-surfaced and fit for heavy vehicles only during the dry season.

Military Region III was influenced by the southwest monsoon, which generally began in early June. The winter dry season ran from November through April. October and May were transition months with unpredictable weather patterns.

Although the areas immediately north of Saigon—the Iron Triangle, Boi Loi Woods, Ho Bo Woods, and the Trapezoid— once were considered formidable base areas, continued allied operations in and around those zones had, by late 1968, reduced their effectiveness as major cache and troop-billeting areas. They still continued to harbor the maze of tunnels that came to be known as the tunnels of Cu Chi and that were among the first targets of Abrams's campaign to "get into the enemy's system." The U.S. 1st and 25th divisions had their hands full eliminating these storehouses, which were so close to Saigon.

At the time covered by this book, two huge base areas remained almost immune to allied action—War Zones C and D.

One hundred kilometers northwest of Saigon, in an isolated corner of III Corps bordered on two sides by Cambodia, lay a vast jungle area known as War Zone C. To the north and east of Saigon, occupying portions of Phuoc Long, Long Khanh, Binh Duong, and Bien Hoa provinces, was War Zone D. These two great base areas combined were equivalent in size and accessibility to the Florida Everglades. Neither war zone had any population center, and occupied hamlets were virtually nonexistant, but both held secret areas where large troop units could hide, rest, and retrain. Additionally, there were enormous storehouses that fed, clothed, and armed the communist armed forces. Abrams's strategy was deceptively simple—destroy the base areas and you concurrently eliminate the armed threat of the VC and NVA.

Map by John D. Talbott

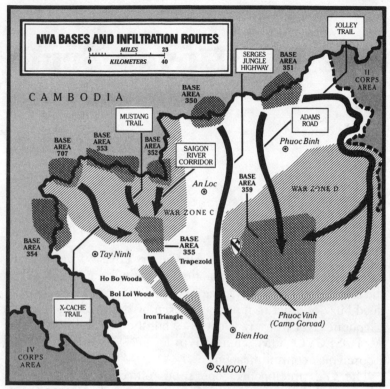

Map by John D. Talbott

Major communist base areas in III Corps in operation when the 1st Air Cavalry
Division was deployed to the region in November 1968. The infiltration routes
were discovered sequentially. The Cav initially targeted the Saigon River Corridor
and the Serges Jungle Highway. The Mustang Trail was discovered in early 1969,
as was the X-Cache Trail. Later in 1969, the Adams Road was interdicted, but
the Jolley Trail was not discovered until December 1969.

1

The Cav Moves South

The operations staff of the 1st Air Cavalry Division was working in the airless root cellar of a tactical operations center (TOC) on the afternoon of Saturday, October 26, 1968. Suddenly the subdued buzz of quiet routine was broken by the insistent ring of a telephone. Not just any telephone, but the phone linked to the AUTOSECVOCOM, an acronym for the system that provided secure voice communications.

The G-2 (intelligence) operations officer, Captain George Long, startled into momentary inaction, stared at it as it rang. As he recalls, the secure phone on his desk had probably rung only once or twice during the three months he had been working in the Cav's Camp Evans TOC. After a moment, he recovered and picked up the receiver. "First Cav tactical operations center," he said.

The voice on the other end said, "This is General Forsythe. Who is speaking?"

"Captain Long, sir," he replied.

The Cav's division commander told Long that he was at XXIV Corps and that the division was moving. He instructed Long to get the word to the chief of staff, Colonel Conrad Stansberry, to assemble the staff.

The entire division staff, along with Brigadier General Richard L. Irby, the assistant division commander for maneuver, was soon gathered in the headquarters briefing room. It took only twenty

minutes for the Cav's commanding general to chopper up to Camp Evans from the XXIV Corps headquarters at Hue-Phu Bai. General Forsythe had no time to waste. Long remembers him striding into the briefing room and announcing, "We're moving to III Corps and the first airplane takes off tomorrow."

The "first airplane," which would leave on Sunday, was a C-130 transport that would carry a forty-man advance party made up of a cross-section of the division staff. Forsythe told the staff that his understanding of the new mission was that the move of the first of the division's combat forces was to commence at 8 A.M., Monday, October 28. Meanwhile, Forsythe, his aide, and a couple of key staff officers would be heading for Saigon later Saturday afternoon on a U-21, a fast, twin-engine turboprop plane. The two staff officers were the division's G-2, Lieutenant Colonel Fred Barrett, and the newly appointed G-3 (operations officer), Lieutenant Colonel John V. Gibney. The U-21 took off around 4 P.M. on Saturday, headed for Bien Hoa, located just outside Saigon.

Earlier on Saturday General Forsythe had been visiting XXIV headquarters just as the Corps chief of staff, Major General Leo H. "Hank" Schweiter, received a call from II Field Force, the corps-level command that ran all allied operations in Military Region III. The caller was Lieutenant General Walter T. "Dutch" Kerwin, Jr., the commander of II Field Force, and he asked to speak to Forsythe. "George," he said, "General Abrams wants the Cav down here right now, and I want you to come see me this evening."

This order came as a complete shock to everyone in the Cav as well as XXIV Corps. There had been no inkling of any kind of move for the division. There had been rumors, of course; soldiers of all ranks thrive on rumors. The 1st Cavalry Division had been involved in pacifying the eastern half of Quang Tri Province, the northernmost province in South Vietnam. As had happened numerous times since the Cav had deployed to Vietnam in 1965, it had been given a mission that was not the most appropriate for the most mobile and lethal fighting force in Vietnam, and General Abrams knew it.

At the time of the movement order, the Cav was engaged in two operations—Jeb Stuart III, which had started back in late

May, and Comanche Falls. The tempo of the operations was slower than earlier in the year when the Cav staged the relief of the Khe Sanh combat base and then fought some vicious battles with North Vietnamese Army regiments in the mist-shrouded mountains surrounding the A Shau Valley. Captain Long remembers that sometimes days would pass without any big firefights. "The most significant thing going on, day after day, was the G-2 log notation 'unknown mine or unknown explosion set off by unknown source resulting in four or five wounded,' " he recalls. "The 1st of the 9th worked its stuff at night and got a lot of reported kills, but we on the desk figured that there probably were a lot of shadows on the ground that were shot up." The Jeb Stuart III area of operations was concentrated primarily in the rice-growing area along the coast between Hue and Quang Tri City. This area was traversed by National Highway 1, the infamous "Street Without Joy" where the principal casualty-makers were mines, booby traps, and occasional snipers.

As the members of the advance party scurried about preparing for their C-130 ride on Sunday, very few had any idea what lay ahead for the division. Most were quite familiar with the terrain of both MR I and MR II, the locus of the original Cavalry battlegrounds from 1965 through 1967. But the MR III situation would be a new experience.

General Forsythe, however, was familiar with the eleven-province MR III that surrounded Saigon. Before taking command of the 1st Cav, he had been the military deputy to Robert Komer, the civilian boss of the pacification operation known as Civil Operations and Revolutionary Development Support (CORDS). Komer had recruited Forsythe specifically for the job, virtually snatching him out of the G-3 slot at U.S. Army Pacific Headquarters in Hawaii in June 1967. Ostensibly, his job was to honcho the development of the Vietnamese territorial forces that were to provide security for the civil aspects of pacification. But Forsythe remembers that a good bit of his time was spent as a buffer between the military members of CORDS and Bob Komer, who had earned the sobriquet "Blowtorch."

George Forsythe was an uncommon kind of general. He was, in the terminology of the sixties, "a pretty laid-back guy." He was under six feet, slight of build, with sandy hair graying at the

temples. The prominent laugh lines around the corners of his mouth made him appear as if he were just about to break into a wide grin, which in the normal course of events he was. Like most senior officers, he could if pushed turn cold and hard, and his temper could flash, but just as quickly subside. Normally, however, his leadership style was to give orders by suggestion. He also gave "mission" orders and left his subordinates the leeway to carry them out. To make a point, he was forever telling stories of Sergeant Donkowski, who had been his platoon sergeant when he was a second lieutenant just called to active duty. This platoon sergeant, in Forsythe's tales, was a paragon of noncommissioned-officer virtue and wisdom, and wise subordinates heeded the Forsythe admonitions offered through these parables.

George I. Forsythe was born on July 21, 1918, in the copper-mining town of Butte, Montana, where he grew up. He graduated from the University of Montana in Missoula in 1939 with a degree in business administration and an ROTC commission. He was first assigned as a second lieutenant of infantry to the 30th Infantry Regiment at the Presidio of San Francisco. He spent more than a year in the Pacific theater, mostly in planning and operations jobs, and had very little troop-level combat command time. After being promoted to lieutenant colonel in 1944, he was transferred to the European theater, where he served out the war as the operations officer of the XIX Corps. After the war, Forsythe became parachute-qualified and in 1954, as a colonel, commanded the 502nd Airborne Infantry Regiment. He graduated from the Air War College in 1958 and did his first tour in Vietnam as the senior advisor for the Army of Vietnam (ARVN) Field Command. He earned his first star in 1963 and his second in 1966. Like his predecessors in command of the Cav, he was an aviator, but unlike them, he earned his wings just before taking command of the division.

How he became an aviator was among his favorite stories, one that he would tell in a self-effacing manner to new arrivals on the division staff. He said that Westy (General Westmoreland) had repeatedly promised him command of a division in Vietnam. But on the day that General Westmoreland called him in and told him that he was getting a division, all of the line infantry divisions had recently been filled. So he was totally unprepared when Westy told him it would be the 1st Cav. Said Forsythe at that point, "Well, that's great news, but I guess you know, sir, that I'm not an aviator." Westmoreland said, "Oh, that's easy. we'll make you an aviator." So off Forsythe went to the accelerated senior officer course at Fort Rucker, Alabama, and then he returned to take command of the 1st Air Cav from the interim commander, Brigadier General Irby.

When the U-21 carrying the Forsythe party landed at Bien Hoa Base Saturday evening, it was met by a sedan that whisked Forsythe to see his new boss, General Dutch Kerwin, the commander of II Field Force, the corps-level command that ran military operations in MR III. Gibney and Barrett talked with their counterparts at II Field Force. That evening Kerwin gave Forsythe a rapid update on the enemy situation and told Forsythe that he would meet with General Abrams the next day. He also would be meeting with Lieutenant General Frank Mildren, the commander of U.S. Army, Vietnam, who has been instructed to ensure that the Cav had whatever it needed to get settled in the northern part of the Vietnam's Military Region III, which was most commonly called, by Americans and ARVN alike, the III Corps Tactical Zone (CTZ).

The next morning, Sunday, October 27, Forsythe headed for his consultation with General Creighton Abrams, commander, U.S. Military Assistance Command, Vietnam (COMUS-MACV). Gibney and Barrett continued consultations with their counterparts at II Field Force. In the course of the briefings, the Cav people learned that the reason they had been brought south in such a hurry was the grave concern about a rapid buildup of North Vietnamese and Viet Cong forces in the twelve provinces around Saigon that constituted the Third CTZ.

As NVA units made serious incursions across the Cambodian border east and north of Saigon, MACV order-of-battle specialists had identified the NVA 7th Division and VC 5th and 9th divisions. (The "VC" in the two latter titles was only a formality. Because of the losses during the Tet and Mini-Tet offensives, these outfits had been rebuilt from the ground up using tough soldiers from the north). The 9th, lurking in the Parrot's Beak area just forty-five kilometers west of Saigon, was a particular threat. These divisions were arrayed in a giant arc northwest, north, and northeast of Saigon. The most recently acquired intelligence also revealed the presence of the newly arrived NVA 1st Division operating out of the Fishhook area of Cambodia about seventy-five kilometers due north of Saigon. What concerned intelligence analysts was not just that those North Vietnamese divisions were formidably strong, but that the transportation and porterage units were frantically moving war supplies into caches ringing the capital city.

MACV had had sufficient strength in the Saigon area to beat back the VC and NVA attacks in May 1968, the second phase of the communist general offensive, which everyone called the Mini-Tet Offensive, as well as the August high point, the third phase of the offensive. But Abrams's staff was not nearly so confident about the next go-round. By this time, communist intentions were well known, and the TCK-TKN offensive still had a fourth phase to go. Some analysts estimated that it could come as soon as the end of November.

The area in the arc south of Saigon was well covered by the 3rd Brigade of the U.S. 9th Infantry Division, the 199th Light Infantry Brigade, the newly arrived 3rd Brigade of the 82nd Airborne, plus the Australian and Royal Thai forces. Abrams had two U.S. infantry divisions, the 1st and 25th, in the northern arc of Third CTZ, but since Tet, he had gradually pulled them back from the Cambodian frontier and into the populated areas around Saigon to aid in the pacification campaign. This new threat presented Abrams with a dilemma. Forsythe said Abrams told him that if MACV redeployed the 1st and 25th divisions forward into War Zones C and D, the pacification areas would be left vulnerable to inroads by the Viet Cong. On the other hand, if Abrams kept the divisions in their positions in the populated area, a lot of towns and villages would get chewed up in the inevitable clash between combatants. The third option was to get another American unit and go up and meet them at the border.

Abrams gave Forsythe this mission: "Ride them with your spurs all the way down to the point where, if and when they do get down to the populated areas, they will be a relatively ineffective fighting force." Abrams didn't expect one division spread over such a vast area to stop the enemy cold, but it could "harrass them, cover, delay, and force them to change their timetable and chew them up as they were coming down."

In his brief conversation with Abrams, Forsythe learned how the Cav had been tagged for the mission, and he caught the sense of urgency. According to Forsythe, Abrams had made up his mind the previous day, Saturday, October 26. He had asked his staff, "What's the 1st Cav doing?" His people said, "They're mining rice up there." ("Mining rice" was Forsythe's terminology for the Cav's rather pedestrian operations in I Corps). Abrams said, "Bring them down," and everybody looked with wide eyes and said, "When?" He said "Tomorrow." Abrams told Forsythe he wanted to introduce forces into northern III Corps the following day, Monday. He also told Forsythe that he wanted the Cav to advertise its move by leaving intact the big yellow-and-black patches that were painted on all the Cav helicopters. The object was to show the enemy that the Americans could move a division six hundred miles in a matter of days.

Meanwhile, back at Camp Evans, the forty-man advance party had been assembled and loaded onto a C-130. When the aircraft arrived at Bien Hoa Sunday evening, October 27, buses took the group to quarters at Long Binh base, where there were showers and real beds. Captain Long recalls the shock of coming from the dirt and stink of Camp Evans to the near-sanitary conditions of Long Binh. "It was like a different war . . . hell, like a different planet," he said.

In its meetings at II Field Force, the Cav's division staff learned just how tough things were going to be in their new area of operations. A week earlier, three battalions of the U.S. 1st Division (the "Big Red One") had been deployed into three fire-support patrol bases (FSPB) in War Zone C just south of the Fishhook. All were mortared and rocketed regularly during that week, and then, just minutes into Saturday, October 26, four battalions of NVA 1st Division violently assaulted FSPB JULIE, which was defended by the 2nd Battalion, 28th Infantry "Black Lions." JULIE was only two miles south of Cambodia, and during the preceding week defenders had heard truck traffic at night just across the border. The NVA infantry breached the wire in several places, and during the hours between midnight and dawn, soldiers of the 28th Infantry fought desperate hand-to-hand battles with the invaders. With artillery support from FSPB RITA a few kilometers south, and Air Force support, the NVA were finally thrown back into the jungle, leaving 128 dead comrades behind. The fact that the NVA was willing to commit four battalions to take out a battalion firebase ended all indecision on the part of the MACV hierarchy. The call went out the afternoon of October 26: "Bring the Cav down, now."

Abrams's concept was to place the Air Cav Division, with its 450 helicopters, at the outer edge of the northern arc, a 150-kilometer-wide and 45-kilometer-deep stretch of the wild frontier country along the Cambodian border. Their mission would be to interdict the three known main infiltration routes leading from Cambodia to VC base areas around Saigon. The focus was not only on the advancing enemy units, but on the substantial logistical system that had already been put in place to support the forthcoming communist offensive.

After his meeting with General Abrams, Forsythe met with General Mildren to outline the logistical and administrative needs of the division as it moved south. Mildren was vastly relieved when Forsythe told him that the Cav had no need for the massive base camps that characterized the other divisions currently working in III Corps. Forsythe said that the Cav would "buddy up against people who were already there, if they'd share." He said the Cav needed revetments for its helicopters, plus fuel, ammunition, and food and not much else. It helped the American logisticians that the Cav had made a fetish of austere living.

Forsythe took this back to the staff, now set up in an interim operations center at the U.S. Army Southeast Asia Signal Training Facility, which had been placed at the Cav's disposal. Here the general and his staff formulated the plan for moving the division. Forsythe's concept of the operation would place his lead brigade heading south into a 1st Division base camp called Quon Loi, located about seven kilometers east of An Loc, the provincial capital of Binh Long Province. This would be the far right sector of the arc. The next brigade to come south, the 1st, would be "buddied up" with the 1st Brigade of the 25th Division at Tay Ninh City. This was the left sector of the arc. The bulk of Tay Ninh Province contained the infamous War Zone C with its triple-canopy jungle, NVA infiltration trails, and myriad hidden caches and bunker complexes. The center sector of the arc would be occupied by the the the Cav's 2nd Brigade, whose headquarters was first to deploy to Quon Loi and later move into available space at the 1st Infantry Division base at Lai Khe, about thirty kilometers north of Saigon on National Route 13, the famous "Thunder Road." For the division headquarters itself, Forsythe chose a former Big Red One artillery base at Phuoc Vinh, which was located about twenty-five kilometers north and east of Lai Khe. Engineers were dispatched immediately to the compound, which had grown up around an old French fort, to begin construction of a division-sized tactical operations center.

The challenge facing Forsythe and his staff on the morning of October 27 was to move a full division almost six hundred miles by air, land, and sea, extracting it from combat at one end of the journey and committing it against a tough and numerically superior enemy in an unfamiliar area at the other. They had less than twenty-four hours to get the show, code-named Liberty Canyon, on the road.

The task was monumental. More than nineteen thousand men, hundreds of vehicles, nearly five hundred helicopters, and tons of supplies had to be moved from one end of Vietnam to the other. A writer in the Cav's Information Office, Michael Harris, summed it up in the Cav's quarterly magazine; "The Cav moved. The equivalent of a medium-sized town tore itself up by the roots, took wings, and landed at the other end of South Vietnam." It was to be the largest, fastest, and by far the most complicated intratheater combat deployment of the Vietnam War.

Brigadier General Irby had remained behind at Camp Evans to oversee the packing and moving process. Two of the brigades, the 1st and 2nd, were fully committed to operations Jeb Stuart and Comanche Falls, but the 3rd Brigade, the Garry Owen Brigade, was less seriously engaged and would spearhead the movement south. The brigade sent an advance party to Quon Loi on Monday, October 28, just ahead of the commencement of Liberty Canyon. The first maneuver battalion headed south was Lieutenant Colonel Frank Henry's 2nd Battalion, 8th Cavalry, the

"Stony Mountain Boys." Thereafter, General Irby sent battalions out at a rate of one a day.

During the next sixteen days, the U.S. Air Force's 834th Air Division flew 437 sorties by C-130 transport from Quang Tri, Camp Evans, and Phu Bai to Quon Loi, Phuoc Vinh, Bien Hoa, and Tay Ninh. The airlift carried 11,550 passengers and some 3,400 short tons of cargo. At the same time, 4,037 passengers and 16,593 short tons of payload were being moved by the Navy's Amphibious Ready Group A and by the aircraft carrier *Princeton*.

On Thursday, October 31, seventy-two hours after he received the order to move from I Corps, Frank Henry sent his Stony Mountain Boys on an air assault into a landing zone named JOE. It was the first combat assault in III Corps by the 1st Air Cavalry Division. The battalion's assignment there was only temporary since JOE was much too far south of the Cambodian border for the division's concept of operations at the time. The area around JOE was peaceful enough to permit the battalion to gather its breath and prepare for subsequent commitment into an area closer to Cambodia. It also got the unit out of the Quon Loi base, which was not developed sufficiently to handle more than one battalion at a time.

On November 1, Lieutenant Colonel Addison Davis's 2nd Battalion, 7th Cavalry, conducted an air assault onto LZ BILLY, just ten kilometers southwest of the site of the 1st Division's Firebase JULIE. Well aware of the danger that lurked in the rain forests surrounding the LZ, the battalion commander's order of the day was "Dig down or build up, but hurry." Although Davis was well respected by his troops, the "dig down" order brought some snickers from the grunts. The site of BILLY looked great on the map, but when the Delta Company grunts leaped from the skids of their helicopters, they plunged into a swamp. Staff Sergeant Stephen Banko, III, a squad leader in Delta's 1st Platoon, called it a "tidal basin." When the troops sloshed to the highest ground, they found that even a shallow hole drew water. So the battalion employed steel planking normally used in building temporary airplane runways, and used prefabricated concrete bunkers, reinforced with sandbags, as fighting positions.

By November 7, the 3rd Brigade had three battalions deployed just south of the Fishhook, and the 1st Brigade had placed three

battalions on LZs in War Zone C north and east of Tay Ninh
City. The pace of moving and getting settled into the new area
of operations, which was code-named Sheridan Sabre, and fighting a tough, determined foe, left most of the division's personnel
only dimly aware that a major event was upcoming in the United
States, the outcome of which would substantially influence the
conduct of the Vietnam War.

2

Forming the
New Team

When Americans went to the polls on Tuesday, November 5, 1968, to elect a new president, they had much more on their minds than the war in Vietnam. News analysts of that period agreed that the new president would immediately have to confront several major domestic problems in addition to trying to solve the Vietnam riddle. An inflationary wage-price spiral, at least partly driven by the war, was threatening the soundness of the U.S. dollar. The costs of Lyndon Johnson's "Great Society" social programs were increasing, and the United States had serious crime problems. A review of the campaign rhetoric of the three major candidates reveals that not much was said about Vietnam.

To be sure, the Democratic candidate, Hubert Humphrey, capitulated to the antiwar wing of his party, and at the end of September made a speech that was, in effect, his declaration of independence from President Lyndon Johnson. Humphrey backers to this day insist that their candidate could have won had he taken an even firmer antiwar stance at the August Democratic Convention. They base this on Richard Nixon's razor-thin margin of victory on election day (a mere half-million votes, less than one percent), and the fact that the Democrats had again captured both houses of Congress.

More objective observers recognized the impact of the Wallace factor. George Corley Wallace, the former Alabama governor running under the aegis of the American Independent Party, polled 9.5 million votes, or 13.5 percent of the total, and carried five Deep South states. Wallace's campaign statements suggested that most people voting for him were protesting the domestic policies of the Democrats—civil rights and Lyndon Johnson's Great Society program. It would have been startling indeed if many of those votes had gone to Humphrey.

Nixon, in his campaign oratory, likewise did not dwell on Vietnam. In fact, in a postelection analysis, *U.S. News and World Report* listed ten campaign promises made by Nixon, and ending the war in Vietnam was not among them. Eight of them dealt with urgent domestic issues. He was given credit for having a "secret" plan to end the war, the result of an overreaching wire-service report of a speech in March 1968, to some New Hampshire textile workers. In fact, Nixon had no plan, secret or otherwise, and he consistently deflected inquiries by saying "I do not believe a presidential candidate now should say, 'This is what I will do in January.' " When he did discuss Vietnam policy, he generally said that there must be greater de-Americanization of the war. (The term "Vietnamization" would come later.)

The announcement by President Johnson on November 1 that he was ending the bombing of North Vietnam undoubtedly defused the Vietnam issue for an electorate already burdened with the need to make decisions about crucial bread-and-butter issues that affected quality of life at home. In his announcement, Johnson listed all the steps that led to his decision, including the chance for peace, which proved to be illusory, and the belief, not founded in fact but fostered by his Paris negotiating team, that the North Vietnamese would reciprocate by lowering the level of violence in Vietnam. He stressed the endorsement of the bombing halt by General Abrams, who had been recalled to Washington, D.C., for consultations with the president. Abrams had arrived in Washington at 2 A.M. on Tuesday, October 29, wearing scruffy civilian clothing to disguise himself. At 2:30 that morning, he met with members of the president's inner circle and told them that a new attack on Saigon could not succeed, basing his response on the fact that he knew, even as he was talking, that the 1st Cavalry Division was deploying into the critical areas north of Saigon. The bombing halt, he told the president, was "the right thing to do."

Abrams was aware that any bombing halt could aid the enemy's infiltration into Laos and Cambodia. But he also had committed MACV to an interdiction and protect-the-population mission. He calculated that a forward-based interdiction campaign could disrupt a great deal of the communist infiltration once it crossed the borders into Vietnam. He was also wise enough to know that the die was cast and opposition to the bombing halt would be futile.

After the election, Nixon set up an interim headquarters in the Hotel Pierre in New York City. On November 25, 1968, he summoned to his suite for an interview a Harvard professor named Henry A. Kissinger. Dr. Kissinger has been characterized by a number of adjectives; the ones that seem to surface the most include "brilliant," "incisive," "egotistical," "abrasive," "ruthless," and "ambitious." During this first formal face-to-face meeting, Nixon and Kissinger discovered they had many ideas and concepts in common. Predominant was a profound distrust of government bureaucracy. Both agreed that the State Department was incapable of formulating bold and imaginative foreign policy. In fact, Kissinger's doctoral dissertation, which earned him recognition among the intelligentsia, had as one of its themes the excoriation of bureaucracy. He wrote: "The essence of bureaucracy is its quest for safety; its success is calculability. . . . Bureaucracies are designed to execute, not to conceive."

Kissinger left the first meeting with the president-elect unsure of his role in the new administration, if indeed he had one. But on November 27, Kissinger was offered the position of national security advisor. After taking two days to "think it over," Kissinger accepted. It was clearly understood that the White House was to be the locus of power and decision-making in the foreign affairs arena, and the National Security Council (NSC) was to be Nixon's instrument to maintain that control. This essentially shut out the State Department from decision-making on substantive issues. The secretary of state for the new team was William Rogers, an affable corporation lawyer who had been attorney general during the Eisenhower administration.

Nixon chose a Wisconsin congressman, Melvin Laird, as his secretary of defense. All historians writing about the Nixon administration agree that Laird was a political animal to his core.

He had carefully cultivated sources on Capitol Hill and a constituency of his own.

On January 20, 1969, just after Richard Nixon was sworn in as president, Kissinger issued National Security Decision Memoranda (NSDM) 1 and 2. NSDM-1 was a technical directive that created two series of presidential directives—National Security Decision Memoranda and National Security Study Memoranda (NSSMs). NSDM-2 informed the bureaucracy how foreign policy and the war were going to be conducted in the Nixon administration. The new order centered power in the White House with the streamlined National Security Council. The decision-making apparatus was designed to minimize the influence of the State Department, including not only the bureaucrats at Foggy Bottom, but also Rogers, the secretary of state. The drafters of the memorandum envisaged that the secretary of defense would be declawed as well, but Laird was a canny veteran of political wars, and he was not about to be left out in the cold. Although Laird and Kissinger respected each other, they often went at each other hammer and tong. Neither emerged as a clear winner. Laird demanded, and got, direct access to the president, but Kissinger finessed him by establishing a direct link to the Joint Chiefs of Staff (JCS). And the JCS did a little finessing of their own later by planting a Navy yeoman in the NSC staff to leak NSC secrets to the Joint Chiefs.

The chairman of the Joint Chiefs still was General Earl K. "Bus" Wheeler. He had been scheduled to leave the job in 1968 after serving two two-year terms, but President Johnson extended his term one year to permit the new president the privilege of choosing his own senior military advisor. Wheeler continued in office, with Nixon's consent, until July 1970. The Army chief of staff was General William Childs Westmoreland, who had taken over the job in July 1968 after turning over the task of running the Vietnam War to his deputy, Creighton Abrams.

The Navy's representative on the JCS was Admiral Thomas Moorer, the chief of naval operations. General John McConnell was the Air Force chief of staff; General Leonard Chapman, the commandant of the Marine Corps, completed the JCS lineup at the time of the inauguration.

Any credible discussion of the "new team" has to include

General Creighton Abrams. Even though Abrams had taken over MACV in July 1968 after he had been interviewed and deemed acceptable by Lyndon Johnson, he has been indelibly associated with the Nixon war. Abrams was born in Springfield, Massachusetts, on September 16, 1914, and graduated from the U.S. Military Academy at West Point in 1936, a classmate of Westmoreland. Abrams established his reputation as a combat leader during World War II, when he commanded the tank battalion that was the point for the breakout from Normandy. Later he commanded the tank-infantry spearhead of the force that rapidly moved north on icy roads to relieve the beleaguered defenders of Bastogne during the Battle of the Bulge. He came out of the war with not one but two Distinguished Service Crosses, the Army's second-highest award for heroism, plus two Silver Stars.

A lot of young officers came out of World War II with medals and excellent combat reputations only to crash on the shoals of peacetime soldiering, but Abrams, whose gruff demeanor cloaked an incisive intellect, moved up rapidly during peacetime. He then ensured his future by a brilliant performance as the major general commanding federal forces deployed to Mississippi and Alabama during the first of the civil rights crises in the early 1960s. His skill in handling those volatile situations earned him the admiration of the Kennedys, President John and Attorney General Bobby, as well as the then secretary of the Army, Cyrus Vance. Abrams was promoted to lieutenant general in 1963, and less than a year later got his fourth star and the job as the Army vice chief of staff. Abrams came to Vietnam as Westmoreland's deputy in May 1967. He doubtless expected to succeed to the top job in a couple of months, since he brought with him as his chief of staff designate one of his trusted associates from his days with the 3rd Armored Division in Germany, Major General Walter Kerwin. The couple of months stretched out into more than a year, and Dutch Kerwin did indeed become chief of staff of MACV, but worked for Westmoreland until July 1968, when Abrams at last became COMUSMACV. Abrams used the time wisely, studying the war as it was being fought by Westmoreland and becoming intimately acquainted with all aspects of the ARVN command structure and combat capabilities.

*   *   *

After receiving the job as presidential advisor for national security, Kissinger was also given authority to recruit his own team for the NSC staff. Key individuals on this team included Laurence S. Eagleburger, a career foreign service officer who initially served as Kissinger's executive assistant; Winston Lord, a Yale graduate and former Pentagon staffer; Morton Halperin, an avowed antiwar and anti-Nixon man who had been deputy assistant secretary of defense under Clark Clifford; and a bevy of bright young men from both inside and outside government.

Among this group was an Army lieutenant colonel named Alexander Haig, who had successfully commanded a battalion in the 1st Infantry Division in 1967 and who had a master's degree in international affairs from Georgetown University. He had been recommended by General Andrew Goodpaster, who had been granted a leave of absence from his post as deputy to General Abrams in Vietnam to serve on the Nixon transition team. (Goodpaster was the principal drafter of NSDM-2.) Haig also came with glowing recommendations from Joseph Califano, who had been Haig's boss in the Pentagon, and Dr. F. G. Kraemer, an advisor to a key member of the Army staff and a friend of Kissinger. Haig had already been selected for colonel when he was drafted by Kissinger.

As the new NSC team was settling into its suite of offices in the executive office building just a few steps west of the White House, the magazine *Foreign Affairs* published an article on Vietnam written by Kissinger before he was hired by Nixon. The article argued that the previous strategy of attrition was futile since the communists could sustain higher casualties than the United States, and as long as they did not "lose" they would "win." The article also stated that the war had to be ended by a diplomatic solution, which Kissinger saw as occurring on three levels—between the United States and North Vietnam regarding a cease-fire and troop withdrawals; between the government of Vietnam (GVN) and the National Liberation Front (NLF) for a political settlement in the south; and, finally, by an international forum to safeguard treaties and agreements arrived at. Although it was not a concrete plan for the future, the article posted some clear guidelines that previously had not been articulated by anyone inside or outside of government. That the main points of the article became the nucleus of the Nixon-Kissinger plan to extricate the United States from Vietnam should not have come as a surprise to any thoughtful observer.

That Nixon devoted little campaign oratory to Vietnam did not mean that he was unaware of the volatility of the issue. He was convinced that his long-range foreign-policy goals of rapprochement with Communist China and easing the confrontational posture with the Soviet Union could not be achieved as long as Vietnam remained a major issue. As he wrote later, Nixon believed that his "first priority had to be to end the Vietnam War in a way that would achieve the goal for which we had fought for so long. . . . The way in which the United States met its responsibilities in Vietnam could also be crucial to the Soviet and Chinese assessment of American will, and thus to the success of any new relationships with those powers." This meant that Nixon had to have some strategy options. Putting together strategic alternatives to the course that had been pursued by the Johnson administration required reliable information. That commodity was in short supply in Washington in early January, 1969.

Kissinger convened the National Security Council for meetings on January 21 and again on January 25. The discussions on Vietnam revealed no new approaches; the hawks wanted to resume the bombing of North Vietnam; the doves wanted immediate, unilateral withdrawal from Vietnam. There was a paucity of information, and what there was Kissinger distrusted. The new team's hunger for information led to the issuance of National Security Study Memorandum-1 (NSSM-1). The confidential study memorandum was sent to a limited list of addressees: the Office of the Secretary of Defense (OSD), the Joint Chiefs of Staff; the State Department; and the CIA in the United States. Overseas respondents were the commander in chief of the Pacific (CINCPAC), the commander of military forces in Vietnam, and the ambassador in Saigon.

NSSM-1 was a massive questionnaire on the status and conduct of the war with twenty-eight major and fifty subsidiary questions. NSSM-1 asked for opinions on the negotiating climate, the nature and status of the enemy forces, the capabilities of the South Vietnamese armed forces, and the progress of pacification. In every case, respondents were asked, "What is the evidence?" or "How adequate is our information?" The administrative instructions of NSSM-1 didn't give the agencies much time for responses. Moreover, the respondents were instructed to complete the questionnaire and return it directly to the NSC without coordination with other agencies and without submitting it to the usual chain-of-command staffing process on which bureaucracies thrive. NSSM-1 perplexed many officials and angered others.

The responses to the questionnaire were returned to the NSC staff by mid-February and were summarized in a forty-four-page report. The responses were predominantly pessimistic and revealed a fundamental schism between the various agencies. One group, which the summary writers characterized as Group A, was somewhat more optimistic on some questions than were the agencies in Group B. Group A consisted of JCS, CINCPAC, MACV, and the ambassador in Saigon; in Group B was State, CIA, and the dovish, civilian staffers of OSD.

The summary noted that in explaining reduced enemy military presence and activities, Group A gave greater relative weight to allied military pressure than did Group B. The improvement in the Vietnam armed forces was considered a little more significant by Group A than Group B, but both groups had fairly gloomy outlooks on the ability of the RVNAF to compete against the Viet Cong straight up and were totally negative about its potential against the North Vietnamese Army. Group A was considerably more sanguine about pacification than was Group B, which was skeptical of the recent claimed advances. The summary did concede that all agencies agreed that the enemy had suffered some reverses, but that Hanoi had not changed its essential objectives and had sufficient forces to pursue them, and that Hanoi's recruitment and infiltration equaled or surpassed the attrition caused by the United States. Finally, all agreed that Hanoi had not approached the negotiating table in Paris out of any sense of weakness. What is interesting in retrospect is that with only a few exceptions, Group A was pretty much on target, proving again that the best way to judge the battlefield is to go smell the cordite.

Kissinger, however, used the disparate responses to demonstrate to Nixon that none of the so-called Vietnam experts in government had the answers, and that Nixon and Kissinger were in the best position to call the shots without consulting the bureaucrats.

This imperious posture was without foundation. Neither had had any real experience with the war—indeed, with any war—although Kissinger had visited Vietnam twice in the mid-1960s. Nixon projected himself as a great war leader who knew more about foreign affairs than anyone else in government. Kissinger fancied himself in the mold of Austria's Metternich or England's Castlereagh. Kissinger's doctoral thesis, which was later published under the title *A World Restored*, dealt with these giants of diplomacy and their work at the Congress of Vienna in 1815, which brought some order to the world after the Napoleonic years. The Paris peace talks, which were stalled when Kissinger came to power as national security advisor and plenipotentiary for Richard Nixon, were to be Kissinger's Congress of Vienna.

Unfortunately for America and South Vietnam, Paris was not Vienna, and the North Vietnamese delegation had no intention of emulating nineteenth-century diplomats. It would take Nixon and Kissinger more than a year to fully comprehend that they were dealing with hardened revolutionaries dedicated to a ruthless ideology, in which the compromises of diplomacy were viewed as a sign of weakness.

In November and December of 1968, while Kissinger began assembling his new team and nurturing his vision of diplomatic triumph, the North Vietnamese were demonstrating on the battlefield their implacable devotion to their goal—the conquest of the south. The communist combat forces had started their movement out of the Cambodian sanctuaries, impeded only by the hastily erected screen of firebases along the border.

3

First Battles Along the Border

The tracers from the five-thousand-rounds-per-minute miniguns mounted on orbiting Cav gunships showered glowing red waterfalls of death on the NVA regiment below, punctuating the eerie light of flares and the muzzle flashes of hundreds of rifles and machine guns on the ground.

It was the night of November 14, nine days after the election of Richard Nixon. Although some soldiers in Vietnam cast absentee ballots, most of the combatants on this night had no such opportunity. Locked in a battle for survival, the 36th ARVN Ranger Battalion was resolutely defending LZ DOT, a tiny firebase just five kilometers south of the Cambodian border near the Fishhook. Equally determined to overrun the small bastion were twelve hundred seasoned warriors of the NVA 95-C Regiment.

This was the first major battle under the aegis of the 1st Air Cavalry Division since it had assumed responsibility for screening the frontier regions along the Cambodian border. But, presaging many battles and campaigns to come, this first big fight was won by a combined arms force of South Vietnamese infantry, a U.S. 1st Infantry Division artillery battery on the firebase supported by 1st Cav gunships and helilifted tube artillery on nearby landing zones, and U.S. Air Force warbirds. The use of airmobility was the pattern of victory established by the 1st Air Cav during its historic Pleiku campaign in the fall of 1965, validated and revalidated in campaigns through 1966 and 1967 in Vietnam's II

Corps Tactical Zone, and proven again in 1968 in the northern combat area, the I Corps Tactical Zone. It mattered little whether the friendly soldiers were ARVN or other free world forces, and if they were American, whether they were division members or not. The Cav and its airmobility techniques inevitably produced the same results.

In this firefight, the ARVN Rangers and the 1st Division's 1st Battalion, 5th Artillery, were working under the operational control of the Cav's 2nd Brigade. Cav artillery from nearby LZs RITA and JAKE pounded the assembly areas and approach routes of the attacking North Vietnamese, as well as bringing in close support fire within fifty meters of DOT's perimeter wire. Following a thunderous mortar and rocket barrage, the NVA's Ninety-Five-Charlie Regiment sent scores of assault teams crashing into the wire of LZ DOT. At one point the enemy was able to penetrate the outer wire, only to be cut down by a hail of fire from the defenders. Artillerymen from Battery D, 1/5 Arty, lowered the tubes of their 105-mm howitzers and fired nearly nine hundred rounds point-blank into the attacking waves. The fight went on for more than seven hours before the NVA broke contact at 6:30 A.M.

Within an hour, three companies of the 5th Battalion, 7th Cavalry, air-assaulted into the vicinity to sweep the battlefield. The three Cav companies found only piles of corpses around DOT—287 total—and heaps of arms and ammunition. But Ninety-Five-Charlie had ghosted back across the Cambodian border to lick its wounds. The ARVN Rangers lost nine killed and forty-one wounded. American casualties were seven wounded.

Captain Frederick L. Kuhns, U.S. advisor for the ARVN force on DOT, told a reporter for the *Cavalair*, the weekly newspaper published by the 1st Air Cav Division, that the support his outfit received had never before been experienced by the ARVN battalion. "It was just fantastic," he said. He was particularly impressed by the speed with which the Cav responded to the threat. He also said that the key to the victory was the "tremendous coordination between the elements on the ground and the air." The aerial rocket artillery, tube artillery, and Air Force strikes kept the enemy off balance throughout the night.

Kuhns also praised the work of the 2nd Brigade's aero scouts for knocking the enemy off balance before the attack, thus making the NVA regiment launch the attack prematurely. On the evening of November 13, while flying a last-light reconnaissance of the area, the scout team spotted a group of NVA soldiers hiding in a tree line near the LZ. The leader of the scouts, Chief Warrant Officer William Autin, said his team engaged the enemy force with M-60 machine-gun fire, killing fifteen or so, then called in artillery on the position. Captain Kuhns said that the unit discovered by the scouts probably was a diversionary force that was to hit the LZ on the opposite side from the main attack. "I think the enemy initiated his attack earlier than originally planned, fearing that the other elements would also be detected by the scout team," Kuhns said.

The brigade aero scouts were a 1st Cavalry innovation. The initial authorized allocation of four UH-1D "Huey" lift ships converted to command-and-control birds for commanders within the brigade had been augmented by four OH-6A Cayuse light observation helicopters (LOH). These scout birds were called "Loaches" by the troops—another case where the users simply refused to use the official Army name. In most instances each brigade scout LOH had a pilot flying the right seat, an observer in the left seat, and hanging out the right door, a gunner armed with an M-60 machine gun. This was a virtual copy of the scout ship configuration originated by the division's reconnaissance squadron. Sometimes the scout birds would be rigged with a fixed-mount machine gun. The brigades used these scouts as the close-in eyes and ears of the brigade, an economy-of-force action that permitted the aerial reconnaissance squadron to assume broader scouting and screening missions.

The air cavalry reconnaissance unit, the 1st Squadron, 9th Cavalry, employed three aero troops and one ground troop, the latter used primarily for road security missions. The three aero troops were 100 percent airmobile in that every fighting man had a seat on an aircraft. Each aero troop had three sections—the gun (Red) section, flying AH-1 Cobra gunships; the scout (White) section, flying OH-6 LOHs, "Loaches"; and the rifle (Blue) platoon. The Blues had long before earned a fearsome reputation as the "Headhunters" and were the scourge of the NVA and VC in campaigns in the northern provinces from Pleiku to Bong Son to Quang Tri. The Red and White sections still used the fundamental high-bird–low-bird concept they had initially worked out in 1965, except that by 1968 it had been institutionalized. Other air cavalry units in Vietnam had adopted the practice, often calling the mode "hunter-killer," but in the Cav, the high-bird–low-bird was called a "Pink Team" because it resulted from pairing Red sections with White sections.

Matthew Brennan, who spent thirty-nine months with the 9th Cav making more than four hundred combat assaults, believed that the change from the old Huey gunship to the high-tech Cobra made for sexy pyrotechnics but the Cobra was not as efficient a killer as the Huey gunship with its door gunners. It is Brennan's opinion that most of the kills notched by the 9th Cav from 1965 through early 1968 were by those door gunners. Their successors in lethality were the door gunners on the scout ships, known within the 9th Cav as "Torques" for reasons known only to those wild and fearless men who wore the black Stetsons of the 9th Cav. In 1968, as the aero troops began ranging far and wide across the wild frontier of northern III Corps, the scout birds with their door gunners proved to be extraordinarily lethal to the NVA soldiers frantically trying to stock the battlefields for the forthcoming general offensive. Because the scout birds worked so close to the ground they were uncommonly vulnerable to ground fire. Brennan recalls that many of the missions of the Blues during the early battles in III Corps were to secure downed aircraft and recover the bodies of crewmen.

Even as the 1st Cavalry Division was completing its monumental move from Quang Tri, allied intelligence was getting a better grasp of the plans of General Tran Van Tra, the COSVN commander, for the communists' Fourth General Offensive, the fourth phase of the TCK-TKN offensive. The COSVN attack plan was simplistic, unimaginative, and fatally flawed. It was drawn up before Abrams had moved the airmobile division south and was based on the presumption that the American command would react to the threat as it had in the past. Because communist military plans tended to be set in concrete, there was no provision for reacting to the change of situation brought about by the deployment of the 1st Cavalry Division into the border areas. In many ways the fourth phase of the TCK-TKN offensive was to be a repeat of the first big attack in February 1968.

The major changes to the original communist game plan were the addition of the 1st NVA Division, a relatively fresh outfit just moved down from the reasonably quiet operations area in the western highlands of II Corps, and the fact that many of the main-force Viet Cong units had been transformed into North Vietnamese regular army units. Knowledge of the composition of the main force divisions arrayed against the allies in III Corps came after the fact, however. At the time, the MACV intelligence and order-of-battle specialists, perhaps reeling under the memory of being burned by overly optimistic estimates before Tet-68, appeared to be very conservative in recognizing the extent of VC losses and NVA replenishment. With Hanoi steadfastly denying having troops in the south, most of the news reports from Vietnam during this period tended to list the VC as the primary threat to Saigon.

The 1st NVA Division was assigned the principal diversionary effort. Its mission was to attack south out of War Zone C through the Michelin Plantation, overrun population centers such as Dau Tieng, and then move down through hamlets and villages into the old base areas of the Iron Triangle, the Trapezoid, and the Ho Bo and Boi Loi woods. This movement, according to the communist strategy, would force Abrams to cut back on his pacification support efforts in the nearby populated areas and commit the large American formations into the threatened areas. This move would increase the vulnerability of Tay Ninh City, where the U.S. 25th Division had a forward-deployed brigade; of Lai Khe, the headquarters of the U.S. 1st Infantry Division, which was secured by a Big Red One brigade; and ultimately, of Cu Chi, the headquarters of the U.S. 25th Infantry Division. This effort would also cause the Americans and ARVN to fight big-firepower battles within the populated areas, which the communists knew would devastate homes and property and cost civilian lives.

Then, according to the COSVN plan, as the regiments of the 1st NVA Division began to draw allied forces into the diversionary battles south of War Zone C, the NVA 7th Division was to move out of its lairs in northern Binh Long Province and push south along National Route 13. This time, however, it would not stop at Chon Than in southern Binh Long Province as it did in February 1968, but continue south into the populated areas of central and southern Binh Duong Province, where the communists hoped they could reestablish control of the countryside and the population. This would force General Abrams's hand and seriously disrupt pacification efforts in those areas. The U.S. 1st Infantry Division had a brigade deployed in firebases from Lai Khe north to An Loc, generally protecting "Thunder Road," the Route 13 ground line of communications into Binh Long Province. The unit chosen to make the main assault on Saigon was the VC 5th Division, whose main area of operations in November 1968 ranged from Cambodia through Phuoc Long Province into War Zone D. It was directed to move into western War Zone D just east of Saigon and attack the capital city from there.

To the west of Saigon, the 9th VC Division had been making periodic forays into South Vietnam from the Angel's Wing and Parrot's Beak of Cambodia. The COSVN scheme for the 9th was for it to march into South Vietnam from Cambodia along National Route 1. In southern Tay Ninh Province at Go Dau Ha was the road junction of National Routes 1 and 22, By seizing this critical terrain feature, COSVN reasoned, the allies would be unsure of the 9th's next target. It could easily swing northwest and attack along Route 22 to Tay Ninh City, a distance of only thirty kilometers. Or it could pivot and move southeast for fifty kilometers and bring Saigon under seige. The communists hoped that the indecision this situation would cause would clear the way for the 5th VC Division to barrel almost unimpeded into Saigon from War Zone D.

To understand Abrams's scheme of defense, it is instructive to understand the North Vietnamese Army's offensive capabilities. Many writers over the years have rhapsodized about the mobility of the Viet Cong and have extended that almost mystical quality to the NVA. To be sure, the Viet Cong in the earlier periods of the war were wraithlike, hit-and-run fighters who could disappear in a twinkling. But the VC mobility still was foot mobility. It is not a difficult feat to travel light and carry only a limited amount of food, water, and ammo when nearly every village or hamlet is a mess hall, rearming point, and hiding place. The North Vietnamese in late 1968 and early 1969 also were foot-mobile, but the NVA, being northerners, no longer had an extensive population base to protect and support them. The North Vietnamese Army already was in its transition from a lightly armed peasant army to a conventional army employing very modern battlefield weapons. But a conventional army has monumental supply problems, and if that army has no truly secure lines of communications to its battle zones, logistics become nightmarish. So the NVA had to depend on the guerrilla mode of stealthily prestocking the battlefield.

Before any of the NVA combat formations could move a step toward their objectives, an ant swarm of porterage units had to move rice, medical supplies, crew-served weapons, and ammunition of all calibers to selected locations. The NVA combat units would travel light, moving by infiltration from one supply and bivouac point to another. But these rest stops and caches were extremely vulnerable to a mobile attacking force. By lopping off large chunks of this "logistical nose," Abrams reasoned, the enemy combat forces could be defeated long before they reached the critical population areas.

The mobile attacking force was, of course, the 1st Cavalry Division. When it completed its move from Quang Tri, it was deployed in a string of mutually supporting firebases from western Tay Ninh Province through the heart of War Zone C, through Binh Long Province and into western Phuoc Long Province. The division was given other assets, both American and ARVN, to help in the screen. In areas adjacent to existing roadways the attached conventionally mobile ARVN and U.S. forces were deployed. The entire operation was given the code name "Sheridan Sabre" by the Cav, and it was part of the overall joint U.S.–ARVN operation named *Toan Thang* II (Certain Victory).

The day-to-day operations of the division were the antithesis of the big battalion-sized operations conducted in some parts of that AO earlier in the war, operations the media generally termed "elephants pursuing ants." In the case of the Cav, it was ants ambushing ants. The biggest formation that moved in the jungle was a rifle company, and often the company was broken down into platoon combat teams conducting reconnaissance in force. And every night across that giant arc there were platoon and company ambushes on trails discovered during the daytime reconnaissance. Those ambushes took a fearsome toll on the NVA rear service units whose job was to push supplies down the trails from Cambodia. Because the pursuing ants could also fly, and some were capable of killing from the air, a numerically inferior force could cover vast amounts of territory and drive the footmobile ants into a frenzy.

As the division settled into its new area of operations and grappled with its interdiction mission, leaders found that they were facing a more numerous and in many ways a tougher enemy. Moreover, many of the techniques that had worked so well in the rugged mountains of I Corps simply were not acceptable in the tangled jungles of War Zone C. The single-file movement of rifle companies that was tolerable on the ridge lines up north was suicidal in War Zone C's tropical rain forests, where the communists, over a period of twenty or more years, had constructed superbly camouflaged bunker complexes that featured interlocking fields of fire. These fields of fire often were cut as tunnels in the underbrush and were thus invisible from the air and virtually undetectable from the ground. An advancing column could have a half-dozen men walk unsuspectingly into the killing zone and be blown away in seconds. "We never moved single file," said Captain Henry "Rocky" Colavita, commander of Delta Company, 2nd Battalion, 8th Cavalry. "I usually had the company in three columns, spread as far apart as I could and still maintain control." The three-column formation permitted the company to immediately begin a flanking action on bunker complexes. Units learned very quickly to avoid head-on charges into NVA bunkers. Tragically, it was a lesson that had to be relearned the hard way by every level of command and by every new commander. There appeared to be no single credible repository of combat lore and wisdom that could be quickly disseminated to incoming units. As a result, much blood was shed as each unit stumbled its way from small victory to small victory, learning to survive in the process. In time, it became generally accepted within the division that since the object of the exercise was to get into the enemy's system, attempts to kill all enemy soldiers in the complex were a bloody exercise in futility.

Commanders in the division gradually learned that it was more important to drive the NVA defenders out and capture what they were defending. Usually it was a supply cache with rice, beans, salt, medical supplies, arms, and ammunition. Moreover, with airmobility, once the NVA units were forced to move, they became lucrative targets for the armed helicopters. Bunker-busting gradually became an art form in which rifle companies and platoons abandoned the traditional role of the infantry in the offense, that of closing with and destroying the enemy in close combat. The new role was that of target acquisition: finding the complexes, sealing them off, then calling in artillery and air strikes to do the actual killing of the enemy. This technique may have brought sneers from macho traditionalists, but it saved lives and accomplished the mission. Commanders also learned that they had to accept the galling reality that their lost point men would have to be left where they had fallen until the complex could be reduced by supporting fires. To send more men to their deaths simply to satisfy the ancient warrior's creed that comrades are to be brought out regardless of cost was, in this time and place, no longer relevant.

The constant pressure from the ground and the air caused the NVA to break their larger combat formations down into small infiltration cells. But once in a while, before an infiltrating company or battalion had been broken into the smaller cells, they made contact with a Cavalry unit. On those occasions, a rifle company or a platoon would, in grunt parlance, "step in shit." The Cav also learned that while big clearings in the jungle made dandy and convenient landing zones, they should be avoided at all costs.

Another lesson was the old truism that commander changes in combat are often costly. The division learned this lesson in a tragic way on December 3, when Delta Company, 2nd Battalion, 7th Cavalry, conducted an air assault at 10:45 A.M. into a large clearing about fifteen kilometers northeast of the 3rd Brigade base at Quon Loi. The purpose of the assault was to launch a reconnaissance in force along a portion of the infiltration trail known as the Serges Jungle Highway. The mission of the Cav forces in this area was to interdict elements of the NVA 7th Division, which was headed south to take part in the upcoming general offensive. The 3rd Brigade had just acquired a new commander, Colonel Karl R. Morton, on November 15, and the battalion a new battalion commander, Lieutenant Colonel George D. Hardesty, Jr., on December 1.

It was a typical Cav air assault, the orchestration of munitions, men, and machines that was the hallmark of its mobility. The full preassault fire by artillery had been delivered on the LZ and the white phosphorus round that signaled the end of the artillery prep brought the runs by the gunships escorting the lift birds that were, at that time, on the final approach to the LZ. As the lift ships settled down into the waist-high elephant grass, the door gunners blazed away with their machine guns at the edge of the jungle. There was no return fire and the message was flashed to the battalion commander that the LZ was "Green," which meant that there had been no enemy fire. Lieutenant Colonel Hardesty choppered into the LZ for a quick conference with Captain Robert L. Fitzsimmons, the company commander. Fitzsimmons had only been with the company a month, replacing a captain who had been killed by a command-detonated mine. But Delta Company was a veteran line outfit. Many of its men had been with the company when it participated in the airmobile minuet that led to the relief of the Khe Sanh combat base and then participated in the bitter battles in the A Shau Valley.

The company, which was loosely organized into a perimeter awaiting the word to move out, was unaware that the Green LZ condition had lulled them into a near-fatal complacency. Efforts to dig in were desultory and frustrated by the hard, laterite soil, baked by one-hundred-degree temperatures. The Skytroopers had no inkling that approximately four hundred NVA soldiers were sheltered in bunkers surrounding the clearing awaiting orders from their commander to open fire. The bunkers had been constructed some twenty meters inside the tree line and had come through the preparatory fire nearly unscathed. As Hardesty's command chopper cleared the trees on its way out, the LZ suddenly was swept with a firestorm of small arms, machine-gun, mortar, and B-40 rocket fire. Dozens of Skytroopers dropped instantly, some dead and many grievously wounded. The detonating mortar and rocket rounds ignited the tall, dry grass and caused it to blaze out of control. Men tried desperately to beat out the flames with their jackets, but this exposed them to the hail of bullets sweeping the LZ and many more became casualties. Some died in the grass fire.

The first blast of rocket, mortar, and machine-gun fire was followed by assaults from the north, west, and southeast, the last-mentioned being the main attack. Under cover of a 12.7-mm machine gun, 60-mm mortars, and B-40 rockets, a wave of attackers in the main assault swept toward the position manned by Delta's 1st Platoon. The leader of the center squad of that platoon was Sergeant John N. Holcomb. He disregarded the enemy fire and personally positioned members of his squad so they could bring effective fire against the attackers. When one of his machine gunners was wounded, Holcomb grabbed the gun and moved to a position where he could deliver accurate fire on the enemy soldiers as they attempted the assault across the seventy-five meters of open clearing. The defensive fires of the platoon beat back the initial attack. As the NVA soldiers withdrew, dragging their dead and wounded with them, Holcomb, a veteran NCO who earlier in his service with the company had earned a Bronze Star for valor, knew with a certainty that another assault was imminent. With the LZ still being raked by NVA supporting fire, he moved back to his men, administered first aid to the wounded, and personally evacuated them to a relatively secure area behind the platoon position. Then he repositioned the surviving members of his squad and again moved forward to man his machine gun. The second NVA attack followed another intensive rocket and mortar barrage and a company-sized NVA element charged toward the platoon's position. Once again, Holcomb's accurate machine-gun fire caused the attack to falter.

By this time, the NVA gunners had Holcomb's position fixed and directed rocket fire at the machine gun, destroying the gun and severely wounding the gallant squad leader. Disregarding his painful wounds, Holcomb crawled back to his squad, all of whom were now dead or wounded. After trying to move his men to a sheltered position, during which he received additional fragmentation wounds, Holcomb moved among surviving members of the platoon, working with another squad leader, Sergeant Stephen T. Banko III, who also had been painfully wounded, to reorganize the platoon into a cohesive fighting unit. With the platoon leader and platoon sergeant incapacitated by wounds, Holcomb assumed command of the platoon and, after crawling to the fallen platoon radio operator, relayed fire-direction information to permit artillery supporting fire to be directed against the North Vietnamese. The company had called for supporting artillery fire and the Redlegs from nearby firebases poured steel into the wood line, keeping the NVA off balance. Sergeant Banko, meanwhile, had taken the radio from his dead RTO and was using it to direct in Air Force tactical air strikes. The combination of Cav gunships and the Air Force Phantoms with their five-hundred-pound bombs and napalm broke the back of the NVA main assault on the embattled LZ.

As Holcomb was undergoing his ordeal other members of the company were being hit hard by the two supporting attacks. The company headquarters was fully exposed in the center of the perimeter and had sustained many casualties. The command effort was held together by Captain Fitzsimmons and his "Six Mike," Sergeant First Class John Allison, the field first sergeant. Allison operated the battalion command radio after its operator, Specialist Four Clarence R. Buss, dropped it to help the company aid man, Specialist Four Jimmie L. Deschields, in caring for the wounded. Under normal conditions, the elephant grass would have provided some concealment for the wounded. But the raging grass fire had burned off most of the grass and the LZ resembled a flat field of charcoal, dotted with blackened lumps, the dead or badly wounded Skytroopers.

The ordeal lasted nearly five hours. When the NVA finally broke contact, Sergeant Holcomb's radio transmissions became infrequent and hard to understand and finally ceased. When the company began its painful reorganization on the LZ, Holcomb's lacerated body was found next to the radio. He was one of the twenty-three Americans killed in the battle. Another fifty-two Skytroopers were wounded in the fight. On March 9, 1971, the Medal of Honor was awarded to Sergeant Holcomb and presented to his father, George N. Holcomb, of Richland, Oregon.

The tragedy is that it need not have happened. The location of the landing zone, which the survivors quickly labeled LZ BLOOD or LZ BITCH, was a mistake. Banko to this day asserts that the actual target LZ was a smaller clearing about one kilometer south of the deadly NVA trap. Two scout teams from Bravo Troop, 1st Squadron, 9th Cavalry, had spotted the bunker complex in the area a day before and one scout aircraft flown by Warrant Officer George Hamilton had bounced an NVA command group moving towards the bunker complex and killed several. The door gunner on the scout bird said it was like shooting fish in a barrel. The scout even landed and snatched a 57-mm recoilless rifle. Warrant Officer Rich Chesson, who had spotted the complex a day earlier, told Matt Brennan in an interview for Brennan's new book on the 1st of the 9th Cav, *Hunter-Killer Squadron,* that he had recommended up the chain of command that a B-52 strike be brought into the area. Instead, the combat assault by Delta 2/7 was ordered. The night after Delta was extracted, a B-52 strike did hit the area. The next day, Chesson was doing a bomb damage assessment of the area and his gunner, Specialist Doug Glover, spotted movement in the bottom of a bomb crater. He fired his machine gun and missed, and then the scout crew realized that the man in the crater was an American. As Chesson recalled, "He was dressed only in his underwear and was covered with dirt and soot. He had survived bullets, artillery, and a B-52 strike and now had survived being shot at by a scout gunner at very short range. That was a miracle in many ways because I never saw Doug Glover miss a shot."

The Cav had not recently been confronted with an enemy with the savvy to recognize that large clearings would eventually be potential airmobile landing zones and the manpower and patience to wait for the opportunity to annihilate a landing force. Inherent in that strategy was the ruthlessness of a leadership willing to risk losing a force to B-52 strikes in exchange for the opportunity to inflict casualties on Americans. As a result of this action, the division became extremely wary of large, inviting clearings, preferring to make do with smaller clearings for feeding in assault forces, which would then assault the NVA ambush force from the rear. The larger clearings, when removed from enemy control, then became excellent locations for firebases.*

Another lesson the Cav had to learn quickly was that the jungle had to be cleared away some distance from the fighting positions of the firebase, a chore that was not necessary on the mountaintop LZs in I Corps. Fortunately, this lesson was not learned through loss of lives. General Kerwin said that when he dropped in on one of the Cav battalions shortly after they had flown down from Quang Tri, he was aghast at the distance between the firebase defensive berm and the surrounding jungle. "I got on the horn to George [Forsythe] and told him to go over to the 1st Division and look at their firebases and see how they do it. I told him, 'You better do something quickly because you could lose an entire battalion out here.'" Thereafter, the Cav choppered in their airmobile bulldozers and cleared out the jungle a respectable distance from the fighting positions on the firebase. The division engineers also packaged a firebase kit that could be flown into a site with a couple dozen Chinook sorties so a functional firebase could be established within twenty-four hours.

During its first forty-five days in III Corps, the Cav established a string of firebases across the extreme northern reaches of the zone, most of them within a few kilometers of the Cambodian border. Given the Cav's mission, at the time of the redeployment from I Corps it seemed like the thing to do. By mid-December the division recognized that the close proximity of its firebases to Cambodia was giving the NVA a free shot. As the NVA units began moving elements south from the border regions, so did the 1st Cav Division. The division began establishing firebases across the middle of War Zone C. The bases were far enough from the border to reduce their vulnerability but far enough north

---

*The 1st Cavalry officially referred to its fire support bases as landing zones (LZs), until September 1969 when ordered to make a change by Lieutenant General Julian Ewell, then the II Field Force commander. At that time all LZs that subsequently were fortified were designated as fire support bases (FSBs) and landing zones became just that, simple airmobile landing zones. In this book, however, the terms are used interchangeably, and an LZ is called that if that was the official title in the division's after-action report, although it may be also be referred to as a firebase in the text. Ewell's order angered the airmobile purists in the division, who disliked the term firebase as being common to the regular infantry divisions and certainly not appropriate for use by the Air Cav.

of the populated areas to provide great freedom of maneuver and fire. Because some early forays into the jungle near the border had yielded large caches and revealed the trails headed south, the 1st Brigade, which had initial responsibility for most of War Zone C, established two firebases, LZs GRANT and WHITE, in the middle of what Colonel Robert J. Baer, commander of the 1st Brigade, believed was a major transshipment area for the NVA. Early intelligence had revealed the presence of a major trail system along the eastern edge of War Zone C, generally following the Saigon River in a meandering southwesterly direction, and another north-to-south trail in central War Zone C, called the Mustang Trail. Both of these trail systems seemed to join in an area just north of the Michelin Plantation that was marked on intelligence maps as Base Area 355.

Because of the interdiction efforts of the Cav battalions in War Zone C, the 1st NVA Division was completely bottled up and deprived of its war-fighting materiel in Base Area 355. Although the 1st NVA Division was floundering in War Zone C, the VC 9th Division was starting to make serious forays out of the Parrot's Beak and Angel's Wing west of Saigon. And to the east, elements of the 5th VC and 7th NVA divisions had broken down into small groups and were methodically working toward Vietnam's capital city. General Abrams had not expected the 1st Cavalry Division to totally stop these four divisions, just slow them down, disrupt their timing, and above all play havoc with the logistical nose that they always had to push out in front of them. So the Cav began a rapid shifting of units to counter the threat. But even as the rapid movement was occurring, a bizarre event was to occur in the jungles of Tay Ninh Province that would capture the attention of the world and draw focus to the capabilities of the communists to manufacture propaganda.

4

Interlude in the Jungle

On Wednesday, December 18, in the Army Security Agency's radio-monitoring facility at Long Binh post just outside Saigon, the routine of listening to the tiresome propaganda broadcasts of the National Liberation Front's clandestine radio changed abruptly with an electrifying transmission. It was a message from the Directorate of Political Affairs for the National Liberation Front (NLF) announcing that the NLF intended to release some American soldiers captured by the communists.

The transcript of that broadcast, which included a lengthy propaganda message about the NLF's humane policy of clemency toward American POWs, was barely on its way to the embassy and MACV headquarters when a second broadcast was monitored. This message was more specific and its originator was the Viet Cong's military command for the area northwest of Saigon, which the communists called "Eastern Nam Bo." This message said that if the United States was interested in the prisoner release it should send an unarmed delegation to meet with the NLF representatives at 3 P.M. on Christmas Day, December 25. The location for the rendezvous, given as map coordinates, was a spot in the jungle southwest of Tay Ninh City in an area within the tactical area of operations of the 25th Infantry Division and a short walk from the Cambodian border. The message concluded by stating that if the United States command was interested it

should respond over its own radio system, the Armed Forces
Vietnam Network (AFVN).

The unexpected NLF proposal presented the U.S. government
with a dilemma. After extensive coaxing, it had within the previous two weeks finally persuaded the government of Vietnam to
participate in the incipient Paris peace talks. One condition was
that the NLF not be recognized as an equal party in the talks.
So the United States was carefully maneuvering through a diplomatic minefield in which it had to talk to the NLF in Paris,
while dutifully not recognizing the front and its claims to be a
legitimate representative of some portions of the South Vietnamese populace.

When Secretary of State Dean Rusk read the cable traffic from
Saigon, he first asked the U.S. ambassador to the GVN, Ellsworth
Bunker, for his recommendation. Bunker strongly recommended
against meeting the NLF in Vietnam. He recognized the NLF
offer for the propaganda ploy that it was and recommended that
negotiations for prisoner release be conducted in Paris. Rusk
forwarded Bunker's reply to Paris and asked chief U.S. negotiator
Averell Harriman for his recommendation. Harriman carefully
considered Bunker's comments and then replied to Rusk that to
make an issue over diplomatic problems with the prisoner release
would be playing into the hands of the NLF. He declared force-
fully that "the American public would never understand the delay
or refusal to accept the release of U.S. prisoners because of our
unwillingness to meet with the NLF in the field." Harriman also
observed that Bunker's suggestion of direct, bilateral negotiations
on prisoner release in Paris would create more problems with the
government of Vietnam than would a meeting of the two parties
in the field.

Rusk, one of the Johnson administration's remaining hard-
liners, studied both recommendations and then cabled Saigon
with instructions to respond positively to the NLF offer. Rusk's
cable said, "battlefield contacts between opposing sides for prisoner release have a time-honored role in warfare." Rusk said that
the appropriate level of field command to handle the actual release was Lieutenant General Kerwin's II Field Force. He reckoned Kerwin's command to be the equivalent rank as the Viet
Cong's Eastern Nam Bo military command. The response was

sent out on AFVN radio every hour on the hour on the afternoon and evening of December 21. The message was carefully phrased and stated that an unarmed team would be sent to meet with the "opposing forces." The term "opposing forces" was used instead of "the NLF."

The MACV staff, after consulting with embassy staffers, told Kerwin that the senior member of the U.S. negotiating team would be a lieutenant colonel. The man finally chosen to head the team was the G-3 (operations officer) of the 1st Air Cavalry Division, Lieutenant Colonel John V. "Jack" Gibney. Gibney said the criterion set forth by MACV was a lieutenant colonel who had already spent six months in command of a battalion. MACV had quickly come up with a computerized list of candidate light colonels and gave it to Kerwin. Gibney said he would have liked to say that his name was tops on the list, but he wasn't on it at all. What finally happened was that Kerwin, already irritated by what he considered micromanagement by the embassy and the staff drones at MACV, looked the list over, pulled his ever-present cigar out of his mouth, and growled to his chief of staff that he "didn't know any of these guys." A guy he did know was Gibney and, after a quick call to General Forsythe at the Cav's headquarters in Phuoc Vinh, the Cav's operations officer was suddenly thrust center stage in the unfolding drama. To Gibney's credit, he seized the moment.

Gibney was a 1952 West Point graduate who had deployed to Vietnam with the 1st Cav in 1965 and stayed. He spent a quick five months at the Armed Forces Staff College in late 1967, then returned to the Cav to command the 2nd Battalion, 8th Cavalry, the Stony Mountain Boys, during the Cav's campaigns during Tet, the relief of Khe Sanh, and the investment of the A Shau Valley. He had been assigned as division G-3 just as the division was beginning its move out of Quang Tri to III Corps. Gibney was tough, smart, and unflappable.

Gibney was the only Cav man chosen for the prisoner release team, the title bestowed on the U.S. negotiating contingent. To be Gibney's interpreter and assistant team chief, II Field Force assigned Major Jean A. Sauvageot, who worked for Civil Operations and Revolutionary Development Support (CORDS) and was fluent in the Vietnamese language. Sauvageot spent most of his time as the primary interpreter for Ambassador Colby, the CORDS boss. Also assigned to the team were three captains— Burke O. Bunts, a communications officer; Melvin R. Chapman, a backup interpreter; and Donald R. Tesch, a medical officer. Another vital member of the overall team was Major Douglas E. Moore, who flew the medical evacuation helicopter that was to come to the clearing on command. Years later, Moore, then a colonel, wrote a paper for the Army War College and later published the paper as an article in the March 1982 issue of *Army* Magazine, the first and only time the complete story was told.

Just prior to the Christmas Day meeting, Kerwin and Gibney attended a briefing and guidance session at MACV headquarters in which the micromanagers attempted to cover every possible contingency. Gibney said as the briefing continued, he "watched the red start creeping up above Kerwin's collar as these guys pussy-footed around what we should or should not do." He said Kerwin was a tough commander who believed in mission-type orders. So when their jeep arrived back at Bien Hoa and dismounted at Kerwin's command post, Gibney tried to get some definitive guidance from Kerwin. Kerwin, pausing halfway up the steps to his office, turned, pulled his cigar out of his mouth, jabbed it in Gibney's direction, and snapped at him: "Hey, look. I picked you because I thought you could do the job. Use your own judgment and I'll back you all the way." With that he chomped back down on his cigar and disappeared into the building.

As Gibney later recalled, that vote of confidence was better than all the stringent instructions he had received from the embassy, which mostly amounted to a basketfull of don'ts—don't shake hands, don't sit down at a table with them, don't permit their photographers to take pictures of the team, and on and on. Gibney knew the mission. Get the prisoners back, but don't give away the store in the process. He also sensed that the game was going to be an exchange of bluffs, but with Kerwin's backing, he was going into the battle of bluffs well armed.

On December 25, a battalion-sized heliborne reaction force from the U.S. 25th Division had its Christmas truce stand-down disturbed as it went on strip alert at Tay Ninh City. Its mission was to go into the jungle to attempt to rescue the negotiating team if it turned out that the NLF offer was a ruse. Kerwin's command, in coordination with the ARVN III Corps commander, established a one-kilometer safe zone around the clearing where the meeting was to be held. The safe zone also included a narrow strip between the site and the Cambodian border. At 2 P.M. Gibney and his team boarded a helicopter at Tay Ninh and flew toward the map coordinates provided by the NLF. When they got to the clearing they spotted a large Viet Cong flag in the clearing. The pilots landed as far away from the flag as possible.

Gibney and Sauvageot walked to the center of the clearing to meet a two-man Viet Cong delegation dressed in ill-fitting khaki uniforms and wearing the standard VC cotton bush hat. The two said their boss was waiting for the U.S. delegation inside the wood line. There Gibney and Sauvageot could see three men seated at a field-expedient table made of bamboo lashed together. Gibney declined, stating, "I am here only to pick up the prisoners."

The VC spokesman tried several times to persuade the American team to sit down and have refreshments. Gibney was firm and stayed put in the center of the clearing. Finally the leader of the NLF team arose from the table and walked to the group in the field. He offered to shake hands and Gibney declined, standing with his hands clasped behind him. Then came a series of verbal thrusts and counterthrusts that the MACV press office later described as "cordial exchanges" but that Gibney characterized as an exchange of bluffs. It soon became apparent that the prisoners were not at the clearing and the VC never had any intention of making a release that day. What they were looking for was a chance to show photographs of Americans and NLF representatives sitting at a table, ostensibly engaged in serious negotiations. It would have been safe to bet the mortgage that any such picture would have surfaced very quickly in Paris and been used to drive a wedge between the United States and the Thieu government. Gibney never gave them the chance. But he had to leave the clearing that day empty-handed.

After nearly two-and-a-half hours of bluff and counterbluff, the negotiating team boarded the waiting helicopter without even setting a definite date for a subsequent meeting. On December 28, however, the NLF radio station broadcast a message that proposed another meeting at the same location, this time at 9 A.M. The United States responded with a series of messages on

AFVN on December 30. The negotiating team remained the same, as did the reaction force at Tay Ninh. One big difference in this meeting was that Gibney's guidance from the embassy had been altered. He still was not to give away the store, or at least all of it, but returning the prisoners was paramount. This might entail his having to sit down with the NLF, the embassy said. To ensure that if he did sit, it would be on American chairs, he brought some GI metal folding chairs with him. Another major difference in this expedition was that a four-man press pool was on a chopper in a trail position. When he got on the ground, Gibney was to decide whether to bring in American reporters. As soon as the team landed, they could see that the clearing was awash with NLF photographers, so Gibney radioed for the press chopper to land. Then he and Sauvageot walked to the center of the clearing. Once again there was the Viet Cong invitation to sit down with the NLF negotiators, and once again Gibney firmly declined. The NLF negotiator who was obviously the boss, a man apparently in his mid-forties, was suffering from a tooth-ache and the lower right side of his jaw was swollen. After some procedural matters dealing with rules for the media representa-tives, the Viet Cong leader indicated that he would outline the conditions for release of the prisoners, but only after both sides were seated. As he was speaking, his aides brought some bamboo stools out for the NLF representatives, and the Viet Cong leader gestured toward the folding chairs, indicating the Americans should be seated in their own chairs.

This was when Gibney ran his final and most daring bluff. He saw that the NLF representatives were going to be seated, leaving him and Sauvageot standing. So he ripped into the Viet Cong officers, saying, through Sauvageot, "If you sit down on your chairs before I sit down, it would be an act of discourtesy. And if you do, I will be forced to turn my back and leave." Gibney's bluff worked; the startled NLF officer abandoned the seating ploy; Gibney knew then that he had won and that he was going to get the prisoners that day. He also credited Kerwin's support for giving him the flexibility to make such a courageous bluff. After their seating gambit failed, the NLF representatives moved into their list of prerelease conditions.

The first demand was a guarantee that the prisoners be returned quickly to their families and not be terrorized or subjected to undue pressure to issue propaganda statements running counter to the NLF's claims of clemency and humanitarian policies. The NLF also demanded that the United States announce that it would not terrorize or harm the people of Eastern Nam Bo. Gibney disposed of the preconditions one by one with devastatingly logical responses; in the end, the NLF agreed to drop the matter of preconditions. Then the NLF leader said that it would take about an hour to get the prisoners to the meeting site, turned abruptly, and left the clearing.

The U.S. negotiating team went back to their helicopter to await the delivery of the three American prisoners. When the hour was up, Gibney and Sauvageot walked back to the center of the clearing. As the NLF team moved back to the clearing, Gibney noticed that a crowd of Vietnamese were gathered near the edge of the jungle. When the NLF leader dramatically raised his arm, the U.S. team could see the three young Americans being moved in single file through the group of Vietnamese, who were jeering and pointing at the prisoners. Gibney again got tough and demanded that these demonstrations cease immediately. The NLF leader issued the appropriate orders and the three young men were allowed to stumble toward the negotiating team. Clad in blue-gray uniforms given them by the Viet Cong, the three American soldiers, all twenty-one years of age—Specialist Four James W. Brigham of Ocala, Florida, Specialist Four Thomas N. Jones of Lynnville, Indiana, and Private First Class Donald G. Smith of Akron, Pennsylvania—stood with their heads bowed as the NLF extracted one last measure of propaganda from the affair. The NLF leader read and then had translated a long statement that, among other things, assured the prisoners that "we wish you will lead a happy life." During the harangue, Smith, who had spent more than seven months in captivity, mumbled, "My God, let's get all of this over with and get out of here." By the time the propaganda statement ended, the medical evacuation helicopter piloted by Major Moore landed and the three young men were helped on board. When Moore's chopper was safely away, Gibney signed a receipt for the three soldiers, looked at his watch and noted the time was 11:05 A.M., and reminded the Viet Cong that the truce would end in three hours. Then Gibney and his team boarded their helicopter and flew back to Tay Ninh for a debrief with General Kerwin.

The press helicopter headed for Saigon, its representatives hoping for a chance to talk to the young ex-prisoners. But it was not to be. With fairly typical wrongheadedness, the MACV Office of Information refused media access to the returnees and relayed a dubious statement allegedly made by a military doctor at a Long Binh hospital that all three were in "generally satisfactory to good condition." Brigham was, in fact, in anything but good condition. He had suffered a head wound during the ambush of his convoy four months earlier. Viet Cong doctors had operated on him but the wound became infected and, at the time of his release, it had developed into a terrible brain abscess that had markedly reduced his vision and balance. Brigham was taken directly to Walter Reed Army Hospital in Washington, D.C., where brain surgeons struggled in vain to save his life. James Woodrow Brigham, Jr., died on January 17 at age twenty-one, never having enjoyed the fruits of the liberty purchased in that small clearing in Tay Ninh Province.

The communists wasted no time in seizing the opportunity to use Brigham's death to flog the United States. They quickly picked up on the MACV statement, which had received worldwide media attention, that all the prisoners were in good shape when they arrived at Long Binh and accused the United States of murdering Brigham, a black soldier, to keep him from speaking his mind about the comparison between racism in America and the egalitarianism in the NLF. But because the media representatives present during the exchange could see Brigham's wound and his obvious distress, this propaganda gambit sank without a ripple.

Another American prisoner got his freedom that same week. One of the fruits of the Vietnamese Army force modernization that MACV had instituted in earnest after Tet-68 was the ARVN 21st Infantry Division, which, with good weapons and good leadership, was taking the lower part of the IV Corps back from the Viet Cong. During a sweep by the newly rejuvenated ARVN division into the U Minh Forest (the "Forest of Darkness"), a long-time Viet Cong stronghold, the guard detail escorting an American Special Forces officer, James N. "Nick" Rowe from a lower-echelon POW camp to a zone camp became badly shaken by the proximity of the ARVN forces. Rowe was able to maneuver himself into a position where he was one on one with a guard, overpowered him, and escaped. Rowe made his way to a clearing in the jungle, signaled a passing American helicopter unit, and was soon winging his way to Saigon. His rescue by the chopper was in itself a miracle; clad in black pajamas, waving the lightest colored cloth in his possession, a faded mosquito net, he looked like a Viet Cong, and only the desire to capture a live prisoner stayed the deadly fire from the air cavalry hunter-killer team.

Rowe, a 1960 West Point graduate, had been a lieutenant when he was captured on October 29, 1963, in the Camau Peninsula at the southern tip of South Vietnam after the Viet Cong had overwhelmed the small combat patrol he was advising. Rowe, knowing the penalty for being recognized as a Special Forces officer, had for the better part of five years successfully fooled his captors with a cover story that he was an engineering officer concerned only with civic action projects in the Delta. In mid-December, he was brought before a senior officer of the NLF, who told him "It is fortunate for us that the peace- and justice-loving friends of the South Vietnam Front for National Liberation in America have provided us with information which leads us to believe you have lied to us." As Rowe recounted in his book *Five Years to Freedom*, the NLF officer methodically recited an accurate dossier on him. Shortly thereafter, he learned he was being transferred to the NLF zone POW camp, which he considered tantamount to a death sentence.

For Rowe, in suprisingly good shape considering the rigors of his captivity, freedom was its own reward. But the Army made it even sweeter. He had routinely been promoted during his five years of captivity, first to captain and then to major, and he had accumulated nearly fifty thousand dollars in back pay. After a debriefing, according to an article published in the December 1989 issue of *International Combat Arms*, Rowe accompanied a combined Vietnamese and American task force into the Forest of Darkness hoping to find other POWs or information about them that could be used to plan further operations. Rowe also volunteered to stay in Vietnam and pass along his knowledge of the Viet Cong to U.S. forces, but the Army would have none of it and sent him permanently back to the states. On April 21, 1989, Colonel Nick Rowe, still fighting communist insurgencies, was gunned down by assassins while serving with the U.S. Military Assistance Group in the Philippines.

Rowe could not understand how an American could betray another American. But then he never had a chance to study the contents of a gaggle of radical journals published during the war in the United States. These journals, the most prominent of which was *Ramparts*, featured a steady succession of authors who urged the American Left to greater efforts on behalf of the NLF and the North Vietnamese, because from their successes would come the reordering of the social and economic structure of the United States. The American Left considered most peace advocates as sincere, naive, and misguided, but nevertheless useful. His incarceration spared Rowe the spectacle of the peace marches where youthful revolutionaries mixed with the crowds of the sincere and naive, waved Viet Cong flags and the red banners of communist revolution, and led cheers seeking a communist victory in Vietnam. It was from this society, one deeply in turmoil, that the young soldiers who fought the battles of interdiction in Vietnam were drawn.

Meanwhile, the Paris peace talks were sputtering along inconclusively. Hanoi had achieved one of its long-standing goals in Vietnam: a talk-fight situation. With a bombing halt in its pocket which had cost it nothing, Hanoi felt that the talking phase was doing quite nicely in Paris. The North Vietnamese were delighted with the recalcitrant stance of the Thieu government and the wrangling over the shape of a conference table, although it could have done better if Hanoi's prisoner-release propaganda ploy had been successful. In Vietnam, the communists were determined to do as well with the fighting phase. Despite the numerous bloody noses inflicted by the allies on the Viet Cong and NVA during the first three phases of the TCK-TKN general offensive, COSVN was determined to have another go at the conquest of Saigon in its upcoming Fourth Offensive. During November and December in III Corps, the communists worked desperately to prepare the battlefields for the combat regiments trying to work their way out of their lairs past the interdiction screens to positions in the populated areas around the capital city.

5

The Defense of Saigon

General Kerwin stood in front of the huge map that dominated the wall of the II Field Force Operations Center in Bien Hoa and gestured toward the area east and slightly north of Saigon. This was the portion of Military Region III that had been known for years as War Zone D. His audience was General Forsythe, commander of the 1st Air Cavalry Division, and Forsythe's two principal staff assistants, the Cav's G-2, Lieutenant Colonel Fred Barrett, and the G-3, Lieutenant Colonel Jack Gibney. Kerwin was disturbed about intelligence reports indicating that, with Tet less than four weeks away, the 5th VC Division was having some success in its attempt to stage an end run through War Zone D toward the eastern approaches to Saigon. He wanted the Cav to deploy one of its brigades into blocking positions in War Zone D just east of Saigon and Bien Hoa to try to slow down the NVA Division.

For most of December and into January, the Cav's 3rd Brigade had been opening and closing firebases in eastern Binh Long Province and western Phuoc Long Province and had had some good luck in interdicting the Serges Jungle Highway and the Adams Road, the major infiltration routes that fed rice and weapons into the secret bases in War Zone D. But most of the 3rd Brigade's battles had been with elements of the NVA 7th Division that kept pushing closer to the eastern borders of War Zone C. The 5th VC Division, after a few encounters with Cavalry elements, had retreated to eastern Phuoc Long Province, and instead of moving southwest along the easier and more direct Song Be corridor, the communist formations had slipped around the Cavalry screen to the east by hugging the II Corps–III Corps border until it reached northeastern Long Kanh Province. At the time, allied intelligence thought that was the hard way to do it, given the logistical requirements of supporting a North Vietnamese division in a relatively unpopulated jungle wilderness. It would be nearly a year before the Cav discovered a major infiltration route that paralleled the corps boundaries and terminated in the depths of War Zone D. When assigning the 1st Cavalry Division its screening mission when it was moved south in November, neither General Kerwin nor General Abrams had expected the Cav, despite its marvelous mobility, to completely halt the movement toward Saigon of all four NVA divisions that threatened to repeat the 1968 Tet investment of Saigon. But, as Abrams had told Forsythe the day after he arrived in III Corps, his mission was to "ride them with your spurs all the way down." It was time to sharpen up another pair of spurs and jab them in the flanks of the 5th VC Division.

The Fourth General Offensive, expected in the spring of 1969, was planned as a rerun of the 1968 First General Offensive, the Tet Offensive. There were, however, some major modifications. First, allied intelligence had nearly the entire picture in advance. Abrams knew that COSVN was planning an attack in three stages, with the campaign to last anywhere from a month to six weeks. This time the communists would be gunning for U.S. installations in the hopes of creating American casualties to help its propaganda campaigns. Another major change was that this time COSVN would have four divisions instead of the three used in Tet-68. But in 1968, in addition to the Viet Cong main-force divisions, several main-force VC infantry and sapper battalions were used in the assault on Saigon and other GVN facilities in III Corps. Myriad Viet Cong platoon and company-sized units had also been used during the 1968 offensives. In 1969, however, the NVA would have to bear the brunt of the offensive; the Viet Cong soldiers, the muscle for the southern insurgency, had been sacrificed for General Vo Nguyen Giap's dream of a great general uprising in the south.

Allied intelligence knew generally that the NVA battle plan called for knocking out key bases and seizing terrain suitable for continued stockpiling of crucial supplies and equipment, with the ultimate intent of forcing the allies to commit their mobile reserves in areas distant from the population centers they were securing.

Implicit in the communist strategy was the destruction of the pacification efforts in III Corps. Ambassador Komer had seen, perhaps better than anyone, that the communists had shot their wads in the countryside during Tet. For the first few months after Tet, the emphasis in Vietnam was on recovery from the devastation of that offensive. But by late summer of 1968, Komer and his deputy, the former chief of station for the CIA in Vietnam, William Colby, reckoned that the time was ripe to combine the reconstruction efforts with the more political and intangible elements of a real pacification program. From that came an intensive three-month program, initiated in November 1968, called the Accelerated Pacification Program. In one of the anomalies of that strange conflict, the part of Vietnam that the North Vietnamese had chosen to make a major battleground—Military Region III —was the region that was the most pacified. In fact, a case could be made that pacification of III Corps probably was the greatest contribution of the legendary John Paul Vann. After the Accelerated Pacification Program got under way, Colby, who had just replaced Komer as the MACV chief of pacification, persuaded Vann to move to Military Region IV, the Mekong Delta region, and bring that area under government control. Vann did precisely that, but his efforts in III Corps loom even larger because they were accomplished without the support that the American and South Vietnamese military and civilian bureaucracies belatedly brought to bear on the process.

When General Abrams assumed command of MACV, he made it clear that the mission of American forces in Vietnam was no longer simply to kill the enemy, but to protect the people. By concentrating on protecting the population centers with the large American formations, training the Regional Forces and Popular Forces, and, with the Revolutionary Development cadres, installing democratic government in newly pacified areas, Abrams and Komer had made pacification work. Working hand-in-glove with the pacification program was Operation *Phung Hoang*, better known by its American name, "Phoenix." The purpose of *Phung Hoang* was to flush out the Viet Cong infrastructure (VCI). The VCI were the hidden leadership elements who ran the communist political apparatus; controlled the guerrilla bands; collected taxes; ordered assassinations; set up front organizations; drafted men and women as soldiers, guerrillas, and laborers in porterage units; spread propaganda; and directed terror campaigns. About eighty-thousand cadres originally were estimated to hold VCI positions in the RVN. In the first eleven months of the campaign that kicked off in early 1968, Operation *Phung Hoang* resulted in about thirteen thousand of these cadres being rooted out of their underground positions in the communist shadow government, although the majority were only low-level operatives.

There probably has been more acrimony over the Phoenix program than over almost any other facet of the Vietnam War. Ambassador Colby repeatedly has had to defend the integrity of the Americans involved in the campaign against accusations of indiscriminate killing and even assassination. It is paradoxical that those things that hurt the enemy the most tended to be the ones that the antiwar protestors howled the loudest about. After the war, Hanoi noted that Phoenix was the program run by the American and Saigon governments that hurt the Viet Cong the most, breaking as it did nearly all contact between the communist political structure and the population of South Vietnam. Ambassador Colby, writing in his 1989 book, *Lost Victory*, said:

In my own view, this was an exaggeration of what Phoenix by itself had achieved. It stemmed from the erroneous impression (prevalent among many who were—and still are—not well informed about the CORDS effort) that Phoenix equated with the broader pacification program conducted by the Thieu Government. The latter, of course, included its stress on territorial security in the villages, the strengthening of local government, in addition to the direct attack by Phoenix against the Communist secret apparatus, the self-defense and Territorial forces, and the programs of local economic and social development. Taken together, these indeed had had results the North Vietnamese ascribed to Phoenix alone. . . .

It didn't take postwar introspection for COSVN to realize that the pacification program had to be disrupted. Its strategy for the Fourth Offensive presupposed extensive combat in the villages and hamlets in the heavily populated provinces around Saigon, thus demonstrating again to the population that the South Vietnamese and American governments were powerless and unable to protect the people. And of course, in the process, the North Vietnamese hoped to stage damaging attacks on Saigon itself. To accomplish this objective, COSVN planned coordinated attacks by all four NVA divisions. The COSVN attack plan was fatally flawed in that it underestimated the impact the addition of an airmobile division would have on Abrams's defensive strategy, and it presumed that the American command would react to the threat as it had in the past.

The constant pressure from the ground and the air by the Cav and the forward-deployed battalions of the U.S. 1st and 25th divisions, plus the ARVN units working in conjunction with the U.S. interdiction effort, caused the NVA to break their larger combat formations down into small infiltration cells. Those cells would be under orders to move to a prearranged supply point, pick up necessary supplies, and reform back into companies and battalions. Many of the kills registered by the air cavalry hunter-killer teams were members of these small groups attempting to infiltrate toward the populated areas. Sometimes, before an infiltrating company or battalion had broken into the smaller cells they would make contact with a Cavalry unit. The result would be violent combat such as occurred with Delta Company, 2nd Battalion, 7th Cavalry, on December 3.

Just six days later to the northwest of Quon Loi, Alpha Company, Fifth Battalion, 7th Cavalry, hit a reinforced rifle company from the NVA 7th Division. Alpha Company was eventually reinforced by Troop C of the 1st Squadron, 11th Armored Cavalry Regiment. The five-hour battle finally ended with the NVA breaking contact, leaving behind ninety-three dead. The fight cost the Americans fourteen killed and seventeen wounded.

The North Vietnamese were well able to retaliate. One of their favorite tactics was to ambush the roadways, knowing that the Army had to send vulnerable truck convoys along those routes to resupply its forward bases. One of the main missions of the 11th Armored Cavalry "Blackhorse" Regiment was to escort convoys on Route 13 from the U.S. 1st Infantry Division's forward Thunder Road security base at Chon Than north through An Loc and Loc Ninh. On January 11, Lieutenant Harold A. Fritz, a platoon leader in Troop A of the 11th ACR, was leading his platoon south along Route 13 enroute to a rendezvous point with a sixty-truck convoy when the platoon was struck by a violent NVA ambush. The platoon consisted of thirty-four men in six armored cavalry assault vehicles (ACAVs) and a brand-new weapons system, the XM163 Vulcan. This was a six-barrel 20-mm Gatling gun mounted on an armored personnel carrier, capable of spewing out one thousand rounds a minute. Four NVA antitank rockets hit Fritz's lead vehicle, killing its crew, setting the vehicle ablaze, and seriously wounding the lieutenant.

Realizing that his platoon was surrounded, vastly outnumbered, and in danger of being overrun, Fritz leaped to the top of his burning vehicle and signaled his remaining ACAVs into the prescribed herringbone defensive pattern. Then Fritz jumped from his track and under withering enemy fire limped back to his other vehicles, where he directed the defense of the position. While the Vulcan's fire down one side of the road broke the back of the enemy force there, North Vietnamese soldiers on the other side of the road assaulted the position and attempted to overrun it. Lieutenant Fritz grabbed a machine gun and helped deliver strong defensive fire that stopped the assault. When an armored relief force arrived, Fritz saw that it was not deployed correctly and again moved through heavy enemy fire to direct the force against the hostile positions. Only after the NVA had broken contact and withdrawn did Fritz permit his wounds to be treated and allow himself to be evacuated. It was later determined that two NVA companies had staged the ambush and thirty-one North Vietnamese died at the scene. Three Americans were killed and fourteen wounded. On March 24, 1971, President Nixon pinned the Medal of Honor on Captain Harold Fritz.

Although the searching by the Cav platoons turned up scores of cache sites, there were still many, many supply points that had been prestocked in the years when the Viet Cong and the North Vietnamese had the run of the countryside. Moreover, no screen spread over the distance that the Cav and its attached units had to cover, could completely stop all materiel infiltration. There were ample munitions stashed throughout the III Corps tactical zone and still enough Viet Cong and North Vietnamese soldiers not directly assigned to the big divisions to make use of them. As a result, nearly every base camp for American and major ARVN units in III Corps was a target for mortar and rocket attacks, and these went on incessantly through the early part of 1969.

In mid-December, allied intelligence picked up the movement of the 9th VC Division's support forces moving battlefield supplies out of Cambodia into western Hau Nghia Province. General Kerwin directed that two battalions of the 1st Brigade redeploy south out of War Zone C into western Hau Nghia and Long An provinces, the area generally between the Vam Co Dong River and the Cambodian border. To distinguish the new operation from the Cheyenne Sabre interdiction activities to the north, the division dubbed the new operational area "Navajo Warhorse." One battalion, Lieutenant Colonel Todd P. Graham's 1st of the 8th, got a chance to work with the U.S. Navy, combining airmobility with the gunboats of the Navy's River Division 553 to disrupt the enemy's prestocking of the battlefield. When the operation moved onto a river in Kien Tuong Province in the IV Corps Tactical Zone, the 1st Cavalry became the first major U.S. Army unit to have fought in all four of Vietnam's military regions. The Navy termed its operation "Giant Slingshot" but the troopers of the Cav quickly dubbed it "Nav-Cav."

Also deploying into the Navajo Warhorse area of operations (AO) was Lieutenant Colonel William Dougald MacMillan's 1st Battalion, 7th Cavalry. The "Garry Owen" battalion had been deployed smack against the Cambodian border in northwest War Zone C. Operating from LZ ANN in the Dog's Head, the companies of the battalion had been involved in several vicious firefights during the last week of November with elements of the 1st NVA Division, which was trying an end run to the west around the cavalry screen. Dougald MacMillan remembers the time in Navajo Warhorse as relatively quiet compared to the tough fighting in War Zone C. During this lull in the fighting MacMillan's battalion displayed some of the qualities that make the American fighting man unique among those who follow the profession of arms—humor, individuality, and a sense of theater. Two days after Christmas the battalion got word that Admiral John S. McCain, the commander in chief of the Pacific, was going to visit their firebase, LZ CLARA. Although cannon salutes were used for greeting high-ranking visitors at major bases, they were discouraged, for obvious reasons, at small, forward outposts. When the gaggle of aircraft bringing Admiral McCain to LZ CLARA landed, MacMillan walked out on the landing pad just outside the wire to greet the dignitaries.

As the admiral's foot touched the ground, a 105-mm howitzer fired. MacMillan reported to McCain, trying, as he said, "to keep a straight face at the sight of this small man with an enormous cigar in his teeth and stars on his collar that disappeared around the back of his neck." As the battalion commander led the admiral through the gap in the wire and the cannons kept firing, McCain took the cigar from his mouth and growled, "Who's that salute for, son?"

MacMillan quickly responded. "Admiral, that's not a salute. That's a fire mission for Alpha Company. It just happens to call for seventeen rounds."

MacMillan remembers the admiral grinning and saying, "Well, I'll be damned; that's pretty good."

"And," MacMillan said, "it was; no parade ground salute was ever more perfect. The chief of smoke [NCO in charge of the firing battery] stood on the berm by the number one gun, looking like a drum major, his arm whipping out to each gun in turn."

Contacts with the enemy in the Navajo Warhorse AO were light, but numerous caches were found. The flat, open, and perpetually wet terrain precluded the communists from handling supply points as they did in War Zone C. Skytroopers of the 1st Brigade found huge quantities of munitions buried in sealed fifty-five-gallon drums. Some of the more significant finds were a complete 120-mm mortar and forty-six 122-mm rockets. The total of small arms ammunition captured totaled more than 150,000 rounds. Rice stores were less frequently found. Hau Nghia Province was, of course, a rich rice-growing area and the NVA believed its combat forces would have little trouble getting food resupply from the villages it overran in its offensive.

Even though the 1st Brigade had moved temporary head-quarters to Cu Chi during the Navajo Warhorse operation, its supporting air cavalry troop, Alpha Troop of the 9th Cav, had continued monitoring movement of NVA forces in War Zone C and wreaking havoc with the members of the 82nd Rear Service Group. This was the NVA organization COSVN had charged with the mission of moving supplies down into the Michelin Plantation area. The lack of contacts in Navajo War-horse and the plethora of targets in southern War Zone C per-suaded General Forsythe to move the 1st Brigade back to the eastern sector of the old Cheyenne Sabre AO. The brigade re-entered War Zone C on January 19 with four battalions for interdiction duty.

One battalion, Lieutenant Colonel James Dingeman's 2nd Battalion, 12th Cavalry, was assigned an area of operations just inside a box labeled Base Area 355 that was drawn on everybody's intelligence maps. A firebase site was picked and LZ GRANT, which had been temporarily closed during the Navajo Warhorse operations, was reopened. The rifle companies of the 2/12 Cav quickly fanned out into the area around the firebase. It was like a bunch of kids being turned loose in a candy store. Almost immediately the companies began turning over cache sites, find-ing and destroying bunker complexes, and finding burial areas, evidence of the lethality of the brigade's and division's aero scout teams. On January 31 one of the 2/12 companies found a rice storage complex that contained ten thousand pounds of rice.

That was only the beginning. The battalion changed com-manders without missing a beat. Lieutenant Colonel Peter Gor-vad pinned on the green tabs of a battalion commander and presided over more rice hauls. In the space of a week, the Sky-troopers of the 2nd of the 12th found more than one hundred tons of rice and thousands of pounds of salt. On February 1, the 1st Brigade extended the screen across the southern part of War Zone C by moving the 2nd Battalion, 8th Cavalry, to LZ ST. BARBARA, about six kilometers due north of Nui Ba Den, and opening LZ DOLLY on the highest hill of the "Razorback," a ridge line that formed the northern boundary of the Michelin Plantation. The U.S. 25th Infantry Division had several firebases ranging west of Tay Ninh to the Cambodian border. Now the

NVA 1st Division was completely bottled up inside War Zone C. And the cork in the bottle was LZ GRANT.

The division didn't yet know it, but the jungle around GRANT was a huge transshipment area where the major infiltration trails from Cambodia intersected. From this part of Base Area 355, porterage units would begin to infiltrate supplies south across the Razorback, through the Michelin, and into caches in smaller base areas such as the Trapezoid and Iron Triangle that were closer to the more populated zones. The NVA organization responsible for infiltration into and protection of Base Area 355 was the 82nd Rear Service Group, a mixture of laborers and soldiers. As the Cav's interdiction of the infiltration trails began to cause attrition among the fighters in the group, more and more combat soldiers from the line units had to be diverted into guarding cache sites and providing security to porterage gangs. The NVA 1st Division was a long way from being in position to stage its assigned diversionary attacks south of the Michelin.

COSVN considered the population area south of the Michelin the most critical for its plans to destabilize pacification in III Corps, so it ordered the NVA 7th Division to work its way westward into the Michelin and take over the mission of the NVA 1st Division.

On February 3, the 1st Cavalry Division, reacting to General Kerwin's concern about the VC 5th Division approaching Saigon from War Zone D, moved two battalions of the 3rd Brigade into the heart of that wild country, establishing the AO the division dubbed Cheyenne Sabre. Lieutenant Colonel George McGarrigle's 1st Battalion, 12th Cavalry, air-assaulted into LZ CINDY. The LZ was located about twenty-five kilometers northeast of Bien Hoa, where the 3rd Brigade set up a temporary headquarters. Paired with CINDY was LZ LIZ, established by the 2nd Battalion, 7th Cavalry. Both firebases were in a heavily jungled area deep in War Zone D and just north of the Dong Nai River. The Dong Nai was analogous to the Saigon River— a major infiltration route out of a nearly impenetrable redoubt aimed like an arrow at the South Vietnamese capital.

The two battalions almost immediately began making contact with the NVA. When intelligence sorted out who was fighting to break through the Cavalry screen, it turned out to be one of the Cav's old antagonists—the 33rd NVA Regiment, the first North Vietnamese regular army unit fought by the 1st Cavalry Division shortly after it arrived in country in 1965 (see *Pleiku: The Dawn of Helicopter Warfare*, St. Martin's Press).

Given that NVA soldiers did not have great longevity, it was unlikely that there were any veterans in the 33rd who could remember the battles in Pleiku Province, but on his third tour with the 1st Air Cavalry Division, Staff Sergeant Martin A. Manglona could. On February 10, Alpha Company, 2nd of the 7th, had established a forward operating base (FOB), set out their ambushes, and settled in for the night. At around 3:30 A.M. the FOB erupted with incoming 82-mm mortar fire. "Quite a few men were wounded by the mortars," said First Lieutenant George F. Dove, leader of the company's second platoon. "Among them were myself and Sergeant Manglona." When the mortar barrage lifted, the NVA assaulted the second platoon position under cover of a barrage of B-40 rockets. One of the rocket blasts temporarily blinded Manglona, so he had another wounded man position him and direct his fire against the enemy. He maintained that position during the enemy assault, refusing medical treatment and evacuation until the situation had stabilized. His were exceptionally valorous actions, and that's how the citation for the Distinguished Service Cross read when he received the nation's second highest award for valor in June.

The two battalions of the Cav, aided by thunderous air strikes, battled the 33rd Regiment to a standstill and eventually caused the regiment to abort its mission and retreat deeper into War Zone D. Further to the south, the 199th Light Infantry Brigade "Redcatchers," deployed along the Xuan Loc–Saigon highway (National Route 1), stopped the advance of the VC 174th Regiment, which had been attached to the VC 5th Division for the assault on Saigon.

This left two organic regiments, the 274th and 275th, and their supporting artillery regiment, the 74th, still moving toward the South Vietnamese capital. The NVA allowed a five-day truce for Tet-69, and even though the South Vietnamese stand-down was not as extensive as it had been the preceding year, there was a dropoff in combat capabilities. Nevertheless, the NVA used this period to maneuver its regiments even closer to U.S. installations outside Saigon.

Early in the morning of February 23, two days after the end of the Tet truce, the 1st Battalion, 275th Regiment, along with D2/U1, a local-force sapper unit, attacked the Bien Hoa City rail yard and were bloodied badly by ARVN defenders. At the same time, the 1st Battalion of the 274th unsuccessfully attacked the American logistical base at Bearcat, about 15 kilometers southeast of Long Binh. The Long Binh post itself was assaulted by the 2nd and 3rd Battalions of the 274th. Following a hail of rocket and mortar fire, the NVA assault forces briefly penetrated the wire into a sector occupied by the 720th Military Police Battalion. A counterattack by the provisional companies formed from support forces at Long Binh threw back the attackers and a sweep of the area outside the compound by the 720th MPs and a troop of the 11th Armored Cavalry Regiment ended the threat. One hundred thirty-two dead NVA soldiers were found in and around the breech in the perimeter wire.

Since the Fourth General Offensive was a countrywide affair, the communists did not neglect other parts of South Vietnam. From midnight on February 23 on through part of the day, the NVA and VC staged a series of attacks by fire, followed by ground probes at U.S. bases throughout Vietnam; none of the attacks had the effect desired by the Hanoi command. Six bases occupied by the 1st Cavalry Division were hit, the heaviest attack occurring at LZ GRANT. That assault was repulsed easily and cost the attackers sixteen dead.

Three days later, on February 26, the 3rd Battalion of the 275th Regiment, along with the 21st Sapper-Recon Battalion, attacked the gates and bunker line at Bien Hoa Air Base. The attack was repulsed after some violent fighting along the bunker line. The area was defended by the 5th Vietnamese Marine Battalion, the 3rd Battalion, 48th ARVN Infantry, and a battalion of the U.S. 199th Brigade. After being thrown back from the bunker line, the 275th was caught in an open field by artillery and Cobra gunships. The NVA fled into the nearby village of Tan Hiep, most of whose civilian residents had already been evacuated. In the fighting to eradicate the remnants of the 275th, in which 214 communists died and 60 more were captured, 86 of the 120 homes in the village were destroyed. On the same day, an element of the 7th NVA Division attacked U.S. 1st Infantry Division defenders at the Dau Tieng combat base and were handily defeated with heavy losses. The VC 9th Division was likewise rendered impotent by the U.S. 25th Division at firebases protecting the western approaches to Saigon.

Thus fizzled out the first stage of the great and much-heralded Fourth General Offensive. The North Vietnamese had failed utterly. Pacification had not been disturbed; only one village had been badly damaged by combat, and that was rebuilt immediately; no American bases had been overrun, and even American casualties were moderate. The Air Cavalry Division in its interdiction campaign, in the period of November through February sustained three hundred killed in action and eighteen hundred wounded. The North Vietnamese losses for the same period as the result of Cavalry actions were over three thousand killed and five hundred captured. The NVA also lost supply caches containing 750,000 rounds of small-arms ammunition, 10,000 large-caliber rounds, and 383 tons of rice.

The firefights that accompanied the interdiction of the attacking NVA forces did not gain a great deal of media attention, but there was enough that Nixon sent Kissinger a note on February 1 stating "I do not like the suggestions that I see in virtually every news report that 'we anticipate a Communist initiative in South Vietnam.' I believe that if any initiative occurs it should be on our part and not theirs." Kissinger and Melvin Laird polled the Joint Chiefs for suggestions on gaining the initiative, but according to Kissinger, the suggestions tended to be reiterations of the familiar desire to resume the bombardment of the north.

A resumption of the bombing was deemed politically inadvisable, but the chairman of the JCS, General Wheeler, came in with a proposal that had been initiated in Saigon by MACV and the embassy. Early in February, MACV intelligence was convinced it had pinpointed the location of the COSVN headquarters complex as just across the Cambodian border in Base Area 353, a heavily jungled area about fifty kilometers due north of Tay Ninh City. General Abrams and Ambassador Bunker wanted to hit the communist headquarters with B-52 strikes, but the proposal went on the shelf as Kissinger advised the president to defer a decision on so radical an action.

Then the communists kicked their offensive into high gear with the attacks on the outposts around Saigon on February 22, plus the countrywide sapper, mortar, and rocket attacks on American installations and major Vietnamese cities. The offensive made headlines worldwide. It took place as the National Security staff was analyzing the responses to NSSM-1, and the day before Richard Nixon was to make his first state visit to Europe, an eight-day jaunt during which he would visit most heads of state, including the irascible Charles De Gaulle. Henry Kissinger termed the offensive a maneuver of "extraordinary cynicism." The timing of the communist offensive made it easy for uninformed observers to declare that it was Hanoi's way of tweaking the nose of Richard Nixon. The *New York Times* editorially lectured Nixon and Kissinger that their new administration had provoked Hanoi by not immediately getting on with the Paris peace talks. The theme was quickly taken up in Congress by foes of the war.

It was, of course, nonsense. The American bases that were attacked were targeted by COSVN Directive 71, issued January 31, 1969. It has been widely speculated that the North Vietnamese Politburo used the attacks to test Nixon's reaction to provocation. Although that may well have been a last-minute ancillary motive, the fact remains that for the North Vietnamese to stage any kind of meaningful offensive, the battlefield had to be prepared well in advance. And those preparations had been underway by the fall of 1968, well before Richard Nixon's election.

The primary targeting of American bases during Phase Four of the TCK-TKN general offensive, which became more popularly known as the Tet-69 offensive, provides a possible clue to the Politburo's real motives. The responses to NSSM-1 were almost unanimous in agreeing that the enemy controlled both side's casualty rates. It really was irrelevant to Hanoi when the offensive took place as long as it inflicted heavy American casualties. The Politburo had learned during 1968 that American casualties were a surefire stimulus to increased antiwar agitation in the United States. Since August 1964, the North Vietnamese had followed unwaveringly the dual strategy of *dau tranh vu tran* (armed struggle) and *dau tranh chinh tri* (political struggle). One of the principal arms of political struggle was *dich van* (action among the enemy), which involved manipulating public opinion throughout the world, particularly in the United States. One of the tools for manipulating public opinion was a weekly English-language newspaper printed in Hanoi and distributed worldwide. A master's thesis by Carl A. Gidlund at the University of Montana in 1967 revealed that Hanoi had started using the paper, *The Vietnam Courier*, as a serious instrument of propaganda as early as 1965 and had pulled out all stops by 1966. Although U.S. currency laws, which precluded subscriptions from North Vietnam, made direct circulation to the United States a little tricky, ample copies for the use of writers in left-wing journals were available from Canada, Great Britain, France, and Sweden.

Another misconception arising from the offensive was that North Vietnam had violated the "understanding" that supposedly was the quid pro quo for President Johnson's decision to halt the bombing of North Vietnam. Lyndon Johnson clearly bought into the American negotiating team's grasping at straws; the natural human desire for peace swayed Averell Harriman and Cyrus Vance into dealing with false perceptions. The most casual perusal of intelligence and operations reports from Vietnam would have confirmed the frantic preparations and threatening posture of the North Vietnamese divisions around Saigon in mid-October of 1968. Even if Johnson declined to take note, the key members of the Nixon team, particularly Kissinger, who thirsted for real knowledge of the war, should have known that the offensive had been planned for months. And that knowledge, coupled with the fact that Hanoi persisted in going through with the operation despite the potential for serious negotiations with the new American administration, should have raised red flags in the consciousness of Laird, Kissinger, and Nixon. Alas, it would be more than a year before they realized that there was no Congress of Vienna in the offing and that the least the hard-core revolutionaries in Hanoi would accept was absolute victory at any cost.

Tragically, that cost involved many lives, and, on March 1, as Richard Nixon proceeded through his European trip, COSVN was putting into motion the next stage of its Fourth Offensive, which would result in more American casualties.

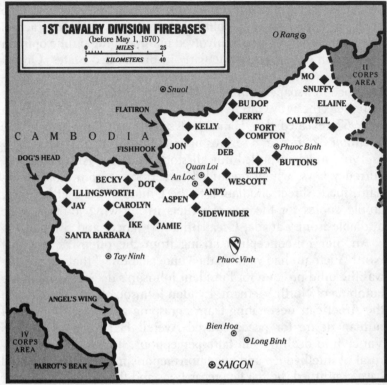

1ST CAVALRY DIVISION FIREBASES
(before May 1, 1970)

0 _____ MILES _____ 25
0 _____ KILOMETERS _____ 40

O Rang ⊙

II CORPS AREA

MO

SNUFFY

⊙ *Snuol*

ELAINE

BU DOP

CALDWELL

JERRY

FLATIRON

FORT COMPTON

KELLY

JON

⊙ *Phuoc Binh*

FISHHOOK

DEB

BUTTONS

Quan Loi ⊙

DOG'S HEAD

ELLEN

An Loc ⊙

BECKY

WESCOTT

DOT

ILLINGSWORTH

ANDY

JAY

ASPEN

CAROLYN

SIDEWINDER

IKE

JAMIE

SANTA BARBARA

C A M B O D I A

⊙ *Tay Ninh*

Phuoc Vinh

ANGEL'S WING

IV CORPS AREA

Bien Hoa ⊙

⊙ *Long Binh*

PARROT'S BEAK

⊛ *SAIGON*

Map by John D. Talbott

This map shows only a fraction of the hundreds of firebases built, maintained, and then abandoned by the 1st Air Cavalry Division and the units that worked under the division's operational control. However, most of the LZs or fire support bases mentioned in the text are depicted on this map.

6

Regaining the
Initiative

The cramped interior of the tactical operations center of LZ
GRANT was hot and stuffy. Lieutenant Colonel Peter Gorvad,
the commander of the 2nd Battalion, 12th Cavalry, had done
all that he and his associates could at the moment. All that was
left was nervous waiting. It was shortly after midnight, March 8.
The men in the TOC were tense, as were all the men on the
base. The firebase was on 100 percent alert, as it had been for
the past several days while North Vietnamese gunners hurled
mortar shells and rockets at its perimeter. But tonight was different. GRANT was the eye of a gathering storm. All intelligence
indicated that the jungle around GRANT was swarming with
North Vietnamese soldiers. In the TOC there was the usual hum
of voices, the hiss and squawk of radios, the monotonous droning
of a fan in a losing struggle against the hot, humid air. Then
there there was a blinding flash and a deafening explosion. An
NVA rocket gunner had gotten lucky and dropped a 122-mm
rocket with a delay fuse directly on top of the sandbagged TOC.
The big projectile sliced through the three layers of sandbags and
detonated inside.

Mortars and rockets give little audible warning before impact,
even for those outside a building. For the men in the sandbagged
TOC, there was no warning at all. Major Billy Brown, the battalion operations officer, had been outside the TOC checking on
the readiness of the base defense when the rocket hit. He raced

back to the TOC and found it demolished. Peering through the smoke and dust of the interior he saw the crumpled body of the battalion commander, Lieutenant Colonel Gorvad. "The colonel was lying just about where I left him, sitting in a chair in front of the map board," Brown said in a later interview. "Our intelligence sergeant was lying wounded under a table. A radio operator was wounded and flat on his back, but still talking on the radio."

One of the men who had been in the bunker was Command Sergeant Major Leland Robinson. Luckily, he was next to the bunker door and was blown outside by the explosion. "It just turned dark for me in there all of a sudden," Robinson recalled, "and I wound up outside on a pile of sandbags." Robinson ignored two shrapnel wounds in his foot and ran back inside the bunker to help the wounded and join Brown in getting things organized. As the senior officer on the firebase, Brown took command and began to orchestrate the defense.

By this time, the men of the battalion's Delta and Echo companies had begun shouting out the well-known phrase that signaled that the up-close and personal defense of a firebase had begun: "Gooks in the wire!" rang out around the perimeter, as the 95-C Regiment of the NVA 1st Division resolutely set about removing the LZ GRANT cork from the War Zone C bottle. Two battalions of Ninety-Five-Charlie charged into the massed small-arms fire of the defenders, while outside the wire, artillery from nearby firebases crashed down among the attackers. On GRANT itself, there were two batteries of artillery, Charlie Battery, 1st Battalion, 77th Artillery, firing 105-mm howitzers, and Alpha Battery, 1st Battalion, 30th Artillery, manning the big 155-mm howitzers. Although some of the artillery was fired in a conventional mode as countermortar and counterrocket fire, most rounds were sent off in a direct fire mode. The Redlegs leveled their tubes and blazed away with either cannister or "killer junior," the macabre nickname for the technique of firing big shells with time fuses set to detonate the high explosive within distances as close as one hundred meters from the perimeter wire. Of the two systems, the killer junior was more lethal because there was no protection from the shrapnel bursting only a few feet above the ground. The cannister, or beehive, rounds were especially effective for final, close-in defensive fire.

Still it was touch and go for a while. Brown had ordered his men to concentrate on using small-arms and automatic-weapons fire initially and to save their claymores for the second assault that he was sure would come after the first wave had shattered itself on the firebase defense. Sappers with 95-C had used bangalore torpedoes to blow sections of wire for avenues of assault to the perimeter bunkers. Now was the time for Lieutenant Colonel Ngo Nhoc Trai, the commander of 95-C, to commit his reserve battalion. But the battalion was in no condition to attack. Unwittingly, Trai had assigned the battalion an assembly area that had been preplotted for a heavy artillery concentration from a supporting firebase, and the unit was hammered badly. Without the added impetus of the reserve battalion, the attack petered out. By 4 A.M. the NVA began breaking contact, and by 6 A.M. the only North Vietnamese left on the battlefield were the 154 dead and some litter parties trying to extract the NVA wounded. The cost to the Cav was the battalion commander and ten other men killed, thirty wounded, and a 155-mm howitzer destroyed.

At first light the brigade commander, Colonel Joseph Kingston, choppered into GRANT to provide some command support for Major Brown, who had been playing battalion commander, fire-support coordinator, and operations officer all night long. Kingston, who had taken over the reins of the "All The Way" brigade from Colonel Robert J. Baer only three days before, was a seasoned warrior on his second tour in Vietnam, and he had extensive combat experience in Korea. He had already directed that the two companies of the 2/12 that were in night positions some distance from GRANT be lifted into blocking positions to try to interdict the retiring NVA regiment. By 8 A.M. the troopers on GRANT were standing around, numb and exhausted.

That's when General Forsythe flew in. When he saw the troops just standing about he demanded that Kingston immediately send them out into the bush to "maintain contact." Kingston told Forsythe that he already had other forces moving to do just exactly that. When Forsythe persisted, Kingston angrily told his boss, "Listen, general, these men have been fighting for hours and they're beat. There's only so much you can ask of a soldier and we've asked enough of these guys right now. If you want them to go out, then you'll have to order them to, because I won't." Forsythe's immediate reaction to this apparent insubordination was anger, and Kingston said later that he was about a millimeter away from being fired on the spot. But George Forsythe was a man of good judgment who could appreciate a sound argument, and he had sincere feelings for the line soldier, so he quickly calmed down, didn't fire Joe Kingston, and let him run his brigade. Kingston said that because he had been assigned to the MACV Personnel Directorate prior to coming to the brigade, he was very familiar with Forsythe's military record. "The truth of the matter is," he said, "General Forsythe had virtually no combat command experience at the troop level in World War II." And like the four Cav division commanders preceding him, he had had no combat experience in Korea.

Kingston didn't have much time to reflect on GRANT, because the 1st Brigade was still operating with two battalions in the Navajo Warhorse AO, and on the night of March 9, Bravo Company, 2nd Battalion, 5th Cavalry, had established two platoon-sized night ambush positions at a location about four hundred meters from the Cambodian border and almost on top of the provincial boundary between Tay Ninh and Hau Nghia provinces. The 272nd Regiment of the 9th VC Division, which had been rearmed and refitted in the Cambodian sanctuaries after it had sustained disastrous losses in 1968, was back on the prowl, seeking to regain the glory that the regiment had won from its attack on Dong Xoai in June 1965. There had been a series of contacts with the regiment by Lieutenant Colonel Jerry Burcham's Second of the Fifth, and all units were warned to be particularly careful when working close to the border.

Bravo Company's 1st and 2nd platoons took the brunt of a massive attack by a battalion of the 272nd in a battle in which more things went wrong than right; there were radio communication failures and a chronic inability to adequately mark front-line traces for supporting helicopters and Air Force gunships. In the end, though, what did go well was the individual fighting man's ability to hang in there and hold the enemy off with individual and squad weapons, plus the heavy concentrations of artillery from LZs TERRI and TRACI that eventually broke the back of the NVA attacks. At daybreak, a sweep of the battle area turned up thirty-one dead North Vietnamese soldiers, but the two Black Knight platoons lost fourteen killed and thirty-one wounded. The exchange ratio, the device by which some senior commanders measured success or failure on the battlefield, was therefore not good. But neither of the platoon positions had been overrun, and these were night ambush positions, not heavily sandbagged firebase bunkers. And the Cav was still in control of the real estate, while the NVA units were back in Cambodia trying to devise a way to get through or around the Cavalry screen.

Even though the first stage of the Fourth General Offensive was fizzling, there was more to come. Part of the communists' master plan called for the NVA 1st Division to fight its way south out of War Zone C and through the Michelin. By early March, at least one regiment of the NVA 7th Division had worked its way into bunker complexes that honeycombed the abandoned rubber plantation. But LZ GRANT was still blocking lower War Zone C, so the 1st NVA sent another regiment, the 101-D, out to eliminate this troublesome firebase.

On the night of March 11, under cover of darkness and a hail of mortar and rocket fire, two battalions of the 101-D attacked down a dirt road known as LTL-13. Lieutenant Colonel Ivan Boon was now the commander of the 2/12, and his Alpha and Echo companies were more than equal to the task. When the 101-D withdrew before dawn, its two battalions had left sixty-two dead in and around GRANT's wire. The regiment also was not as clever in evading 1st Brigade pursuit as was the 95-C, which had escaped to the north with virtually no further contact with Americans. On the other hand, Kingston was three days further in command and his brigade forces were probably more responsive to his direction. At any rate, scout birds and gunships of the 1st Squadron, 9th Cavalry, and infantry ambushes accounted for fifty-one more 101-D soldiers. And the LZ GRANT cork was still in the War Zone C bottle.

Throughout Vietnam, during the first two weeks of March, the communists continued attacks by fire. Villagers in other parts of Vietnam were not as fortunate as those in III Corps. An estimated twenty-five thousand South Vietnamese, primarily in the

populated areas of Military Regions I and II, were rendered home-
less as a result of the fighting. Despite the efforts of the allied
forces guarding the mortar and rocket belt around Saigon, VC
rocket gunners got off a couple of salvos. One occurred while
Defense Secretary Melvin Laird was making his first visit to Vietnam. The second attack, after he had returned to Washington,
slammed into a residential area, killing thirty-four men, women,
and children.

For Richard Nixon, this was the last straw. He had been vac-
illating on the question of retaliation against North Vietnam ever
since the offensive kicked off on February 22. He desperately
wanted to punish Hanoi, but for practical political reasons ruled
out resuming bombing of the north. Other than unleashing a
full-scale invasion of North Vietnam, obviously out of the question, the only recourse was to bomb the Cambodian sanctuaries.
Nixon made his decision to hit Base Area 353 with a B-52 strike.
But before the decision was transmitted to Saigon, there ensued
a great deal of pushing and pulling among his advisors, despite
the fact that Nixon had created a National Security Council
apparatus to prevent the wrangling that occurred in the Johnson
White House. Nixon reached a sort of consensus in a lengthy
meeting in the Oval Office on Sunday afternoon, March 16.
Henry Kissinger, in his book, *The White House Years*, remembers
the meetings, memoranda, and discussions leading up to that
Sunday meeting in the Oval Office: "These deliberations are
instructive: A month of unprovoked North Vietnamese offensive,
over a thousand American dead, elicited after weeks of anguished
discussion exactly *one* American retaliatory raid within three
miles of the Cambodian border in an area occupied by North
Vietnam for over four years. And this would enter the folklore
as an example of wanton 'illegality.' "

At that meeting Nixon also made a fateful decision: the raid
would be kept secret. Nixon said in his memoir, *No More Vietnams*, that he made this decision for two reasons: to avoid the
domestic uproar that could result from a publicized strike, and
the desire to avoid antagonizing Prince Norodom Sihanouk, the
Cambodian head of state.

On March 18, B-52s struck a zone in Base Area 353. The
code name for this bombing was "Breakfast," a name all writers

condemned as tasteless, which begs the question of what constitutes a tasteful code name for a combat operation. That the strike was successful in hitting ammunition and fuel storage areas was evidenced by aircrews' reports of something like seventy-three secondary explosions. Whether COSVN was hit was not known, but later it was confirmed that COSVN had indeed been in the vicinity of the strike. The next day, March 19, the various sections of the headquarters complex moved out of that base area. The White House held its collective breath awaiting a formal protest to the strike. None came; not from Sihanouk, not from the National Liberation Front, and certainly not from Hanoi, who had been denying for years that there were North Vietnamese troops in Cambodia.

Despite all of the setbacks to the COSVN scheme in February and March, allied intelligence believed that the NVA was still going to try to pull off the second stage of the offensive, which would probably occur in late March. So General Kerwin cranked up a big offensive in the old base areas inside the Trapezoid and the Michelin Plantation as well.

This rubber plantation was one of two owned by the Michelin Company. It was by far the largest rubber plantation in Vietnam, sprawling over thirty-five square miles east and northeast of the principal rubber-processing town of Dau Tieng. The plantation was laid out in neat five-hundred-square-kilometer blocks, with trees planted at ten-meter intervals. The average rubber tree is between six and eight inches thick at the base and is clear of limbs to its first main fork about fifteen feet above the ground. When the plantation was being tended and was productive, all of the undergrowth was cleaned out and the plantation resembled an enormous orchard, with neat aisles between the trees stretching for ten to fifteen kilometers. The French laid out access roads running north–south every thousand meters, so all the trees in the huge plantation were accessible. After the Viet Cong seized control of the plantation in 1964, jungle undergrowth sprang up between the orderly rows of trees. The communists established a labyrinth of camouflaged bunkers in the plantation and mined the access roads to deny their use to American or ARVN forces.

The mission statement for Kerwin's operation, called "Atlas Wedge," read, "Inflict heavy losses on the main force units while they are still concentrated and drive them away from the populated areas." The operation was somewhat reminiscent of the multibattalion actions run in the same general area earlier in the war.

It was also the last hurrah for Dutch Kerwin, who was scheduled to go home soon. Interdiction was a reasonable strategy, but once in a while old soldiers still yearned to unleash a big thunderbolt. Three battalions of the U.S. 25th Infantry Division attacked suspected enemy bunker complexes in the jungled areas west of Dau Tieng and the Michelin complex. The U.S. 1st Infantry Division deployed a battalion into the old Trapezoid stronghold and placed a couple more battalions in blocking positions just south and east of the Michelin. The Air Cav's 2nd Brigade deployed a battalion into blocking positions north of the rubber plantation.

These were all anvil forces. The hammer was provided by Colonel George Patton's 11th Armored Cavalry Regiment and the Big Red One's 1st Squadron, 4th Cavalry. These two armored units were ordered to roll right through the interior of the rubber plantation. Going into the rubber on an offensive operation was something new. Previously, the American command, fearful of damaging the valuable rubber trees and mindful of the eight years it takes for a seedling to become a productive tree, had declined to take the war to the enemy inside the plantation.

The operation kicked off on March 17. The tanks and ACAVs began rolling north through the neat rows of trees looking for a fight, using their superior firepower to neutralize any enemy opposition. The elements of the Viet Cong and NVA main-force units in the plantation bunkers were doubly surprised, first by the fact that the Americans had chosen to carry the battle to the enemy in the rubber, and second, by the shock action of the armor. The NVA and VC defenders were routed. When the three cavalry squadrons reached the northern boundary of the plantation, the formations wheeled to the west and then back toward the southern boundary. The armored cavalry units systematically swept the plantation for a total of four days, then finished with a sweep up a provincial road to Minh Thanh, to cut off any retreating groups of NVA soldiers. The four-day operation cost the NVA 7th Division 366 men, 88 weapons, and 6 tons of rice.

After Atlas Wedge, the North Vietnamese ceased most of their offensive operations in lower III Corps. The Fourth General Offensive had come to naught, the North Vietnamese and Viet Cong had been cuffed around, and the Americans had demonstrated by the operations in the Michelin and the bombing of Base Area 353 that the old rules were not necessarily applicable any more. So it was time to put some emphasis on the talk part of the "talk-fight" strategy. Hanoi ended its diplomatic foot-dragging in Paris as its delegate responded favorably to the U.S. proposal for private sessions.

But the allies kept the pressure on. The U.S. 1st and 25th Infantry Divisions kept pushing into the old base areas south of the Michelin to flush out Viet Cong and North Vietnamese mainforce units still lurking in the jungle redoubts. To the north of the populated area, across the northern rim of the Corps boundary, the 1st Air Cavalry, whose units had been systematically disrupting the enemy's logistics system, racheted the intensity level up several notches. On March 29, the division initiated operation Montana Scout in honor of the Montanan who commanded the division and whose tour of duty was scheduled to come to a close by the end of April. The 1st Brigade turned over its firebases in the old Navajo Warhorse AO to the U.S. 25th Division and air-assaulted its 2nd Battalion, 5th Cavalry into an area 22 kilometers northwest of Tay Ninh City. The target was a suspected base area harboring the NVA 1st Division's 101-D Regiment. The companies of the Second of the Fifth fought several vicious battles and eventually captured enough real estate to build LZ JESS.

On April 11, the 11th Armored Cavalry Regiment was placed under the operational control of the 1st Cavalry Division and assigned a search mission into the southwestern corner of Base Area 355 east of Tay Ninh City. The 11th ACR, now commanded by Colonel James Leach, was given an airmobile infantry battalion, the 1st Battalion, 8th Cavalry, to help provide close-in security to the armored vehicles as they ploughed through the jungle of the part of Base Area 355 commonly called "the Crescent." When the armored sweep of the Crescent was completed, the division changed the name of the operation to "Montana Raider" and redeployed two squadrons of the 11th ACR (the third squadron remained in the Saigon area as part of the mobile defense of the capital region) to an area just east of the Fishhook and agaïn assigned an airmobile infantry battalion, the 2nd of the 7th, to work with the armored task force.

Throughout the division area, the NVA avoided contact as much as possible. When a patrolling cavalry unit came across a cache site, the NVA troops in the complex would leave a small covering force to engage the exploitation forces while the main body evaded to another bunker complex.

While the main force units avoided decisive combat, the rear service groups still were working like beavers to move food and ammunition down the infiltration trails. By now the 1st Brigade commander, Colonel Joe Kingston, had a pretty good handle on the major infiltration trails being used by the NVA. Interrogation of captured enemy soldiers revealed the presence of a major trail complex that had not previously been detected. Those captured soldiers told of various cache and supply sites identified by "X" numbers: X-1, X-2, X-7, and so on. It was not long before this trail was known as simply the "X-Cache Trail." It started in Cambodia just north of the Dog's Head and snaked southeast to terminate in Base Area 355 a little north of the Michelin. The porterage units would orient on the high ground of the Razorback, the highest peak of which rose some three hundred meters off the jungle floor.

Kingston had an S-2 (intelligence officer), Captain Dave Milton, whom he considered the best in Vietnam. Milton visited every unit that had operated in War Zone C, American or ARVN, combing records for information about trails and cache sites and contacts. He began building a comprehensive system of overlays that depicted the trail system used by the communists. Kingston and his staff used this trail trace to direct the search and interdiction operations of the brigade in War Zone C, with particular emphasis on ambushes. They knew that the communists tended to use the same trails repeatedly, gambling that the Americans, if they ambushed a trail one night, probably would not be back.

So, night after night, the 82nd Rear Service Group would send its bicycle convoys south. The NVA used bikes, rigged with sticks as extensions for steering and for balancing the load, to carry heavy and cumbersome loads. But bicycles need well-developed trails to move on. And that was the major vulnerability that the Cav exploited with night ambushes.

"The name of the game was ambushes," said Captain Henry "Rocky" Colavita, commander of Delta Company, 2nd Battalion, 8th Cavalry. The 2nd of the 8th, now commanded by Lieutenant Colonel Richard Wood, was operating out of a firebase named CAROLYN that had been built adjacent to an abandoned Special Forces camp at Prek Klock, directly astride the X-Cache Trail.

Kingston also opened up another firebase, LZ IKE, almost exactly halfway between GRANT and CAROLYN. This gave him three firebases, about ten kilometers apart, paralleling the X-Cache Trail. He also had a fourth base, LZ DOLLY, located on the highest point of the Razorback, which overlooked both the Michelin to the south and the terminus of the War Zone C infiltration trails, Base Area 355, to the north and west.

The heavy traffic on the X-Cache Trail led to differing conclusions by the allied intelligence community as to North Vietnamese capabilities. The fact that the X-Cache Trail originated in extreme northwest Tay Ninh Province indicated fairly solidly that the communists were bringing in war materiel from a source other than the Ho Chi Minh Trail. Yet for most of 1969, the Central Intelligence Agency continued to maintain that the Ho Chi Minh Trail was the communists' primary supply pipeline. Bill Colby, in his book, *Lost Victory*, admits the CIA was slow to recognize the significance of the Cambodian port of Sihanoukville (Kompong Som) as it related to direct supply of communist forces in both Military Regions III and IV. He wrote that the CIA's analysts carefully measured what they thought was the required logistical support of North Vietnamese and Viet Cong operations in South Vietnam and determined it was so small that it could easily be carried over the Ho Chi Minh Trail. Of course, many CIA analysts and most Department of Defense civilians still believed the war in Vietnam was a native insurgency. Other than the military forces in contact, few seemed to be aware that the North Vietnamese had committed the bulk of their regular army to the "liberation of the South."

A regular army, whether a "people's army" or a South Vietnamese army or an American army, has a voracious appetite for war materiel. For the NVA, the Ho Chi Minh Trail as it was constituted in 1969 was incapable of delivering an adequate volume of supplies. But the port of Kompong Som had the capability, and after Sihanouk was overthrown, evidence of the massive shipment of supplies came to light in the form of bills of lading and records of trucking companies that carried the supplies to the border sanctuaries.

It was a smooth operation until the NVA had to cross the border into Vietnam, but running truck convoys in the face of American airpower would have been suicidal. So the NVA, once it crossed the border into War Zone C, had to conduct itself as a guerrilla army and attempt to infiltrate its war-making materiel down the thousands of trails and paths in advance of its combat units.

The one advantage the communists had going into this mortal struggle for control of the infiltration trails was that they had had virtually uncontested control of War Zone C for nearly fifteen years and had used the time to build hundreds of bunker complexes and food and ammunition caches. The three thousand square kilometers of the War Zone were honeycombed with these complexes. Finding them in the first place and then rooting them out after their discovery was a tough and dirty job. But as long as the Cav kept the NVA totally occupied in just trying to push its logistical nose down into positions where it could threaten the populated areas and disrupt pacification, Dutch Kerwin was happy, and so was General Abrams. Both realized that the best measure of success in this war in III Corps was the security of the people. Kerwin was less interested in body counts than he was in weapons counts and rice hauls. He had confidence in the Cav, and because of his own aversion to being told how to accomplish missions, generally left General Forsythe and the other division commanders alone.

Then Kerwin went home and a new II Field Force commander arrived on the scene, breathing fire and expressing vocal disapproval of the way the American units in III Corps were fighting the war. His name was Julian Ewell, who had just been promoted to lieutenant general from his command of the U.S. 9th Infantry Division in the Delta. He brought with him a deserved reputation as a big body-count man, and he promptly began to make life miserable for the commanders of American units in III Corps, probably no one more so than General Forsythe of the 1st Cavalry. If George Forsythe had been writing a Chinese play, he would have titled the act starring Julian Ewell, "Enter the Dragon."

Ewell was a 1939 West Point graduate, a classmate of the Cav's first commander, Harry Kinnard. And like Kinnard, he threw in his lot with the new airborne concept and fought in Europe as a battalion and regimental commander for Maxwell Taylor's 101st Airborne Division. He became a protégé of Taylor, ultimately serving as his aide when Taylor was recalled to active duty to be the chairman of the Joint Chiefs of Staff. It was a powerful sponsorship that served Ewell well throughout his career. In the 9th Division, Ewell and his chief of staff, Colonel Ira Hunt, had contrived statistical devices to "get a management handle on the war." He had charts and graphs that measured everything that conceivably could be measured and some things that seemingly defied measurement.

In a postwar monograph coauthored with Hunt, *Sharpening the Combat Edge*, Ewell adopted a moderate tone that indicated he realized that the statistical analysis devices force-fed to the "Old Reliables" of the U.S. 9th Division were not nearly as valuable and relevant at the corps level of command. But when he arrived at II Field Force headquarters in Bien Hoa in early April, he exhibited none of that moderation. He immediately began comparing the U.S. units in III Corps with the division he had just left and concluded that none could measure up. In a 1979 interview for the Senior Officer Oral History Program at the Army War College shortly after his retirement, Ewell was caustic: "When I went to II Field Force, there was no doubt, although I didn't say so publicly, that the divisions there were not really carrying their weight and they were having a lot of trouble in the jungles. I'd say the kill ratios were around 10–1, which was about the traditional Vietnamese level." Ewell went on to point out that at this rate, for every thousand enemy killed, one hundred Americans would die. He said one cause of the high casualties was units' trying to retrieve dead and wounded. He established an absolute rule that units would not attempt to retrieve their dead point men until the bunker complex had been taken; by following this rule, he said, the American units were able to get their kill ratio in solid jungle up to twenty-five to one.

Ewell felt a particular antipathy for the 1st Cavalry Division. Coming from a division where helicopter assets were scarce, Ewell thought the helicopter-rich 1st Cavalry, despite its reputation and record in III Corps, was squandering its riches. The Cav, under Forsythe, although maintaining nominal body count statistics, didn't have anything close to what Ewell deemed minimum acceptable production. "They liked to fly around and look at the top of the jungle, but as far as coming to grips with the enemy was concerned, they just fiddled around," he said in a more recent interview.

In one of his first briefings by the Cav, after he asked for results from the number of helicopter assaults made in the preceding twenty-four hours, Ewell exclaimed in his distinctive American Southwest twang, "Goddamn, if the 9th Division had put that many insertions in, they [the enemy] would have come out like corn out of a popper." It went downhill from there. Within a couple of weeks after taking over, Ewell took the western part of the War Zone C area of operations from the Cav and assigned it to the 1st Brigade of the U.S. 25th Division, which also had a base in Tay Ninh. Then he did what no senior commander had ever dared do to the Cav before: he stripped out a helicopter lift company and attached it to the 25th Division. "You don't deserve these assets," he twanged. "You're not killing any gooks."

Forsythe was fit to be tied. But his only recourse was to mark the final few days on his short-timers calendar and head for the relative sanctuary of command of the Infantry Center at Fort Benning, Georgia.

Elvy Benton Roberts always felt that his age would be a hindrance in his Army career. He entered West Point after attending college in western Kentucky and graduated from the academy in January 1943 at the age of twenty-six. He was four years older than most of his classmates. He also had gone the airborne route after commissioning, ending up in the 501st Parachute Infantry Regiment of the 101st Airborne Division, where he made the jump into Normandy on D-Day. His service with the regiment continued through five major campaigns, including the combat jump into Holland and the defense of Bastogne. Despite Roberts's often asserted reservations about the hindrance of his age, he moved up steadily in his career, and as a colonel was the second man on the morning report of the fledgling 11th Air Assault Division at Fort Benning, Georgia, in January 1963. Roberts served as chief of staff for Major General Harry Kinnard during the testing of the airmobile division and then took command of the 1st Cav's airborne brigade when it came time to deploy the division to Vietnam in September 1965. A leg injury that led to his hospitalization prevented him from participating in the historic Pleiku Campaign. He was promoted to brigadier general in September 1966, and when the tall, lean, gray-haired Kentuckian returned to Vietnam, it was as the assistant division commander of the U.S. 9th Division, working for the man he had served under while in the 501st Parachute Infantry in World War II— Julian Ewell. Despite Roberts's impressive background with the Air Assault Division and the Air Cav, he, like Forsythe before him, did not become an aviator until he was nominated for command of the 1st Air Cav. At the time, he was serving as deputy chief of staff for operations at U.S. Army, Vietnam, at Long Binh. Like other 1st Cavalry Division commanders, he had not had a combat assignment in Korea.

On May 5, Major General Elvy B. Roberts assumed command of the 1st Air Cavalry Division in a fairly subdued ceremony at a little open area near division headquarters that doubled as a mini–parade ground and the chopper pad for the division's senior officers. The ruffles and flourishes by the division band and the cannon salute echoed over the old French fort at Phuoc Vinh that was now named Camp Gorvad in honor of the fallen commander of LZ GRANT. General Roberts, during his assumption-of-command remarks, said all the right and obligatory things about the division's fame and reputation. But, as he was walking General Ewell back to his chopper, Ewell pulled him aside. Roberts remembers the exchange well. "Julian had a style of getting right up in your face and he told me, 'That's the biggest bunch of bullshit I've ever heard in my life. This is the sorriest goddamn division in Vietnam and it should be the best. You have three months to straighten it out or I'll relieve your ass.' "

Ewell was guilty of more than a little hyperbole with that assertion. All things considered, the division's performance had been pretty good. Many of the Cav's soldiers, who already had heard most everything the three-star general had to say to Roberts, bitterly resented the Ewell slurs. Even Roberts's hand-picked chief of staff, Colonel Robert Shoemaker, said later that he never believed the division was as bad as Ewell painted it. The division's record spoke for itself. During Operation Thoan Thang II, which ran from November 12, 1968, through February 16, 1969, the division killed 3,103 enemy soldiers, at a cost of 279 Skytroopers killed. The exchange ratio of eleven-to-one probably drew a sneer from Ewell. But this was also the first time any American unit had gone deep into the jungles of War Zones C and D and stayed there, operating with only companies and platoons. Moreover, unlike in some of Ewell's more favored units, there were weapons to go along with the enemy bodies. Nearly eight hundred individual and crew-served weapons were captured, and nearly three-quarters of a million rounds of small-arms ammunition.

Most important, especially for a "weigh the rice" man like General Abrams, was the 383 tons of rice that were captured. The best estimate at the time was that it took 1.7 pounds of rice per man per day to keep a communist soldier healthily fed in the field. The Cav's rice haul meant 450,588 man-days of meals that communist soldiers would never eat. And with pacification in the rice-growing areas denying food to the communists, hunger within the ranks of the VC and NVA fighting units was a growing concern for Hanoi. In the final analysis, this so-called "sorry" division had moved six hundred miles while concurrently conducting combat operations in opposite ends of the country, then began to harass and interdict the offensive plans of four NVA divisions, and with superior mobility and firepower whittled down the NVA offensive capabilities so that General Abrams never had to sacrifice the security of the populated areas to defend against the communist attacks.

Although the division's staff and commanders were united in

indignation about Ewell's slurs against the division, a number of officers, particularly those serving their second tour with the Cav, recognized that the division still was not as good as it could be. Aviation maintenance was less than what it should have been. Captain George Long, the G-2 operations officer, remembers the division as being less mobile that it had been when he served as a charter member of the Cav in 1965. But the division was in a dilemma. Its firebases tended to bog the units down and lead to a static "French fort" state of mind. Yet the nature of the mission required physical occupation of much of the territory along the Cambodian border to deny the enemy use of his infiltration trails.

All of this notwithstanding, General Roberts came into the division with Ewell's admonition ringing in his ears, and sat through the first day's round of senior staff briefings with ill-concealed skepticism. He planned to start his next full day in command by lighting fires under commanders and staff officers. But while Roberts slept in his air-conditioned mobile home in the division's headquarters compound, Lieutenant Colonel Ngo Nhoc Trai, the commander of the NVA 95-C Regiment, was in the process of changing Roberts's itinerary.

7

Tightening the Noose

Junior Captain Nguen Ban Luong and his small reconnaissance party had spent two days late in April carefully moving around the jungle clearing that contained LZ CAROLYN. Luong was deputy chief of staff of the 95-C Regiment, and the NVA had targeted CAROLYN for a major assault. Luong was responsible for visual reconnaissance of the firebase to note its defenses and select probable areas of vulnerability. Now, after two days of reconnaissance, Luong was confident he knew enough of the layout of the firebase to return to the base area of his regiment and construct a sand-table layout for the detailed planning of the assault.

The 95-C Regiment was in a training base area in dense jungle about ten kilometers northwest of CAROLYN. In that reasonably secure environment, the regiment rehearsed its attack plans on the firebase.

The basic NVA assault force was composed of interlocking three-man cells. There were sapper and wire-breaching cells; automatic weapons base-of-fire cells; rocket-propelled grenade (RPG) cells; and straight infantry assault cells, whose primary weapon was the AK-47 supplemented by hand grenades or satchel charges. The North Vietnamese Army's extravagant way of expending its human assets often gave rise to the erroneous belief that the NVA engaged in "human-wave" assaults, a mass of humanity rushing wildly across a clearing toward a bunker line.

In truth, while there were a lot of men concentrated in a relatively small area, there was nothing haphazard about the methodology; it was the principle of mass concentrated at a narrow point of attack. Each of the assault elements had a carefully rehearsed plan of action. But during the battle, when leaders were killed or wounded, some of the initial sense of purpose and determination was inevitably lost and the younger and less trained soldiers tended to become disoriented. Moreover, as is the case with all totalitarian armies, NVA soldiers, although superbly conditioned and trained, were never noted for initiative and resourcefulness once the basic attack plan had come unraveled.

The proposed attack on CAROLYN was not a single spasmodic lashing out; rather, it was part of a larger designed offensive. February, March, and April had been a very trying period for the communists. Despite all efforts, a truly effective offensive had not been launched in February and March, particularly against III Corps targets. Then there was the B-52 strike against Base Area 353 in March. Nixon, emboldened by lack of reaction from either Hanoi or Phnom Penh, ordered another strike on the "Breakfast" area (BA 353) in April. It too was secret and took place without reaction from Cambodia or North Vietnam.

Despite these bombings, or perhaps because of them, Hanoi needed some sort of offensive action to keep the pressure on Nixon and Kissinger. So the North Vietnamese planners devised a mini-offensive they termed the "Ho Chi Minh Emulation Campaign" because it would fall close to the birthday of the North Vietnamese leader. It would feature countrywide attacks by fire on American installations, but the major effort would take place in Tay Ninh Province, where COSVN planned to attack and seize Tay Ninh City, the provincial capital. Tay Ninh City offered many possibilities as an objective. First, the city was easily accessible to large forces. It was only a short march from the Angel's Wing of Cambodia and from Base Area 355 to the city's northeast. From those two places a converging attack could be made. Inside the city there were only headquarters and service elements for the 1st Cav and the U.S. 25th Division and some Regional Force and Popular Force units. These weaknesses seemingly made the city an easy target. Another big bonus for Hanoi in seizing Tay Ninh City was the potential for widespread destruction in the city. Tay Ninh City had thus far been spared the ravages of war. Large-scale destruction of the city in house-to-house fighting could cause the Cao Dai, a religious sect that harbored considerable animosity toward the Catholic-dominated Thieu government, to abandon the Saigon regime completely and remain totally neutral in the war pending resolution of the conflict. COSVN had no illusions that the Cao Dai would actively join the VC cause; a neutral stance would be all that was necessary to seriously undermine government control in Tay Ninh Province.

Curiously, while COSVN was putting the final touches on this attack plan, it issued its famous Directive Number 55, which stated, "Never again, and under no circumstances, are we going to risk our entire military force for just an offensive. On the contrary, we should endeavor to preserve our military potential for future campaigns." The reality of events, however, proved that it was never wise to accept at face value any of the various manifestos that constantly were being issued by COSVN or Hanoi. In Directive No. 55, which was a preliminary document, and its follow-on, Resolution No. 9, issued in July 1969 following a North Vietnamese Politburo vote of approval, the term "offensive" had different meanings to different people. Both documents were written and intended for internal audiences, predominantly southerners. It was Hanoi's way to reassure the remnants of the NLF that their lives would not be squandered in any more big, flashy, futile exercises like Tet-68.

The documents also embodied the basic strategy switch of the Politburo; theoretician Truong Chinh had won the power struggle and the new strategy was a return to protracted warfare. Chinh had argued that the traditional three stages of revolutionary warfare, which had won the day for the communists in their 1945 –54 war against the French, were no longer correct in the south. The loser in the struggle was Giap, who had initiated the Tet Offensive in the belief that the time was ripe for the third (general uprising) stage. Some historians have interpreted Directive No. 55 and Resolution No. 9 as clear indications that there were going to be no more offensives. And if the conventional wisdom declared there were not going to be any more offensives, those that occurred could be ignored, which may be part of the reason the battles in III Corps have been overlooked by many. Shelby Stanton, in *Rise and Fall of an American Army*, is one of the few historians to devote more than a couple of pages to the vicious battles in 1969 that were an integral part of Abrams's interdiction strategy.

The protracted war strategy set forth in Resolution No. 9 was implemented in a tactical document, Resolution No. 14, which directed that main-force regiments and battalions be broken into small sapper teams that could conduct a souped-up guerrilla war, concentrating on American installations. Aside from manpower economy, the chief advantage of sapper attacks on American bases was to create casualties that would result in headlines in the United States. This, in turn, would aid Hanoi's *dich van* program (political action among the enemy's people).

But as always, overlying all resolutions and directives were the pragmatic political considerations of the communists' "talk-fight" policy. While professing on one hand to eschew large offensives, Hanoi dictated that a fair resemblance to an offensive take place in May 1969. The reasons were entirely consistent with the "talk-fight" policy. On May 8, in Paris, the National Liberation Front was scheduled to lay a ten-point peace proposal on the round table. Hanoi was continuing its charade that the NLF called the shots in the conflict. It would have been an exquisite political stroke if, as the NLF was making the peace proposal, it could also announce to the world that Tay Ninh City had suddenly become the seat of a provisional revolutionary government.

While small-unit attacks on American installations might have been the order of the day in other parts of Vietnam, sappers alone couldn't cut it in War Zone C or in the southern approaches to Tay Ninh City. In mid-April the 9th VC Division lost five hundred men in futile attempts by conventional infantry assaults to overrun Trang Bang, which was an outpost on National Route 1 between Tay Ninh City and Cu Chi, and FSB FRONTIER CITY, which guarded the southwestern approaches to Tay Ninh City. Both outposts had been manned by infantry battalions of the U.S. 25th Infantry Division. Meanwhile, the rifle companies of the 2nd Battalion, 8th Cavalry, continued to disrupt the X-Cache Trail traffic. By overrunning LZ CAROLYN, the COSVN planners reasoned, the pressure on the supply points around Prek

Klok would be relieved and the flow of supplies to the caches in Base Area 355 would be freed.

Lieutenant Colonel Ngo Nhoc Trai, the commander of the 95-C Regiment, believing he had learned some lessons from his futile attack on LZ GRANT in March, wanted a larger force for the attack. He asked for and received the attachment of a battalion from the 101-D Regiment. He planned to assault CAROLYN from two locations. Both assaults would be violent and focus on a small perimeter frontage. The first attack would be directed toward the northernmost bunkers on the perimeter by the K-1 Battalion, with a company from the 9th Battalion, 101-D Regiment, as a reinforcing force. The main attack would be directed against the southernmost bunkers and would be by the K-2 and K-3 battalions. The lead battalion would be responsible for the shock action in penetrating the wire and taking out perimeter bunkers, while the follow-up battalion would exploit the breach. The commander, his staff, and the regimental political officer were confident that the regiment could overrun CAROLYN in a night attack and be dispersed and back in the jungle before daylight brought the inevitable swarms of helicopter gunships and Air Force fighter bombers.

Lieutenant Colonel Dick Wood's Stony Mountain Boys had built CAROLYN out of the debris left over from the abandoned Prek Klok Special Forces camp. The worn-out and shell-pocked steel planking from the nearby airstrip was salvaged and used to construct bunkers and firing positions for the artillery batteries. Rusting empty fifty-gallon fuel drums were filled with dirt and used as revetments. CAROLYN bore a striking resemblance to a landfill dump. To provide fire support for the maneuver elements working the X-Cache Trail system, the 1st Brigade had assigned Battery A, 2nd Battalion, 19th Artillery (105-mm) and Battery B, 1st Battalion, 30th Artillery (155-mm). The infantry garrison on the firebase was Company C, 2nd Bn., 8th Cav., and the mortars and reconnaissance platoon of the battalion's Echo Company. Counting the battalion headquarters company, there were 231 infantrymen on the base on the evening of the brawl, plus 156 artillerymen and 35 engineers and logistical support personnel. Altogether, 328 Americans to defend against an enemy force that exceeded a thousand men.

Lieutenant Colonel Wood said the configuration of CARO-LYN's perimeter, which was formed in a zigzag circle of broad, inward-pointing Vs, was used because a lot of space separated the protective wire and the edge of the jungle. Another reason was to confuse the enemy by not following precisely the trace of the old Special Forces compound. Wood said the zigzag trace was a tough sell to the troops at first. The firing apertures in the bunkers at the points of the inverted Vs were at the side, rather than facing full front. The immediate front of the bunker was protected by a short length of steel cyclone fence fabric, which provided a stand-off detonation barrier for incoming RPGs. Wood said that the NVA had become almost extravagant in their use of the RPG, which generally was fitted with an 82-mm warhead, and the side-looking apertures reduced the vulnerability of the fighting positions to RPG fire.

Just after the Cav's last-light recon birds had made their sweep around CAROLYN, Ninety-Five-Charlie began moving toward the firebase. The battalion moved furtively but swiftly. Its movement did not go undetected. The 2nd of the 8th's Delta Company was in its night position on the east side of a large clearing about four kilometers northwest of the firebase. For two hours the men of Delta could see the heavy movement through the small breaks in the jungle on the west side of the clearing. Obviously a lot of men were headed somewhere, and CAROLYN seemed the likely target. Captain Rocky Colavita reported the movement to the battalion headquarters, but made no attempt to take the NVA column under fire. It was a prudent decision. The NVA obviously were looking for a fight; it was better to oblige them with a bristling firebase. It would be a reversal of roles in Vietnam, the Americans luring the NVA into a fight on American terms at a place of American choosing.

An hour and a half after midnight, a trip flare outside the wire went off and a B-40 rocket slammed into the perimeter. The signal explosion was followed by an intense barrage of 107-mm rockets, 82-mm and 60-mm mortars, and RPG rockets, that continued unabated for about a half-hour. Then from the north came the initial assault, with the blue-green fireballs of NVA tracers from base-of-fire automatic weapons zipping toward the firebase, mixing with the fiery red American tracers. The torrent of machine-gun fire was followed almost immediately by the crashing explosions from the bangalore torpedoes blasting gaps in the wire. Then small dark figures in twos and threes darted through the wire and onto Bunker 11. A satchel charge was thrown into the bunker, the deafening explosion blinding and dazing the occupants and eliminating resistance. The NVA had a breach in CAROLYN's northern defenses to exploit.

But Wood's problems were only beginning. The 95-C launched its main attack on the south with two battalions. This was where the main road from the airstrip entered the firebase and was also the boundary between bunkers 1, 2, and 3, manned by Charlie Company, and bunkers 19 and 20, manned by the recon platoon. The same assault pattern was used as on the north perimeter: bangalores to shred the protective wire, a violent automatic weapons base of fire, and a hailstorm of RPG warheads. The overwhelming mass of NVA assault cells finally forced a breach in the defenses, occupied bunkers 1, 2, and 20, and penetrated past a burning fuel dump to within a few meters of the base defense command post manned by Captain Harry Taylor, the commander of Charlie Company. There, a spirited defense and counterattack held the NVA temporarily in check.

On the north, the NVA, having overrun Bunker 11, penetrated to the 155-mm howitzer in the number 6 gun position. Private First Class Jerry Peck, the assistant gunner in the gun pit, later said "four of them jumped up on the berm and prepared to throw satchel charges. But I killed three of them before they could make it." Despite the efforts of Peck and other artillerymen, the NVA forced the defenders out of the gun pit. There followed a seesaw battle for control of the gun as the NVA and a combined force of American infantry and artillery soldiers attacked and counterattacked under the glare of flares and the flickering yellow-orange light of blazing ammunition and fuel dumps. Despite their gaining control of the howitzer three times, the North Vietnamese soldiers were never able to destroy it, and when the penetration was finally pinched off around Bunker 11, the gun was back in action, firing as part of the battery protective fire.

The tight coordination between the two artillery batteries and the infantry's mortar platoon played an enormous role in the successful defense of the base. While some of the 81-mm mortar tubes fired preplanned countermortar fire, most concentrated on spitting out flares to illuminate the battlefield. Some 105-mm tubes fired counterbattery fire at NVA mortar firing positions, which had been pinpointed by countermortar radar. However, most of the eight hundred rounds fired by the two batteries were killer juniors. Other fire support came from "Blue Max," the Cav's aerial rocket artillery battalion, as the Cobra gunships sprayed minigun and 2.75-inch rocket fire at enemy indirect firing locations and at the big antiaircraft machine-gun positions. The Air Force gunships, "Spooky" (AC-47) and "Shadow" (AC-119), were on station during most of the fight, raining down their incredible firepower on NVA positions.

Dick Wood, orchestrating the defense of CAROLYN from the TOC, dispatched his operations officer, Major James Bramlett, to take charge of the counterattack to seal off the penetration of the south perimeter, where the last reserve of medics and cooks and engineers had gone into the breach to seal the doom of the North Vietnamese soldiers, who had just begun to sense a possible victory. The zigzag nature of the defensive perimeter was critical as it allowed flanking fire and attacks directly on the base of the penetration, ultimately trapping many of the attackers.

By 4 A.M. the NVA tide had receded. Lieutenant Colonel Trai knew he was beaten and ordered a withdrawal. When he broke contact at 5:30 A.M., he left 172 of his soldiers dead, 30 captured, and a truckload of arms and ammunition. He also left behind Junior Captain Luong, his assistant chief of staff, who was captured when the southern penetration was sealed off. Captain Luong, appalled at the carnage, was receptive to a suggestion by psychological operations people to go aloft and broadcast appeals to his former comrades to give up the unequal struggle. Later, under interrogation, Captain Luong told intelligence people everything he knew of the 95-C Regiment, which was considerable, as he had been assigned in a position of trust and authority since before the attack on FSB DOT in November.

Under the direction of Kingston and Wood, airmobile infantry companies were airlifted into positions where they could interdict the retreating regiment. The pursuit operations cost the NVA sixty more dead and fragmented what had once been a formidable fighting machine.

Shortly after daylight, General Roberts, who had hastily dressed after the attack started and monitored the battle in the division tactical operations center during the night, flew into CAROLYN with a fistful of Silver Stars and Bronze Stars for impact awards to soldiers who had distinguished themselves during the fight. Also arriving in droves were the news media. The battle on CAROLYN had been monitored in Saigon and the command was anxious for the media to see the site of a major victory by an American force. Incredibly, despite the intensity of the assault, only ten Americans were killed, although another eighty were wounded. All three networks flew in, as did reporters for the wire services and major newspapers. Young soldiers became instant celebrities and their comments became fodder for the insatiable appetite of the television cameras. The Skytroopers were interviewed near the bunkers that had been overrun. Clearly showing in the background were crumpled bodies of little men in khaki clothes, with sandal-clad feet and short black hair, lying amid stacks of the paraphernalia of death.

The failure to knock out CAROLYN did nothing to dissuade COSVN and the level of enemy activity swung sharply upward throughout the Cav's area of operations as the communists continued preparations for the Ho Chi Minh Emulation Campaign. Infantry companies searching for supply caches began making frequent contacts with NVA main-force units rather than with their more usual foes—the soldiers assigned to provide security to the supply and service units. Ground-to-air firing incidents rose to as many as thirty a day as the NVA tried to protect troop movements from observation. The decisions to fire on Cav helicopters usually were ill-advised and invariably fatal to the individuals firing when the choppers belonged to the brigade scouts or the Air Cavalry squadron, whose lethality was legendary. The communists achieved the high point of their May campaign between May 12 and 14, hitting most of the 159 targets nationwide on the night of May 13. The majority were attacked by fire (rockets and mortars) and limited ground probes by sappers. Forty-eight of the enemy attacks were directed at U.S. installations and cost the lives of one hundred American soldiers. The headquarters of five of nine U.S. divisions were targets of attacks by fire, including all of the divisions in Military Regions III and IV. The air bases

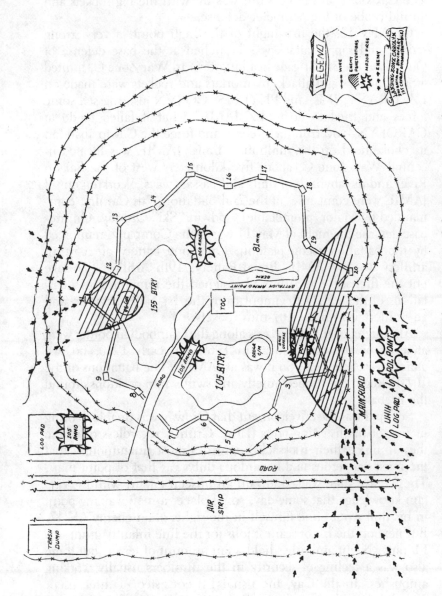

This is the original sketch map of LZ CAROLYN that accompanied the unit's recommendation for a Valorous Unit Citation.

at Bien Hoa and Tan Son Nhut were struck by 107-mm rockets. The Cav's base at Phuoc Vinh was hit with the big rockets and a mild probe of the perimeter defense.

On May 12, the first night of the high point, a very strong mortar and sapper attack was launched at the base defense of Quon Loi, the 3rd Brigade headquarters. In War Zone C, limited ground attacks and attacks by mortars and rockets were made on LZs GRANT, IKE, and PHYLLIS. COSVN also massed some forces and tried to do to LZ JAMIE what it failed to do at CAROLYN—overrun the firebase and force the Cav to abandon its choke-hold on the infiltration trails. JAMIE was located in central War Zone C, about five kilometers west of the Saigon River and its labyrinth of trails and passageways. Working out of JAMIE were companies of the 2nd Battalion, 7th Cavalry, commanded by Major (promotable) Godwin "Ski" Ordway. On firebase defense the night of May 11 was Delta Company, reinforced by the battalion recon platoon. Only one battery of 105-mm artillery was on JAMIE: Bravo Battery, 19th Artillery. To take out the firebase, COSVN had assigned the remaining two battalions of the 101-D Regiment from the 1st NVA Division and an artillery unit firing 107-mm rockets.

Although dozens of firebases along the Cambodian border were attacked by the communists in 1969 and early 1970, no two attacks were identical. So it was at JAMIE. The battalions of the 101-D Regiment slipped quietly and swiftly into positions around the firebase.

So rapid was the envelopment that Ordway was unable to bring in five of his listening posts (LPs). Grunts, regardless of where they humped their rucksacks, agreed almost unanimously that the most dangerous and hazardous duty was that of point man. These brave men walked toward an unseen enemy with the certain knowledge that some day, some place, a man walking point in his unit would find himself in the sights of an enemy AK-47. But next on the list of scariest jobs for the line infantry grunt was LP duty. Night ambushes held a fair amount of terror, but there also was a feeling of security in the numbers usually working ambushes. In the Cav, the usual LP consisted of three men, armed only with rifles, grenades, and a radio. They would move out of the firebase after dark and set up in a position where they hoped they could hear the approach of an enemy yet not be so obvious that the NVA probe would be tipped off and get them first. The favored position was in a bomb or shell crater, which were never in short supply around a firebase. The three would hunker down and sweat out the jungle noises and peer out into the spooky darkness of the bush. The men worked a two-on four-off shift, and slept when they could, rarely worrying about the man on duty going to sleep. GI lore abounded with stories about how the NVA or VC could creep up and slit a sleeping sentry's throat; the fear of dying proved a most effective stimulant. Radio communication was whispered. If contact was imminent and even a whisper could betray a hidden position, the LPs would simply push the press-to-talk button, breaking squelch on the firebase radios. On this night, once the NVA had bypassed the LPs and cut them off from the firebase, the sounds of JAMIE's LPs breaking squelch was similar to the sizzle and pop of bacon in a hot frying pan.

For this attack on JAMIE, the NVA tried a new approach. Instead of the usual practice of starting an attack on a defensive position with a mortar and rocket barrage, followed almost immediately by an infantry attack, the NVA opened up first with automatic weapons fire from the jungle edge. This happened at around 2 A.M., which drew the artillery and mortar crews into the gun pits for fire missions. At 2:40 A.M., the first of more than two hundred rounds of rockets and mortars hit the firebase. Hardest hit during the initial barrage, which was devastatingly accurate, were the gun crews caught in the open at their guns. As the barrage continued, the NVA sappers with bangalore torpedoes blasted gaps in the protective wire. In the midst of the deafening mortar and rocket barrage, even the explosions of the bangalores were lost, and the snap, snap, snap of the AK-47s was barely audible.

From three sides the North Vietnamese regulars poured toward the perimeter. The fact that the NVA had diluted their main attack from the east to mount an assault on the south side of JAMIE with sappers and satchel charges was to Ordway a small triumph. JAMIE had been constructed with two sets of artillery positions, giving it an elongated, rectangular look. But, because 155-mm batteries were hard to come by and were needed more urgently elsewhere, the gun pits at the south end of the firebase were empty. So the battery commander of the 105-mm battery hatched up a deception scheme. Each night he towed a couple of the light howitzers to the south end of the base and fired some missions from there, then towed them back to their normal positions in the morning.

During the assault, the wire at the south end was breached, but as the NVA assault teams closed to the bunkers, red signal flares were fired, the defenders got their heads down, and the NVA assault teams were blown away by the two tubes firing beehive rounds. The MX546 beehive round contained eight thousand flechettes, small steel-finned darts about the size of a one-inch nail. The shell burst open at predetermined distance from the gun muzzle, liberating the darts that flew forward with the shell's velocity. A grunt under the shower of flechettes described the sound as similar to that of a million whips snapping in the air above him.

At one point during the fight, the northernmost bunkers were overrun and occupied briefly by the NVA. Captain William Lacey, the assistant S-3 of the battalion, who had just left command of Delta Company, was gathering up reinforcements to counterattack and regain control of the bunker line. After ascertaining that no Americans remained in the captured bunkers, Lacey ordered the artillery to fire point-blank at the bunkers, and the blast completely demolished one of them. Lacey then led a counterattack that ejected the last of the NVA from inside the firebase; he was subsequently awarded a Silver Star for his gallantry and leadership.

For the LPs caught outside the wire, the night seemed to last an eternity. When calling in fire support, Ordway had no way to protect his listening posts. Miraculously, none of the men outside the wire received so much as a scratch, even though hundreds of rounds of artillery impacted around the base and the aerial support from the Cav's Blue Max and the Air Force had rained death down on the jungle surrounding the perimeter.

Finally, just before dawn, the NVA battalions withdrew, leaving the Cav still firmly in control of the infiltration routes along the Saigon River corridor. The battle for JAMIE was another example of how the combination of firepower and fighting spirit could bring victory to a force that was heavily outnumbered. It also was just one of a series of battles the NVA conducted throughout the summer and fall in a vain attempt to force the Cav to remove its firebases from deep within War Zone C. COSVN seemingly never comprehended that airmobility had changed the game and that the Americans were determined to maintain their forward bases and had the firepower and determination to defend them against anything the NVA could throw at them.

Once again, when daylight came, General Roberts choppered in to talk to the soldiers and pass out impact awards. Also coming in was Don Webster of CBS-TV, the one TV newsman who always seemed to be on hand when the Cav was involved in serious action. Once again there were pictures of the seventy dead North Vietnamese soldiers, no longer fierce, but like most of their American counterparts, simply nineteen-and twenty-year-old draftees who had fought bravely and well. They would fill an unmarked mass grave near where they fell. On the American side, seven young men wrapped in ponchos lay in a ragged line, waiting for their final helicopter flight in Vietnam.

By May 15, all was quiet in War Zone C and in the Cav's AO in and around Quon Loi. When Ho Chi Minh observed his birthday on May 19, all that COSVN had to show for its efforts to blast the 1st Cavalry Division out of War Zone C and away from its infiltration routes were six hundred killed and another 140 tons of rice lost to marauding Cav patrols.

Although the war quieted down in III Corps, a fierce battle was being fought about 450 miles due north of Saigon on a three-thousand-foot peak named Dong Ap Bia. When the smoke had cleared on May 22, and weary "Rakkasans" from the 1st Battalion, 187th Infantry of the 101st Airborne Division, clawed their way over the crest, the mountain had earned the name "Hamburger Hill." Because of the number of American casualties, it became one of the most notorious battles of the Vietnam War and brought widespread criticism cascading down on the heads of the generals who directed the operation.

In the United States, Senator Edward Kennedy led the attacks on the military leadership. He was joined on the Senate floor by several Senate doves who insisted it was their prerogative to be involved in the tactical direction of the war by being consulted prior to any future combat operations. Major General Melvin Zais, who commanded the 101st Airborne at the time, was subjected to a blistering attack by Senator Kennedy. Zais defended his tactics by saying that his orders directed him to find and destroy the enemy wherever he found him. Colonel Joseph B. Conmy, Jr., commander of the division's 3rd Brigade, the immediate tactical commander, who also took some heat from in-country media, defended his decision against backing off and pounding the mountain with B-52 strikes by saying that if he had withdrawn his men to a safe distance, the NVA would have broken contact and escaped into Laos.

General Abrams found himself having to publicly defend his battlefield commander, Mel Zais, for an operation clearly more attuned to the outdated strategy of attrition than to his current strategy of interdiction. That he did so speaks volumes about an army's institutional inability to admit it might have screwed up. Abrams defended Hamburger Hill while being well aware that Marine General Raymond Davis had just run a highly successful interdiction operation (Dewey Canyon) through the upper part of the A Shau Valley just weeks earlier, and that the 101st's operation, Apache Snow, also was to have had an interdiction mission.

While defending Zais, Abrams, according to the *Fighting for Time* volume of Boston Publishing Company's *The Vietnam Experience*, nevertheless told reporters, "Since the beginning of last fall, all our operations have been designed to get into the enemy's system. Once you start working in the system that he requires to prepare his offensive operations, you can cause him to postpone his operations." What happened on Dong Ap Bia can probably best be summed up in an old barracks phrase: "Somebody didn't get the word."

Colonel Harry Summers, in his book *Vietnam War Almanac*, cites the intense public reaction to publication by *Life* magazine of pictures of 217 of the 242 American soldiers who died in Vietnam from May 28 through June 3. Although *Life* did not directly state that any of these men had perished on Hamburger Hill (the inclusive dates did not coincide), it did quote a dead soldier's last letter home, allegedly written on Dong Ap Bia. He wrote: "You may not be able to read this. I am writing it in a hurry. I see death coming up the hill." According to Summers, as a result of the public reaction to the article, General Abrams "was ordered to avoid such large-scale battles." Other writers have also indicated that Abrams was ordered to hold down casualties. There is, however, no evidence that if Abrams received such orders at that time, he passed them along to subordinates. Dr. Lewis Sorley, author of *Thunderbolt,* the biography of General Abrams, has interviewed scores of commanders who worked for Abrams in Vietnam. "I asked them if they had ever received any instructions from Abe to hold down casualties or to avoid getting seriously engaged," Dr. Sorley said. "None of them said so. In fact, they all say specifically that they didn't get any such guidance. But they all quickly add that they, and all other prudent commanders, understood it was necessary to hold down casualties as much as possible." One author, writing about Hamburger Hill, claimed that in the aftermath of the battle the U.S. Army had orders to fight only when threatened by the enemy.

Certainly no such orders were directed at the 1st Cav. Its interdiction campaign continued unabated, and the NVA was unrelenting in its attempt to break the Cav's stranglehold. The 95-C Regiment was still determined to get into a position where it could attack Tay Ninh City. With intelligence provided by the captured Captain Luong, Colonel Joe Kingston's staff could track the regiment all the way, even though the unit had broken down into small infiltration packets. Ninety-Five-Charlie reassembled in a heavily jungled area in the southwest corner of Base Area 355 that was known as "the Crescent."

Once it had massed, Kingston took advantage of Abrams's philosophy that if one B-52 strike was good, massing the strikes at a lucrative target would be even better. Kingston had seven infantry companies lifted into ambush positions around the Crescent and, with a tank company from the 11th Armored Cavalry Regiment, set in motion a series of events that resulted in the virtual destruction of the 95-C as a viable combat unit. He first put in a drop of powdered tear gas that brought the NVA soldiers out of their bunkers, followed by a leaflet drop that said, in effect, "Welcome back to the meatgrinder, Ninety-Five-Charlie." Then came the Arc Lights (B-52 strikes). The death and destruction was awesome. The encircling rifle companies pounced on the survivors that straggled out of the killing zone. The operation put 95-C out of action for at least two months while it rebuilt itself in its Cambodian sanctuary. The cost to Kingston's brigade was three men killed; an RPG round struck an armored vehicle on which the men were riding during a sweep of the objective area. The area was turned over to the 25th Division, which promptly brought in the Rome Plows and ended the enemy's use of that part of the old base area.

Later in June, LZ IKE, the home of the 2nd Battalion, 5th Cavalry, located halfway between CAROLYN and JAMIE, was hit by the K28 sapper battalion, and thirty-seven sappers were killed before the battalion broke off the attack without having breached the wire or gotten close to the perimeter berm. On June 20, the 2nd Battalion of the 18-B Regiment had a go at IKE and got badly bruised for its efforts, leaving sixty-three dead soldiers, most of them dying in the wire. The attacking battalion retreated to its regimental base only to find that the 1st Brigade had tracked it to its lair and encircled the base with companies from the 2/5th and 2/7th Cavalry. The encircled enemy was pounded by air strikes and barrages by 155-mm howitzers. Those elements of the 18-B Regiment that attempted to break out were ambushed and wiped out by the waiting Cavalry companies. When the operation terminated on June 23 the 18-B Regiment was so badly battered that it remained out of action until August.

General Roberts's exposure to the fighting abilities of the division's battalions and companies during his first six weeks in command pretty much persuaded him that General Ewell did not have a fair measure of the Cav's fighting ability. Not that everything was all sweetness and light within the division. Roberts was understandably concerned about the mediocre aircraft availability rate in the division; in a unit whose method of operations is driven by helicopters, the higher the availability rate, the better the combat capability. Early on, Roberts gave Brigadier General Frank Meszar, the assistant division commander for support, the mission of getting a handle on aviation maintenance. Roberts later said, "I called Frank in, and, incidentally, he was one of the really fine aviators in the Army, and I told him, 'I don't want to see you up on any firebases. I want you to spend all your time back with the aviation maintenance units.'"

The unfairness of Ewell's assessment of the Cav's fighting abilities was banged into Roberts's skull when the Field Force commander flew into Tay Ninh and was briefed on the results of the "meatgrinder" operation. Both Roberts and Kingston were justifiably proud of the achievement of the 1st Brigade and expected at least a modest "Atta-boy," if for no other reason than the astounding casualty exchange ratio. They got nothing but Ewell's twanging, "Well, you shouldn't have let them get through you in the first place." Kingston was stupefied and started to react angrily, but Roberts shushed him before a combination of his mouth and temper got him into serious trouble. Elvy diplomatically hustled Ewell out of the briefing bunker and onto his chopper for the trip back to Bien Hoa. At that point both Roberts and Kingston realized that Ewell did not understand the nature of combat in War Zone C and probably never would, and there was precious little the Cav could ever do to please him.

Nevertheless, the 1st Cav continued into the summer constantly tightening the screws on the NVA infiltration routes. No one outside the MACV hierarchy knew it yet, but the time was rapidly approaching when American forces would be fighting, and dying, not for victory in a conventional sense, as they had been led to believe was their mission, but for political objectives. Political realities in Washington had set in motion initiatives that would seriously disrupt morale and fighting efficiency in even the finest outfits, and present to American commanders leadership and motivation challenges that no commanders since the waning days of the Korean War had faced.

8

Beginning the Stand-Down

Throughout the latter part of 1968, official and semiofficial speculation, reported and amplified by the news media, about possible American withdrawal from Vietnam intensified. Only the most obtuse soldier could not have known about the possibility of the withdrawal of combat forces as part of the general winching down of the Vietnam War.

However, soldiers tend to be realists and probably recognized that most of the talk was just that. Those who had been in-country for a period of time, who had been in combat units, and who knew that U.S. forces were regularly clobbering the VC and NVA, assumed that any withdrawal would be tied to a general peace agreement. But peace is an elusive concept more fitting for diplomats than soldiers, particularly those fighting in a war with fuzzy goals and objectives. For everyday soldiers, rumors of withdrawal focused on faint hopes that the 365-day tour might be shortened. Most soldiers' conversations centered around the Army's policy on "drops." A "drop" was a curtailment of the normal tour for any number of bureaucratic reasons. The most common was the Christmas drop, which permitted soldiers whose DEROS (Date Estimated Return from Over Seas) occurred during the holiday season to be given a fifteen-day drop so he could be back home by Christmas. Fifteen days doesn't sound like much when measured against 365, but if you're a grunt, it can be a life-or-death matter. Generally, soldier-level discussions of withdrawal centered around speculation that tours would be curtailed, not that major combat units would be sent home. In the Cav, when media types relentlessly asked their questions on attitudes and opinions, one soldier was heard to respond: "The Cav withdraw? Hell no. The Cav will be here longer than the ARVN!" The question of withdrawals was not yet a major issue.

But, on June 8, 1969, on Midway Island, President Nixon announced that he had ordered the withdrawal of twenty-five thousand combat troops from Vietnam. Moreover, it was a unilateral withdrawal. In the past, all official discussions of withdrawal had been tied to a mutual reduction of outside forces, which meant that North Vietnamese Army units would have to match withdrawal numbers with the American Army. The Midway announcement was a stunning development. Now the rumors were no longer just idle chatter. The president had officially started the inexorable progress toward a stand-down. Although Nixon tried to sugar-coat his decision, tying the withdrawals to a new concept he called "Vietnamization" along with further successes in pacification and a hoped-for breakthrough in negotiations, the stark fact remained: America had started its retreat from Vietnam. In his memoirs, Kissinger reported that Nixon was jubilant after he reached an agreement of sorts on a withdrawal stategy with President Thieu. He said Nixon considered the announcement a political triumph, one which would buy him the time to develop U.S. strategy on the war. Kissinger went on to say, rather ruefully:

His advisors, including me, shared his view. We were wrong on both counts. We had crossed a fateful dividing line. The withdrawal increased the demoralization of those families whose sons remained at risk. And it brought no respite from the critics, the majority of whom believed that since their pressure had produced the initial decision to withdraw, more pressure could speed up the process, and who did not care—nay, some would have rejoiced—if accelerated withdrawals produced a collapse.

And while Kissinger rightfully recognized the anguish of families, there was a more immediate problem in Vietnam. Virtually overnight, America had to deal with a draftee Army whose members, unwilling participants in the war to begin with, now asked themselves, "Why should I be the last to die in a war we're not trying to win?" But because that question was not asked loudly, early on, very few commanders and fewer key staff officers recognized the true scope of the problem.

Unlike the history of the war itself, the road to this sorry state of affairs was not long. It started with the inauguration in January of Richard Nixon, the self-styled hard-liner on communism who surrounded himself with cabinet advisors of varying persuasions, all of whom had their own agendas concerning the Vietnam War. One of the most influential was Defense Secretary Melvin Laird, the pragmatic politician who saw the war as a losing proposition for the Republican Party and who wanted to get the United States out of Vietnam as quickly as possible. He didn't much really care what happened to Vietnam in the process. Laird made a typical whirlwind VIP visit to Vietnam on March 5. He received a round of briefings from MACV, culminating in a session with General Abrams. Abrams briefed him on the MACV planning for "T-Day" redeployments. (The "T" signified termination of hostilities.) In all of the scenarios, MACV planners had assumed a cease-fire and a withdrawal of North Vietnamese forces from South Vietnam and the border regions of Cambodia and Laos. Abrams told Laird that he felt strongly that those preconditions for withdrawal were sound and should be observed. Laird agreed with Abrams in their face-to-face encounter, but told the general that he should start trying to firm up some numbers for a first-increment withdrawal. Laird suggested that forty-four thousand men would be a good start; the administration's honeymoon period was fast running out, and he reckoned that political pressure would require some action within six months, possibly four. Laird also told Abrams that he was satisfied with the progress in the war effort as well as the modernization program for the Republic of Vietnam Armed Forces (RVNAF).

What Laird told Abrams and what he reported to Nixon in his trip memorandum were vastly different. Even though the senior civilians in the Defense Department, a dovish lot altogether, were pessimistic about the ability of the RVNAF to survive even the much weakened Viet Cong, much less the combined strength of the North Vietnamese and VC, Laird either convinced himself that the South Vietnamese could hang on without the American

Army, or more likely, really didn't care. Laird also reported that Abrams had told him that an American military victory was improbable. Abrams knew that U.S. forces had consistently clobbered the communists, but he also knew that, given the restrictions under which he had to operate, he was essentially fighting for a draw. The 1st Cav's first commander, Major General Harry Kinnard, once described the U.S. military situation in Vietnam as similar to a football game where the other side doesn't have to play by any rules at all and your side has stringent rules and cannot cross the fifty-yard line. "The best you can hope for," Kinnard observed, "is a scoreless tie."

Laird also complained to the president that MACV did not have any realistic plan to withdraw forces without a corresponding reduction in North Vietnamese forces. It was rather bizarre that Laird really expected a subordinate military command to initiate planning for unilateral withdrawal when no one in the Department of State or Defense or the White House had even hinted of guidance in that direction. Political bosses usually do not cherish presumptuous generals.

Laird also told Nixon in his trip report that American military leaders in Vietnam tended to be heavily oriented on U.S. operations, rather than assisting in the upgrading of the RVNAF. In this perception he was on target, but he could have similarly indicted all the senior military in the Pentagon, including his Joint Chiefs of Staff. Laird concluded his report by strongly recommending the creation of a withdrawal plan for up to seventy thousand American troops by the end of 1969 and that the withdrawal be tied only to the improvement of the RVNAF.

The defense secretary did not simply write a memo and let events take care of themselves. Laird distrusted Kissinger's ability to suppress the sometimes bellicose tendencies of the president. So he endlessly lobbied Nixon and Kissinger on behalf of his concept of turning the war over to the South Vietnamese, a process for which he coined the phrase "Vietnamization."

Ultimately his efforts carried the day. In early April, Kissinger's staff in the Executive Office Building brought draft withdrawal guidance plans to the White House. This draft won the president's approval and was issued as National Security Study Memorandum 36 (NSSM-36) on April 10. NSSM-36 instructed the Defense Department to develop plans for a phased withdrawal of American forces until only a residual advisory and support force remained. The process would start July 1, 1969, and continue through 1970 and 1971. NSSM-36 specifically discounted a withdrawal of North Vietnamese forces and any sort of major increase in the number of South Vietnamese under arms. It envisioned that American forces would be able to rapidly turn over the major ground combat duties to the RVNAF, despite the fact that almost every response to Kissinger's NSSM-1 in February had firmly asserted that the South Vietnamese could not then or in the foreseeable future handle the combined armies of the Viet Cong and North Vietnamese. Had NSSM-36 been issued in 1966 and carried a longer-term time line, it would have been a splendid strategy document, but coming as it did in 1969 and driven as it was by an administration fearful of public pressure and strongly motivated by its instincts for political survival, it was a document of extraordinary cynicism. General Abrams was not going to be allowed to even play to a tie.

The chairman of the Joint Chiefs, General Earl Wheeler, had kept Abrams reasonably well apprised of developments, including the potential for an early, unilateral withdrawal. Although Abrams's messages back to the Pentagon pleaded that the timing and size of the withdrawals be based on his assessment of the military situation, he began preparations for the inevitable.

With a prescience typical of perhaps the most cerebral general in the Army, Abrams had in January 1969 cranked up a small and very secret planning force headed by an armor branch colonel named Donn Starry. The study group consisted of Starry and four majors, two Army, one Air Force type, and one Marine. Only Abrams and his chief of staff, Major General Ellias C. Tounsend, knew what Starry's study cell was up to. Starry later said "I worked for Eddie Bautz [the J-3] for six months before he knew what I was doing." Initially, the group worked on contingency plans for redeployments. As the message traffic from Wheeler heated up before NSSM-36 was issued, Abrams knew it was inevitable that combat forces be included in the redeployments. His guidance to Starry was that any redeployment packet had to contain major U.S. combat forces. That philosophy was also expressed in messages to Wheeler, but Dr. Jeffrey J. Clarke, a Department of the Army historian, in *Advise and Support: The Final Years*, asserts that the records left by the Joint Chiefs of Staff note that the redeployment of combat forces was Laird's idea alone. However, General William Rosson, Abrams's deputy, said in an interview for the Military History Institute of the U.S. Army War College that Abrams insisted that initial planning for any withdrawals of American forces always have at the heart of each increment major U.S. combat units stationed in areas of prime significance. Abrams believed this was important to give the withdrawal credibility with the American public. Based on subsequent developments, it is likely that while Abrams planned for redeployment of certain combat forces, he opposed their withdrawal until the bitter end in order to buy as much time as possible for preparation of the ARVN.

So it came about that when the number twenty-five thousand announced by Nixon was translated into unit designations, MACV decided to deactivate the 1st and 2nd brigades of the U.S. 9th Infantry Division in IV Corps and redeploy the brigades and division headquarters to Fort Lewis, Washington. But nothing was as simple as it appeared. While the unit's colors were to be redeployed, the Army had no intention of sending back to the States soldiers who had just arrived in country. So there began a major shifting of personnel; short-timers from throughout the division were transferred into the redeploying brigades, while soldiers with much of their tour yet to serve were shifted to either the division's remaining 3rd Brigade or to other divisions.

The personnel turbulence wasn't particularly critical during the first increment of the withdrawals, but later, in 1970 and 1971, there was wholesale shifting of soldiers between units, and morale plummeted. Starry, whose career eventually took him to four stars, later said that he had written a memorandum to General Abrams giving his opinion that this indiscriminate shifting of personnel would eventually be destructive to the command. Starry recommended that all soldiers in a unit be redeployed and those that had a lot of time left on their hitches be reassigned to stateside or European units that were part of a badly depleted strategic reserve. He said that Abrams was receptive to the idea, even though at the time it was unthinkable to take even one American soldier out of Vietnam and not have the war effort collapse. Abrams floated the idea to the Pentagon, but the generals there, including Westmoreland, who, Melvin Laird notwithstanding, still believed there should be more American soldiers in Vietnam and not fewer, shot it down.

Starry also remembered one of his early conferences with Abrams in which the general told him, "I think we're about to get stampeded out of this damn place. I'm not trying to delay this thing, but I am. I don't want to seem to be obstinate, but I've got to slow things down so the ARVN have got the best chance. We've got to boot the ARVN in the ass and boot our own commanders in the ass and let the ARVN start picking up the tab." This ruminating with a trusted planner manifested itself as MACV policy on April 16 when Abrams informed Julian Ewell, the II Field Force commander, that he didn't have a prayer of getting any more American units to run the interdiction campaign and would have to work with the ARVN II Corps commander, Lieutenant General Do Cao Tri, to get the three ARVN divisions in the III Corps area moving. On April 20, at the MACV commanders conference, Abrams reiterated his guidance. The Army book, *Advise and Support*, reports that a memorandum for the record by Ewell, still on file at the Army's military history branch, states that Abrams told Ewell to devote his main efforts to the "less glamorous areas" of population security and "upgrading the RVNAF." Ewell was also instructed to continue "working the system."

Ewell quickly got together with his III Corps counterpart, General Tri, and hatched a program called *Dong Tien* (Progress Together). The concept behind the program was to "marry up" a Vietnamese Army unit with an American counterpart so that the American unit could provide training as well as tactical and logistical support. The concept was not original to III Corps. The "buddying up" of American and Vietnamese units had had some success in I Corps, and at I Field Force in the II Corps area, Lieutenant General William R. Peers, had pioneered the big-brother approach in the Highlands. Both Ewell and Tri wanted to get the ARVN battalions out of their garrisons and into the field and had the goal of forcing at least half of the rifle companies to stay in the field day and night. For the ARVN divisions in III Corps, this was unheard of. Ewell also made it clear to his commanders that they were not to take control of the ARVN units. At his commanders meeting at II Field Force headquarters at Plantation in Bien Hoa, Ewell told his commanders that the whole purpose of the *Dong Tien* program was to provide training and support for the ARVN units so that they could take over their own independent operations as rapidly as possible. General Tri also sent a message to his commanders endorsing Ewell's approach and exhorting them to upgrade their intelligence, operations, and leadership shortcomings and get their forces out of their static role and into an aggressive, offensive posture. And, with Do Cao Tri, an aggressive and offensive spirit was the name of the game. A smart, capable, and courageous commander with a charisma and flamboyance that enhanced his leadership, Tri perhaps was the best field general to have been developed by the ARVN.

The early pairings of American and Vietnamese units occurred in or near the populated areas. One of the first was to colocate the headquarters of the U.S. 199th Light Infantry Brigade with the headquarters of the ARVN 18th Infantry Division, considered by all Americans and most knowledgeable Vietnamese as the sorriest ARVN division in Vietnam. The ARVN 25th Infantry Division divided its units between the 3rd Brigade of the U.S. 9th Division southwest of Saigon and the U.S. 25th Division. Major General Ellis Williamson, commander of the "Tropic Lightning" division, moved a brigade into southern Hau Nghia Province to work with the ARVN 49th and 50th regiments. The ARVN 5th Division buddied up with the U.S. 1st Division.

In most cases the joint operation missions were aimed at tightening security in the populated areas. The Big Red One had the vital mission of securing National Highway 13, the logistical lifeline to 1st Cav operations along the Cambodian border. Working with its ARVN counterparts, the 1st Division targeted Viet Cong attempts to move supplies down through the Michelin into base areas in the Trapezoid. Because the rice-growing areas around Saigon had come almost completely under government control, the guerrilla units needed food as much as war-fighting materiel. Much of the Big Red One's interdiction resulted in rich rice hauls, guaranteeing hungry times for Viet Cong and NVA units still at large in Binh Duong Province. Units of the two divisions also worked over the VC Dong Nai Regiment, which occasionally sent raiding parties out of War Zone D into southern Binh Duong Province. The 1st Cavalry Division eventually became involved in *Dong Tien* in October when the Air Cav was paired with the ARVN Airborne Division, which until that time had hung around Saigon as anticoup insurance for President Thieu.

All of the *Dong Tien* activities being devised by Ewell and Tri were still in the planning stage when the president announced the withdrawal. And on July 9, just nine days after the official kickoff of *Dong Tien*, some eight hundred men wearing 9th Infantry Division shoulder patches stood in parade formation behind a panoply of flags and banners that signaled that this was the 3rd Battalion (Riverine) of the 60th Infantry of the 9th Infantry Division. This was the first combat element being redeployed. There was a lot of pomp and ceremony with Creighton Abrams and President Nguyen Van Thieu trooping the line and making speeches as MACV struggled to put a favorable spin on the withdrawal, but the news media focused on negative statements from the homebound soldiers.

Meanwhile, commanders of the forces still in Vietnam began to recognize that there were some morale problems associated with the withdrawals. In Boston Publishing Company's *The Vietnam Experience* series, the volume *Fighting For Time* asserts that "short-timer fever" broke out and was virulent in 1969. The volume overstates the case. There were indeed some symptoms of morale-sapping attitudes in mid- and late 1969, but the virulence referred to didn't really occur until mid-1970. But because of those early manifestations of morale problems associated with the redeployments, the military's internal information machine went into high gear.

Command information (CI) is the term the Army and MACV had given to its internal information program; it is officially defined by the Army as "those command activities which seek to improve the effectiveness of the Army by providing the soldier with information on military and civil events, conditions, policies and actions in order to increase his understanding of his own role in the Army and the importance of the Army to the defense of the nation."

A small unit commander who gathers his people around him and says, "Listen up. Here's. the straight poop from the head shed," is engaging in face-to-face communications, which is the best and most reliable channel of command information. But that method doesn't get repetitive messages to the masses, so the people who ran the CI programs in the various commands supplemented this with a plethora of mass-communications media —pamphlets, posters, newspapers, magazines, motion pictures, radio, and television. In Vietnam, every military command, regardless of size, had some sort of in-house publication. From Tokyo came the Pacific edition of the *Stars and Stripes*, part real newspaper and part house organ. At the top of the heap in Vietnam, MACV published the *Observer*, U.S. Army Vietnam (USARV) the *Reporter*. Both were tabloid-format newspapers. MACV also oversaw the operation of Armed Forces Radio and Television. II Field Force had a quarterly magazine, the *Hurricane*. Each division published a newspaper and a quarterly magazine. In the 1st Cav Division, the newspaper was a weekly tabloid named *Cavalair*. A quarterly magazine featuring generous use of full-color pictures was entitled *First Team*.

An analysis of the publications of units in III Corps that came out in 1969 shows that they very rarely acknowledged a budding morale problem arising from withdrawals. There were editorials and CI messages about the risks of marijuana use and some indication that race-relations enhancement was underway. All copy for the house organs had to receive prior clearance from a MACV clearance officer, the command's euphemism for a censor. The MACV censors ensured that never would be seen or heard a discouraging word. All the house organs of the units in III Corps bubbled happily about the wonderful cooperation between the ARVN and American forces and how this all would bring ultimate victory. The sheer weight of these propaganda messages, combined with other devices within commands to raise and maintain morale, kept the lid on for most of 1969 and early 1970.

But the so-called short-timer fever was not caused solely by the sense of abandonment brought about by withdrawals. Each new batch of replacements brought with them attitudes influenced by problems in American society of the late 1960s—racism, drug use, and the antiestablishment attitudes of youthful revolutionaries. In a few organizations in Vietnam, this volatile combination produced some of the highly publicized incidents that have led historians to report that the Army in Vietnam fell apart in 1969. Units that had strong, resourceful programs to enhance morale were not as vulnerable to these external infections as others. The reputation of the unit and its type of mission played a key role in how its members perceived the unit's worth . . . and their respective worth within that unit.

The sense of being with an elite unit and the nature of the mission tended to immunize the 1st Cavalry Division from the virus. Since the division had arrived in Vietnam in September 1965, its helicopters and some colorful commanders had quickly made it a media darling. It soon became known as the most publicized unit in Vietnam, a status it never relinquished.

In addition, the division had long established a reputation among its members that "the Cav takes care of its own." This was accomplished by doing a lot of little things, services to the members that sent subtle but unmistakable signals that the division leaders cared about the welfare of the men. These services included placing liaison NCOs at all the field hospitals where wounded Skytroopers were sent for recuperation. These NCOs would make sure that each member of the 1st Cav had a placard over his bed that signified that he belonged to the Cav, and then worked diligently to get the man's mail forwarded to him and to handle any personal problem the man had. Each Sunday, the three general officers of the division flew to the hospitals and visited the Cav wounded. Often they had a photographer armed with a Polaroid camera accompany them to take pictures of the soldier being given his Purple Heart and any other medals that might be due him. Other units did this too, and although some ex-GIs sneered at the practice, the fact remained that for the majority of the men, this gesture helped alleviate the feeling of being a very small and helpless member of the giant Green Machine. The Cav also had liaison NCOs at the replacement depots and the R and R centers for the sole purpose of taking care of Skytroopers. General Roberts, recognizing the value to soldiers' morale of the U.S. 1st Division's association, "The Society of the Big Red One" and its affiliated scholarship program, directed that the 1st Cav start up a similar program. The seed money for the scholarship fund had to come from the active division, and eventually nearly one hundred thousand dollars was raised through raffles and sale of watches and 1st Cav memorabilia. Through all these efforts, many of them just outside or on the borderline of military rules and regulations, the word spread through the ranks and became an article of faith in the division—"The Cav takes care of its own."

When Roberts came back to the division he further liberalized an already liberal award and decorations program so that he could better reward his soldiers. To criticism that the awards were being cheapened, his rejoinder was that a handful of medals was a small price to pay for a division that retained its fighting spirit. He said he considered every soldier in Vietnam to be a volunteer. "But," protested a staff officer, "most of them are draftees." "That's true," said Roberts, "but you have to remember, many of them had a choice. They could have run to Canada or Sweden, or they could have wriggled out of the draft by being clever, or getting some kind of deferment." Roberts also knew that in any good infantry division, a brutal and terribly unfair filtering process existed that ensured that only the most highly motivated men finally ended up in line companies. The drones, troublemakers, and cowards were "punished" by being sloughed off into rear-echelon jobs because line-company leaders, from squad leaders to company commanders, could not take chances with undependable and unmotivated soldiers. The good soldiers tended to be the sons of working- and middle-class families where values were taught and retained. That is why author Arthur Hadley once wrote that in line units in Vietnam, "it is the best of the middle class that gets blown away."

Even though the commercial news media still flocked to the Cav, Roberts had the unique concept that any publication, whether it was produced by the government or not, was to be considered external media. He believed that Skytroopers expected the Cav house organs to say nice things about them, but when they read stories about their exploits in the *Stars and Stripes*, the MACV *Observer*, and the USARV *Reporter*, they accorded those stories a higher level of credibility with a corresponding enhancement of morale. Roberts also had another motivation for dominating the house organs in Vietnam. He reasoned, correctly as it turned out, that when staff officers at supporting headquarters constantly read about the Cav being engaged in meaningful operations, it made it easier for the division to obtain additional allocations of scarce supplies, and would guarantee a stream of top-notch replacements.

Although it is difficult to entirely quantify good morale, one method of measurement is that of disciplinary actions. Shelby Stanton, in his book, *Anatomy of a Division*, reported that from October through December 1969, the Cav had thirty-seven men confined in the USARV stockade, the "Long Binh Jail," which was a rate of 1.85 per thousand, the lowest in Vietnam of any division or equivalent command. Stanton went on to note that even a year later, for the same three-month period of 1970, the Cav's confinement rate was 4.68 per thousand, still the lowest in Vietnam. Stanton concluded his discussion of 1st Cavalry Division morale and discipline by stating: "These statistics are astonishingly low, even for a peacetime garrison division in Europe or the United States, and a tribute to the leadership and men of the division."

Although the government media played a crucial role in the Cav's morale-boosting efforts, the division maintained excellent relations with most of the commercial news media representatives. The same could not be said for the relationship between MACV and reporters. Day after day, at the 4:45 press briefing, which everyone still called the "Five O'Clock Follies," briefers working for the MACV Office of Information (MACOI) held a pack of reporters at bay. The MACOI press briefing on April 27 was at once typical yet unique. A couple of days earlier, without explanation, the air briefer had stopped providing bomb damage assessments (BDA) for B-52 strikes. At one time, the list of BDA had been quite extensive. Then, late in April 1969, nothing. The briefing of April 27 started with the air briefer announcing that eight B-52 missions had been flown in northern Tay Ninh and Binh Long provinces, but he provided no BDA from the strikes. In their habitual places in the front row were George Esper of the Associated Press, one of the tigers of the press corps, and Joseph Fried (pronounced Freed) of the New York *Daily*

News, the acknowledged king of the briefer baiters. This is how the briefing proceeded:

Esper: Major, earlier this week there were eleven B-52 strikes. I asked the question at the time, why were the B-52 strikes put in? Was there anything unusual? I was told that no information was available. Do you have any further information on the strike?

Briefer: We still have no information to pass on. Any information like that would be termed intelligence information and we do not discuss that data.

Esper: How can that be current intelligence information when it's several days old?

Briefer: Intelligence information is information which the command used as a basis for a scheme of maneuver. We do not pass that along; it's part of our ground rules.

Fried: It was announced yesterday that we put twenty B-52 bomber raids in Tay Ninh Province and I asked if we had had any secondary explosions reported and I was told that there were no such reports. Now I see we have put in four more and that makes twenty-four B-52 raids in approximately three days. Have you any reports that there are none or several or hundreds of secondary explosions?

Briefer: The question is again, reference B-52 strikes in northern Tay Ninh Province, do we have any additional BDA to report, like secondary explosions. I have no BDA to report at this time.

Fried: You say "additional," Major. To my knowledge, you have told us of none. Now isn't it unusual that we don't get a report of one secondary out of twenty B-52 raids in three days?

Briefer: The question is whether it isn't unusual to have no BDA from these missions. I still have no BDA to report on this and I have no further comment to make on BDA on the B-52 missions.

Esper: Major, in your release on page five, regards the B-52 bombers, it lists targets such as troop concentrations, base camps, weapons positions, bunker and tunnel complexes and supply areas. How do we know this? Do we comb the area after the raids? How do we know there were troops there?

Briefer: The question is, how do we know that it is in fact that type of target. Information is made available to the command what type of target it is and that information depends upon where the strike goes. These are general statements, certainly not current intelligence by the fact that it's not minute or individual pieces of information. We're just giving you general information; generally what targets the missions are targeted against.

Fried: I still want some answers on all these B-52 strikes with no reported BDA. After putting in eleven raids, then following up with another thirteen raids, certainly there must have been a report to General Abrams on the results of the earlier raids. Otherwise why would he order in thirteen more raids?

Briefer: Once again, I have no information on BDA to report and I have no further comment on BDA.

Question from the audience: You say you have no comment. Does that mean you don't know, or you know and won't tell?

Briefer: Once again, I have no comment.

By the time the air briefer escaped and turned the podium over to the ground briefer, the pack was in full cry, smelled blood and went for the briefer's jugular. First there was a controversy over whether American troops fired into Cambodia, then whether there were raids into neutral Laos and whether the Marines fired across the DMZ into North Vietnam. The reporters questioned the accuracy and honesty of some casualty figures and generally challenged every assertion made by the briefing officer. In every case the briefer dodged and danced without ever confirming or denying any of the media assertions. The term "stonewalling" hadn't come into vogue yet, but it accurately described the MACV press policy in 1969.

The fascinating aspect of this particular briefing was the decision by MACV to suddenly suspend announcement of BDA of B-52 strikes. Until that sudden turnabout, the MACOI evening handout had lavishly described the meters of trench line destroyed and bunkers shattered, the number of secondary explosions recorded, and the estimated enemy casualties—all in an attempt to justify the use of a weapons system that many reporters had challenged as less than cost-effective. Suddenly there was silence, allegedly for security reasons. Despite the acrimony at the briefing, very little was reported in the United States, as those in charge of MACV's press policy most certainly knew would happen. About a week after the wrangling over the BDA had stopped, a story was bruited about Saigon that the *real* reason for the shift in release policy was that the command had been embarrassed and angered over some story in a stateside magazine that toted up the cost of B-52 strikes and calculated that it cost the taxpayers X thousands of dollars per meter of destroyed trench line. It was a measure of the distrust and suspicion the press corps harbored about MACV that this story was accepted at face value. The reporters figured it was typical of the lying SOBs and let it go at that. And besides, there were always fresh targets to shoot at in the nightly briefings.

Plenty of circumstantial evidence supports the hypothesis that stopping public announcements of bomb damage assessments of B-52 strikes was a necessary prelude to the massive secret bombing of Cambodia. When it had become obvious that Washington was going to press for immediate withdrawals regardless of the shape of the ARVN, Abrams told General Wheeler that more cross-border B-52 strikes would help justify the withdrawal from a military standpoint. Abrams was thinking of publicly acknowledged strikes into the Cambodian sanctuaries, but Nixon and Kissinger didn't want to upset their fragile relationship with Cambodia's Sihanouk and most definitely did not want to risk the public uproar they were certain that on-the-record bombings of Cambodia would bring. So Abrams got his bombing, but the price he had to pay was to establish an elaborate system of deception. The B-52s were reported as bombing targets in South Vietnam while they were actually striking base areas across the border. The bombings carried the code name "Menu" apparently because the targets were all given code names such as "Breakfast," "Dinner," "Lunch," and "Snack." The way the system worked was that all B-52s would be given legitimate Vietnamese target designations when they took off, but as they approached Vietnam, some would be given coded target designations by radio that switched their targets into Cambodia. However, these Cambodian strikes were reported as strikes in Vietnam, usually as strikes in northern Tay Ninh, Binh Long, and Phuoc Long provinces, where there were ample legitimate strikes to cover the deception. Obviously, it was easier to maintain the deception by not reporting any BDA than by manufacturing phoney BDA to satisfy the press corps.

Dr. Sorley, in his biography of Abrams, contends that while Abrams had to lie as part of the White House–imposed secrecy plan, he did not consider it a serious breach of Abrams's well-known code of ethics. Sorley says that deception plans have always had a place in warfare, and placed the Menu bombings in that category. General Bruce Palmer, a West Point classmate of

Creighton Abrams, in *The Twenty-Five Year War*, strongly condemned the Nixon decision to conduct the Cambodian B-52 strikes covertly. He said the decision "placed the military in an impossible position, having literally to lie publicly about a perfectly legitimate wartime operation." He asserted that it was wrong for political leaders to place their military personnel in a position where they had to dishonor their personal and military code of ethics.

Nevertheless, whatever the ethical implications of the secrecy, the bombings of the Cambodian sanctuaries and routes to and from those sanctuaries started in earnest in May, and by August had started paying dividends, although none of those who would benefit knew it at the time.

9

Battle of Binh Long— The Quiet Phase

The small sheet of paper drifted slowly through the jungle canopy, the silence broken only by the rapidly diminished *whop-whop* of a helicopter, strewing a cloud of white chaff to the wind. The young Viet Cong soldier watched the paper drift in his direction and, recognizing it as an American *Chieu Hoi* leaflet, reached out and snatched it just before it touched the jungle floor. He glanced about furtively and thrust the leaflet into his shirt. He would study its contents later when his superiors and political officers could not observe him.

For about a week Nguyen Van An thought about the prospects of becoming a *Hoi Chanh* (the term for the voluntary returnee to the government's side), weighing the alternatives offered by the American and South Vietnamese *Chieu Hoi* (Open Arms) program and the claims of his political officers, who told him that to surrender to the Americans meant certain death. But An was on a mission that he believed would result in his death anyway. So he decided to take a chance.

At 6 P.M. on July 29, An walked up to a soldier of the 214th Regional Force Company and with great trepidation, expressed his desire to *Chieu Hoi*. An was taken from the village of Binh Minh to the *Chieu Hoi* center in the Binh Long Province capital city of An Loc, about three kilometers west of the site where the young Viet Cong made his decision for freedom.

On July 31, the interrogation team from the 11th Armored

Cavalry Regiment (ACR) made a routine stop at the *Chieu Hoi* center and started talking to An. He told them an incredible story. He said he was nineteen years old and had been forced to become a laborer for the VC 9th Division, which he claimed was operating in the Fishhook area of Cambodia. He said that the 9th Division, the VC 5th Division, and the NVA 1st and 7th divisions were going to stage coordinated attacks on key targets throughout the border regions, with a concentration on Binh Long Province. An was obviously intelligent and cooperative but the list of "AKAs" (Also Known As) he gave the interrogation team was about two years old. Moreover, the VC 9th Division, although it had operated out of the Fishhook earlier in the war, was known to be located in the Angel's Wing of Cambodia adjacent to Hau Nghia Province.

The young Viet Cong could have been dismissed as a crackpot, but Lieutenant Thomas R. Kelley, the intelligence analyst for the 11th ACR, believed there was more to An than met the eye, and convinced his bosses, Colonel James Leach, the commander of the 11th ACR, and his S-2, Major Robert D. Foley, that they should continue with An's interrogation. Leach said that Kelley told him that it was like a Harvard MBA trying to convince people he was only a humble laborer.

It was August 2 before Kelley and his team got back to the An Loc *Chieu Hoi* Center. When they arrived, An ran out to greet them and started blurting out the real story. An told them his first cover story was concocted because he believed he would receive better treatment if he pretended to be a simple forced laborer. His attitude had changed because of the friendly treatment he had received at the hands of Kelley's team, who had taken him out to eat on one occasion during the initial interrogation. The story he told still was incredible, but at least parts of it could be double-checked for credibility.

An was, in reality, a platoon leader in the H21 Sapper Recon Company of the 272nd Regiment of the VC 9th Division. He was one of the few remaining true Viet Cong in a unit that was now almost entirely filled by northerners. He had been fighting for five years without ever being allowed to return to his home for a brief visit, and he believed the forthcoming combat action would kill him. He had memorized as much information as he could, based on what he could glean at his level of operations.

He stuck with his original story: that the VC 9th Division had moved two regiments from the Angel's Wing to the Fishhook and that these two regiments, along with the VC D368 Battalion, a local unit, were targeted against American and South Vietnamese bases in the An Loc area. He said that the NVA 7th Division was sending its 209th Regiment against Quon Loi and LZ ANDY, the sprawling base that was headquarters of the 1st Cav's 3rd Brigade and the 11th ACR. He said that COSVN also had ordered attacks on the Bo Duc district headquarters in extreme northeastern Phuoc Long Province; the 101-D Regiment of the NVA 1st Division had the mission of interdicting National Highway 13 in the vicinity of Chon Thanh, near the southern boundary of Binh Long Province. The only information that An did not have was the date of the attack. An knew only that it was to be fairly early in August. He knew that his platoon had nearly completed its mission of reconnaissance for attack positions for the 272nd Regiment.

Kelley was convinced that An was telling the truth. His team could corroborate enough of An's background to determine his basic credibility. But his story by itself was not enough to bring about a wholesale change in allied defensive posture in the province. What followed at 11th ACR headquarters was a frantic sifting of all available intelligence information. One solid piece of evidence came from a battle site about ten kilometers southwest of An Loc on July 28. Papers found on the bodies of two enemy soldiers killed in the contact identified them as belonging to elements of the 271st Regiment of the VC 9th Division. Intelligence analysts at the time had assumed they were hospital patients who had been reassigned to the 101-D Regiment. An's story began to look more credible. At the very least it decreased the giant leap of faith it took to recognize that two regiments of an NVA infantry division had moved, absolutely unbeknownst to the allies, more than eighty-five kilometers from the Angel's Wing to the Fishhook.

An August 1 contact by the 1st Battalion, 7th Cavalry, east of Loc Ninh resulted in the capture of a prisoner who told interrogators that the NVA 7th Division was going to attack Quon Loi. Another piece of evidence came from another *Hoi Chanh* who rallied on August 2. He told of two companies of the 9th VC Division reconnoitering the area west of An Loc between July 18 and 31. He also reported that about forty men from the D368 Local Force Battalion had moved into the areas west of An Loc on July 31.

By August 3, Jimmy Leach believed he had enough evidence to make a credible case that the portion of Binh Long Province that it was his mission to defend was due for a major attack. He dispatched his S-2, Major Foley, to Camp Gorvad to brief the 1st Cavalry division intelligence people, and from there to Bien Hoa to inform the G-2 of II Field Force. Intelligence specialists at both headquarters greeted the story with substantial skepticism. But at 1st Cav headquarters, even the faint possibility of a threat of this nature was viewed seriously enough to initiate contingency planning.

The Cav's hierarchy at this time consisted of the division's chief of staff, Colonel Bob Shoemaker, who was on the brigadier general's list awaiting his September promotion, and Brigadier General George Casey, who had just returned to the Cav as its assistant division commander for maneuver and who at the moment was the 1st Cav's acting division commander. The 1st Cav commander, Major General Elvy Roberts, had suffered chest seizures a few days earlier and was recuperating in a field hospital near Saigon. Because Casey had just assumed his position, he leaned heavily on the advice of Shoemaker, who counseled maximum planning and preparedness, including a modest increase in the planned B-52 strikes in the area west of An Loc, which was about all the division could do at the time.

As he evaluated the nature of the threat, General Casey knew he would need some reinforcements from outside the division. Shoemaker and G-3 Dick Wood had already given him the grim news: the Cav was nearly overextended. The three battalions working for the 3rd Brigade had their hands full dealing with elements of both the VC 5th Division and the NVA 7th Division, and based on the perceived threat, had to maintain their positions astride the Song Be corridor as well as reinforce the district town of Bo Duc. The 3rd Brigade and two battalions had spent part of April and May in War Zone D east of Saigon, beating back the last attempt of the VC 5th Division to penetrate into the populated areas around Saigon. The VC 5th Division spent most of June and July pulling back into Phuoc Long Province, where it began reinforcing the VC's hold on that province's population base and working to reopen the clogged infiltration routes. One of the Cav's infantry battalions was fully occupied trying to provide security for the Phuoc Long Province capital of Song Be City. And even though the violence in War Zone C had subsided somewhat, the lid was kept on only by the presence of the 1st Brigade.

Then the gods of war smiled on the Cav. On August 7, General Creighton Abrams made a routine visit to 1st Cavalry Division headquarters at Phuoc Vinh. His briefing by the Cav's G-2 and G-3, usually a pro forma affair, was anything but routine this time. The briefers told Abrams about An the *Hoi Chanh* and the evidence they had gathered to substantiate his story. Abrams chomped down on his cigar as the briefing unfolded. "It was obvious," Shoemaker recalled, "that General Abrams hadn't had a clue about this from his MACV intelligence staff." What his staff had told him was that there were general indications that the enemy was about to launch another of the so-called "high points" sometime in August. That the communists would mass the equivalent of two divisions against Binh Long Province made sense, given their continual post-Tet efforts to overrun a province capital and control enough territory around it to proclaim the area a "liberated zone" and the province capital as the capital of their newly created Provisional Revolutionary Government.

Although the evidence was not overwhelming, Abrams, years removed from the turret of a tank, retained the tanker's basic philosophy of "let's get the show on the road." He had not gotten where he was by waiting for technicians to present him with a picture-perfect analysis. It was the strong endorsement by Colonel Leach that probably sold Abrams. Leach had worked for Abe in World War II, commanding a tank company in the legendary 37th Tank Battalion, and Abrams trusted Leach's judgment totally. When the briefing concluded and the staff and commanders waited for Abrams's verdict, he unwrapped another cigar, fired it up, and told them that the Cav needed to get serious about the threat, promised them reinforcements, and strongly suggested that they radically increase the number of B-52 strikes targeted against the avenues of approach to the critical bases in Binh Long Province. Then he flew back to Saigon where he put in motion directions for strong reinforcement of the allied forces in Binh Long and also ensured that the secret B-52 bombing of Cambodia would be intensified to match the strikes being scheduled by the 1st Cav.

The Cav opted to deploy a small staff group under General Casey to Quon Loi as a forward coordinating group. In Army parlance, it was known as a "jump CP" and it was colocated with Colonel Jack Barker's 3rd Brigade TOC. As the various staffs began planning for the enemy's August offensive, they recognized that the geography of Binh Long Province presented the defenders with both problems and advantages.

Binh Long was a relatively long and narrow province, averaging fifty-five kilometers in length, running north-south, and thirty kilometers in width. The province's eastern boundary was composed almost entirely of the Song Be River, which during the waning period of the monsoon in August was roughly thirty to forty meters in width with a swirling, dangerous current and steep, overgrown banks. The Cambodian border provided the western boundary of Binh Long for nearly half the north-south length of the province. The balance of the western boundary between Binh Long and Tay Ninh provinces was the Saigon River. The critical terrain feature of Binh Long Province was National Route 13, which ran north-south up the center of the province, connecting Chon Thanh, An Loc, and Loc Ninh. It was a hard-surface, all-weather road, nicknamed "Thunder Road" by the U.S. 1st Infantry Division, who had fought for its control for nearly four years.

The relative proximity of established communist bases in Cambodia to key population centers in Binh Long was a definite defensive liability for allied forces. The straight-line distance from the Fishhook to An Loc was about twenty kilometers. The terrain between the Cambodian border and An Loc for some thirteen kilometers was extremely thick and sometimes marshy bamboo and jungle. But for about seven kilometers to the west of An Loc and virtually surrounding it was the second-largest rubber plantation in Vietnam. The plantation extended for twelve kilometers north to south and twenty-two kilometers east to west. Eighteen kilometers north of An Loc was the district headquarters town of Loc Ninh, also surrounded by seventy square kilometers of rubber plantation.

The rubber plantations were still quite productive, even at this stage of the war, and their neat rows of trees provided a canopy that prevented both undergrowth and good aerial observation. For the NVA, an added bonus was that the trees were planted in perfect north-south and east-west rows, which made ground navigation, even on the darkest night, a simple matter. But rubber plantations also presented advantages for the allies. Foremost was that they were superb terrain for armor; the distance between the trees allowed easy movement of tanks and armored personnel carriers. Additionally, the lack of undergrowth permitted armored units to bring their vastly superior firepower to bear on enemy forces more effectively.

The geography of the province made it logical that the 11th ACR had the responsibility for most of the province, its rubber plantations, and Route 13, while the 3rd Brigade of the 1st Cavalry was aligned on both sides of the Song Be River, working interdiction patterns along the Serges Jungle Highway, a major infiltration route from Cambodia, which generally followed the Song Be River south into War Zone D.

The frantic preparation of the 1st Cavalry Division and its OPCON units was little noted outside of the division's AO. Washington, D.C., had certainly no cognizance of the situation. For most of June and July, which were quiet militarily in Vietnam, the political processes in Washington churned away, with President Nixon and Henry Kissinger trying vainly to get some sort of dialogue started with the North Vietnamese. The May high point had been followed by quiescence as the communists rested and retrained their formations. The summer lull in which American casualties dropped was regarded by Washington as a signal that the North Vietnamese might be receptive to some peace initiatives. For some reason, it appears that no one ever told the White House about the ebb and flow of military action by the NVA and VC. Out of a discussion on July 7 between the president and his advisors over the meaning of the lull came a decision to officially change the mission statement for the American forces in Vietnam. The old statement, promulgated by the Johnson administration for General Westmoreland, spoke of defeating the enemy and driving him from South Vietnam. The new statement, which was to go into effect August 15, focused on providing assistance to the South Vietnamese armed forces, supporting pacification, and reducing the flow of supplies to the enemy. The politicians, particularly Mel Laird, wasted no time in claiming credit for the change of mission to MACV, disregarding the reality that General Abrams had, in fact, been doing exactly that for nearly a year without any formal "guidance" from Washington.

At any rate, Kissinger, using the good offices of Jean Sainteny, the former French delegate-general in Hanoi, arranged for delivery of a private letter from Nixon to Ho Chi Minh. The letter, dated July 15, was a strong commitment to peace through negotiations and concluded with the statement—a plea, really—"Let history record that at this critical juncture, both sides turned their face toward peace rather than toward conflict and war." After writing and dispatching the letter Nixon left for his around-the-world trip, which included the *Apollo 11* splashdown at Guam and his visit to Vietnam on July 30. Nixon was still waiting for Ho's reply when the *Hoi Chanh* came to An Loc with his story of an August offensive.

Once General Abrams got into the act, it didn't take II Field Force and the ARVN III Corps headquarters long to begin scratching up reinforcements. Since the 11th ACR had the most significant defense positions between the Cambodian border and the towns and villages along Highway 13, the bulk of the reinforcements sent up by generals Julian Ewell and Do Cao Tri were directed by General Casey toward Leach's two squadrons. An indication of the seriousness with which MACV and II Field Force viewed the threat to the Highway 13 corridor was the level and quality of reinforcements pumped into the An Loc and Loc Ninh areas and the speed of their dispatch. Suddenly there were convoys on Highway 13, all protected by armored calvary units, and the skies were filled with transport planes bringing troops to the airstrips at Quon Loi and Loc Ninh. Then there were more convoys carrying the airlifted troops to defensive positions.

The 9th Regiment of the ARVN 5th Infantry Division, commanded by Lieutenant Colonel Ma Son Nhon, which had been working with the U.S. 1st Division as well as with the Cav's 3rd Brigade, was deployed to take up defensive positions in and around An Loc. The ARVN 15th Armored Cavalry Squadron was sent to reinforce allied forces as deemed necessary by Casey. The ARVN 36th Ranger Battalion was deployed to reinforce Loc Ninh, teaming with Major John Bahnson's 1st Squadron, 11th ACR, to form Task Force Wright, named after Lieutenant Colonel Larry Wright, the executive officer of the 11th ACR. Leach's main line of resistance in the attack corridors that led from Cambodia to the An Loc and Quon Loi areas was reinforced with two companies of Lieutenant Colonel Ken Cassels's 1st Battalion, 16th Infantry, a mechanized infantry battalion from the U.S. 1st Infantry Division. Leach put the "Iron Rangers" plus the 4th Battalion, 9th ARVN Regiment, into FSBs ALLONS II and THUNDER IV along Highway 13 just north of An Loc and northwest of Quon Loi. To defend An Loc and Highway 13 from the south were fire support bases, ASPEN and SIDEWINDER, which were located in mutually supporting distances of each other just a half-dozen kilometers west and slightly south of An Loc. Additional artillery support came from Charlie Battery, 2nd Battalion, 33rd Artillery, a towed 105-mm howitzer battery from the 1st Division, which Leach placed on FSB ASPEN to provide additional fire support for the elements of his 2nd Squadron, which garrisoned that firebase. SIDEWINDER finally ended up with elements of the ARVN 15th Armored Cav and the 1st Battalion of the 9th ARVN Infantry. To handle the expected assault at Chon Thanh was a squadron of the 1st ARVN Armored Cavalry. The Big Red One also contributed a troop from its divisional armored cavalry squadron, Alpha Troop of the 1st Squadron, 4th Cavalry, more popularly known as the "Quarter Horse" Cav. This unit was directed to take up hasty defensive positions deep within the rubber plantation about three kilometers south of LZ ANDY.

Even as the reinforcements were moving into positions and establishing the hastily developed defensive plan, the counterattack plans were being drawn up. Two rifle companies were pulled back to help handle base defense at LZ ANDY, one of the companies being designated as a reaction and pursuit force for the counterattack phase. Also programmed for a reaction were two companies of the 2nd Battalion, 5th Cavalry, which was pulling palace guard at division headquarters. Additionally, every unit in the 11th ACR was given a counterattack sweep mission. Artillery fire support plans were prepared for both the defense and the counterattack phase.

Most of the preparations and planning were completed by nightfall of August 9. Now it was a matter of waiting until COSVN fired the starting gun. But the time spent waiting would not be wasted. Heeding Abrams's admonishment, the Cav scheduled massive B-52 strikes in the heavily jungled areas adjacent to the Fishhook. Later, debriefed POWs indicated the decisive weapon in the campaign to cause attrition among the advancing NVA regiments was undoubtedly the BUF (the crew's acronym for Big Ugly Fella . . . or whatever other "F" word seemed appropriate). This was the Strategic Air Command's eight-engine bomber, which was flown out of Guam and U Tapao in Thailand. One BUF could carry a massive conventional bomb load of 108 500- or 750-pound bombs that, when impacting, spread a carpet of death and destruction that unrolled at a rate of more than four hundred kilometers per hour. Moreover, the strikes on the Vietnamese side of the border had counterparts just inside Cambodia. In the dry season, a dust pall hung over a five-hundred-square-kilometer area.

The Arc Lights wreaked a terrible toll on the North Vietnamese formations. Survivors told of entire companies being decimated by the strikes, with dazed soldiers reeling out of the strike zone, blood streaming from their nostrils, eardrums shattered, and minds muddled. A great deal of disinformation about the B-52 strikes was circulated during the Vietnam War, stories discrediting the efficacy of the strikes. Critics claimed there was little evidence that the BUFs were doing more than spectacularly cratering the countryside. One of the favorite stories late in the war, and one that has been picked up and parroted as gospel by writers since, is that the enemy knew when the strikes were coming and was thus able to escape the full force of the bombing. For example, in his 1986 book, *The Army and Vietnam*, Andrew F. Krepinevich wrote, "There is also evidence that the VC developed an early warning system against ARC LIGHT attacks." Yes, there was an early warning system. It is true that Russian trawlers off Guam or in the Gulf of Siam could get a fix on the number of bombers taking off and their general flight heading and could flash that warning to Hanoi. The warning would then be relayed to field units, whose members would presumably escape from the target areas. In fact, however, there was no way the average North Vietnamese soldier in the jungle, particularly the tangled jungle of War Zone C, could escape. For American units, the minimum safe distance from an Arc Light box was three kilometers; any number of strikes were aborted because American units could not get out of the danger zone in time. If a North Vietnamese unit knew that B-52s were inbound, how far could they move in the limited time between their warning and when the bombs dropped from a silent sky? And in what direction?

The VC and NVA in South Vietnam did know when a B-52 strike was about to occur, particularly in the case of a daylight raid. There was sudden quiet; no scout helicopters, no aircraft of any kind, just an eerie silence. The B-52 was a weapon of sheer terror, and probably was the greatest creator of enemy defectors of any weapon in the American arsenal. A former Viet Cong official, Truong Nhu Tang, in a 1985 book, *Journal of a Vietcong*, made it sound as if evading the BUFs was child's play and their impact on the VC and NVA was minimal. He apparently never discussed the issue with Colonel Bui Tin. In 1989 in Hanoi, CBS reporter Morley Safer talked to a retired North Vietnamese colonel, Bui Tin, and verified what every prisoner interrogator and psychological operations officer in Vietnam long ago knew absolutely. In his book, *Flashbacks: On Returning to Vietnam*, Safer recorded that Bui Tin recalled the terror of the B-52 raids: "I had no wounds from the B-52 raids, but the psychological problems for me and my men were terrible. You cannot understand what it was like unless you've lived through it. The bombs came out of absolute silence. And because you had no warning and could see nothing because of the dust, you did not know which way to run until the second stick of bombs exploded."

Whatever the critics' long-term view of the Arc Lights, in the incipient August offensive, the air attacks thinned down some rather formidable NVA formations. Those who survived the raids became sitting ducks for the marauding gunships of the 1st Cav and 11th ACR. Soldiers not killed by the gunships were scooped up by the aero rifle platoons of the air cavalry unit. In their dazed condition, the prisoners talked readily and confirmed the presence of the VC 9th Division in a forward attack position targeted against the An Loc area. The mental and emotional state of the prisoners was preconditioned with an extensive psychological operations program. Two leaflets, in particular, were very effective. The first stated:

Soldiers of the 9th VC Division: Your leaders have foolishly led you back to Binh Long Province. The last time your unit was here, death lived in your camps. From March, 1966, to November, 1967, 1,800 of your comrades died useless at Loc Ninh. 400 of your brave soldiers were left on the battlefield at Du Dop in November, 1967 and 400 more were buried at Sroc Con Trang in January, 1968. Death and misery await you and your comrades in Binh Long Province. Your leaders have again led you into the valley of death.

The second leaflet featured a picture of *Hoi Chanh* Nguyen Van An and said:

Soldiers of the 9th VC Division: On 29 July 69 Nguyen Van An, a platoon leader from H21, Sapper Recon Co., 272 Regt., 9th VC Div., rallied to the GVN at An Loc. An's mission had been to recon the An Loc area in preparation for future attacks. But after completing his mission, An rallied to the GVN. Perhaps what An saw on his mission made him realize that any attack on ARVN and Allied forces could only bring death to him and his comrades. An found a way to escape death. You must find a way out also. Rally or surrender to the GVN before death claims you.

The big bag occurred on August 9, obviously the date the NVA had chosen to move their formations into forward attack positions. After the Arc Lights of the night before, the air cavalry units found large groups of enemy soldiers wandering around in the open. Near the Fishhook, B Troop of the 9th Cavalry killed twenty-three NVA of an even larger group milling around in an open field; the rest escaped to safety. A positive unit identification was not obtained. But a few minutes later, just south of the southernmost point of the Fishhook, the Air Cav troop of the

11th ACR spotted another large group of NVA in a clearing. When the firing stopped, another thirty-three communist soldiers were dead. This time, the unit identification was certain. The dead soldiers were from the 271st Regiment of the VC 9th Division and the 101-D Regiment of the NVA 1st Division. In the same general location, the aerial rifle platoon of the 11th Air Cav Troop snatched a group of dazed NVA soldiers. Van Ngiah, one of the prisoners, said that he was a member of the 1st Battalion, 101-D Regiment, and that his battalion base area had been hit by a B-52 strike the night before. He had stayed in his bunker all night and when he came out in the morning he found that only five others remained alive in the area.

But the sizable number of NVA combat formations that survived the strikes and the air cavalry sweeps did an admirable job of concealing their approach to their targets. Only minor contacts were noted in the operational logs of committed units on Monday, August 11—with one exception. The NVA opened up prematurely on LZ BECKY in central War Zone C. At 3 A.M. on August 11, a sapper unit tried to work its way through BECKY's wire. The barefoot sappers, clad only in shorts, started cutting a path through the three rows of concertina wire. Wrapping rubber bands around the trip flares so they wouldn't ignite and carefully neutralizing other anti-intrusion devices, they had only penetrated the outer ring of wire when they were detected. When the bunkers started blazing away, the NVA dropped a couple dozen light and medium mortar rounds into the base perimeter to cover the withdrawal of the sappers. The attack was easily beaten back, but the indirect fire cost the base defenders four killed and fourteen wounded. The 1st Cav's entire AO was on a hundred percent alert, but all was quiet for the remainder of the night. For the thousands of American soldiers who had been on alert for night after night, there was widespread bitching that the whole exercise was a case of overreaction by the brass. Fortunately, no one paid any attention to the griping, and on the night of August 11, all the bases in the Cav's AO went back on full alert. They needed all their physical faculties. That night was an unusually black one. The moon was in its dark phase, and the sky was overcast. The troops manning bunkers on firebases could barely see a dozen meters through the gloom. It was a night made to order for enemy sappers.

10

Battle of Binh Long—
The Killing Phase

At one hour after midnight on Tuesday, August 12, Hanoi dropped the hammer, not only in the Cav's AO but throughout Vietnam. The communists assaulted 16 allied camps during the night and struck 137 others with rocket and mortar barrages. These countrywide attacks have been classified by historians as just another of the communists' high points and thus not a repudiation of the July 9 COSVN resolution about no more big offensives. The same could not be said about COSVN's effort in Binh Long, where elements of three NVA divisions were sent out to conquer a province. Big stakes were on the table when Hanoi rolled the dice.

The opening act took place on LZ ANDY, the massive and almost undefendable base camp for the 3rd Brigade and 11th Armored Cavalry Regiment. The base sprawled over the crest of a large flat-topped hill some three kilometers long and one-and-a-half kilometers wide. The perimeter covered nine full kilometers and had eighty-two bunkers and nine towers.

Unlike other very large base camps in Vietnam, which used full infantry battalions for base defense, the LZ ANDY "Green Line" (perimeter bunkers) normally had but one rifle company, which was rotated in from one of the line battalions. On this night, however, a second rifle company had been brought in to beef up defenses by acting as a brigade ready reaction force.

But even though ANDY was larger than some division-level base camps, the bulk of the defense was provided by what almost everyone called the "ash and trash" elements. These were the cooks, clerks, and supply, ammunition, and transportation specialists—everyone who had a role in providing logistical and administrative support to the line outfits. In general these were reluctant warriors who detested Green-Line duty, regarding it as a waste of their leisure time, a part of which, by mid-1969, was spent in a haze of marijuana smoke. Others who got bunker duty were the personnel from the battalion and company rear elements of the battalions working for both the 2nd and 3rd Brigades, some of whom were good soldiers doing legitimate and vital jobs in the rear. But there also were a significant number of soldiers who were assigned to positions in company and battalion rears because they couldn't cut it in the bush. They, too, were reluctant warriors. On the other hand, a portion of the rear area strength was made up of transient grunts—troopers returning from rest and recuperation (R and R), or who were on the base for dental appointments, or even those who had recuperated from wounds, returned from hospitals, and were awaiting reassignment back to their units. This group comprised the pros, who knew what an NVA attack was all about and knew what to do about it.

Aggravating the personnel situation was the physical layout of the base. Many of the Green-Line bunkers were not sited to provide mutual support. Even a first-rate infantry battalion would have been hard-pressed to defend the base and repel all invaders. The Quon Loi base was sited right in the middle of the Terres Rouge Plantation, which, despite the war, still was a working rubber plantation. Many of the workers had been recruited by the Viet Cong to plot bunker locations. Base defense planners assumed that the VC probably knew the base's defensive characteristics better than the defenders.

The NVA attack plan was designed to exploit these weaknesses and maximize its own strengths. It called for a three-pronged sapper attack, using stealth and cunning on the west, east, and southeast portions of the base. After the sappers were inside the wire and racing toward their targets with satchel charges, the NVA would then unleash a mortar and rocket barrage on the revetment areas of the airstrip, followed immediately by a major assault on the southeast sector with one battalion of the 272nd Regiment of the VC 9th Division.

As always in war, the best-laid plans need a lot of luck to ensure perfect execution. The luck COSVN had at Quon Loi was all bad. The first piece of bad luck was its choice of sectors for its sapper attack. The western attack was directed at a portion of the perimeter called the "Blue Sector," which encompassed bunkers 10 to 24. This sector was the responsibility of the rear elements of the 1st Battalion, 8th Cavalry, the "Iron Dukes," whose line units had just finished trouncing elements of the VC 5th Division in War Zone D. The defense coordinator was the battalion executive officer, Major John Blake, a hard-bitten professional soldier who had served in the airborne brigade of the 1st Cav in 1965.

The Quon Loi base had begun to beef up its defenses right after intelligence learned of a potential attack on the base. Blake's solution was a step-by-step textbook approach. He asked the brigade for an additional allocation of the "ash and trash" support people, but made sure he had a hard-core infantry base. He guaranteed himself a supply of tough, well-trained grunts by holding the floating manpower pool for an extra day or so before returning them to the field. He broke out an 81-mm mortar from storage and scrounged up some illumination rounds for it, along with some high explosive rounds; trying to go through base defense for regular illumination took much too long, he said. And he had his own on-call artillery. He had a watchtower in his zone, and on it he stationed a crew with a Starlight Scope, which he dubbed "Green Eye." On the night of the attack, however, there was no moon and the sky was overcast, so there was hardly enough illumination to make the night vision devices work. The troopers in the bunkers could barely make out the first strand of the concertina just twenty meters away.

About a hundred meters behind Blake's command post was a maintenance shop for the 11th Armored Cavalry. Blake coordinated with the shop chief, and each night the Cav vehicles capable of moving and shooting would be a standby firepower reserve. On the night of August 12, "Blackhorse" was the radio call sign for the 11th ACR maintenance shop, which had a

Sheridan tank and two ACAVs in for maintenance, and all could move and shoot. Blake also had nearly one hundred men to defend his sector with its fifteen perimeter bunkers and provide a fifteen-man reaction force at his command post.

Blake later recalled that by the time his people had been going through this exercise for nearly two weeks, "They were tired of the bullshit and didn't really believe there was going to be an attack." Around midnight on August 12, however, Blake remembers, "I could tell there was a hell of a firefight out toward An Loc. You couldn't hear anything, but the night sky was glowing with the reflection of explosions and tracers going in all directions." This put his force in the bunkers in a higher state of alert. At about a half-hour after midnight he got a call from Green Eye in the tower.

"Duke Five, this is Green Eye. Movement at the edge of the rubber in front of bunkers 10 and 15."

Blake then called for some backup.

"Blackhorse, Duke Five. Send 'em down."

Blake positioned the two ACAVs with his reaction force and brought the Sheridan tank down to a preselected position. The perimeter contour allowed the tank to be sited so that its 152-mm main gun could fire almost parallel with the part of the wire in front of bunkers 11 to 15. Blake said it was a "gunner's dream," with the long axis of the beaten zone over the long axis of the target. Blake got up on the turret with the tank commander and told him to load a round of beehive. By this time Green Eye was reporting a lot of movement, now as close as the "tanglefoot" wire on the perimeter. Bunkers were also reporting seeing movement in the gloom. Duke Five called all the bunkers and told his people to get down inside the bunkers because beehive was coming. Then he called his mortar section and told them to prepare to hang six illumination flares over the sector. It was now near 1 A.M., almost an hour since the first movement was spotted, which indicates the time and patience that trained sappers were willing to spend to infiltrate without detection.

As soon as Blake got a "roger" back from his bunkers, he ordered the mortar to fire. When he heard the first round hit the bottom of the tube, he tapped the tank commander on the shoulder. The TC kicked the gunner and the beehive round went down range. Said Blake: "The results were unbelievable. Before the illumination round had a chance to light up, those flechettes hung about thirty bad guys in the wire, and set off about a hundred trip flares. The place lit up like a night game at Yankee Stadium. For the guys in some of the bunkers it was a daylight turkey shoot." But, Blake noted, the NVA hung tough and kept coming. The wire-breaching assault was made by the K33 and K37 sapper companies, part of a crack sapper unit controlled by COSVN. The volume of return fire from the enemy surprised the troopers in the bunkers. The tenacity and courage of the sappers earned the admiration of old soldier Blake. Despite the fact that the invaders were taking terrible casualties from the now not-so-reluctant warriors manning the defenses, many of the sappers cut a swath through the wire and fanned out to assault perimeter bunkers. Bunkers 15 and 16 bore the brunt of the NVA assault and the responsibility fell to Lieutenant Gary Farrington, who assisted Blake in the command of the sector, to coordinate the defense in the area until the sector reaction force could arrive.

While the fight was raging in Blake's sector, the NVA bit into their second piece of bad luck on ANDY when they undertook the probe at Bunker 61 on the Green (east and southeast) sector, which was defended by Bravo Company, 1st Battalion, 7th Cavalry. Quite coincidentally, earlier in the day an engineer unit had improved the wire in front of this bunker. It had been discovered that erosion had eaten out a four-foot ditch under the wire through which the enemy could move almost to the bunker line without being seen. The sappers doubtless were surprised to find the gap gone, and among all the probes against ANDY, this was the only place where bangalore torpedoes were used to blow gaps in the wire. Bunker 61 also was directly east and the closest bunker to the 3d Brigade TOC. The use of the bangalores, of course, alerted the defenders to the presence of the sappers, but the enemy still managed to penetrate the wire around bunker 61.

Bob Shoemaker, in remembering those desperate battles on 1st Cav firebases during the interdiction campaign, said that in almost every case, there was an individual who rose to the occasion and whose actions turned the tide of battle. On this night it was Lieutenant Barry G. Hitner of the 919th Engineers, a unit attached to the 11th ACR. Hitner commanded one of the reaction forces, which he had dubbed "RF All Glory." His orders were to stay put until he received commitment orders from the brigade base defense commander. Hitner heard the fighting at Bunker 61 and, because he had lost commo with the base defense TOC, decided on his own initiative that it was time to move out. Hitner's decisive action was the next piece of bad luck for the NVA.

Hitner deployed two of his Combat Engineer Vehicles (CEVs), along with the rest of his reaction platoon. The CEV, as it was configured at ANDY, was a fearsome machine with bulldozer blade, two M-60 machine guns, and a 165-mm gun that fired softball-sized plastic explosive rounds. The CEVs and the remainder of the All Glory reaction force did not take long to plug the gap and the situation was stabilized. Four or five enemy sappers, however, had escaped the counterattack and reached the interior of the perimeter, and they were to be heard from later.

In the meantime, on the western side of the base, in the Blue Sector, Lieutenant Farrington was fighting a desperate battle to hold the line at bunkers 15 and 16. Bunker 15 was taking RPG fire from all directions. The RPG screen to the front of the bunker was stopping the rockets coming from that direction, but some of the sappers had penetrated behind the bunker and were firing from there. The bunker was sufficiently solid and it stood up under the explosions, but the three troopers inside were shaken up and decided that if they made it to Bunker 16, six or eight Americans together might have a better chance of holding off the NVA onslaught. Specialist Four Grenville Braman, a Harvard graduate, was in 16. He remembers that when the occupants of 15 made their run for it, the area between the bunkers was clear for a minute and they made it. He said, "They told us there were dinks behind us, but we couldn't see them because of the berm behind our bunker. So we put a few frags out and the firing seemed to stop for awhile." Over on Bunker 15, Braman could see NVA soldiers running all around the bunker. "We couldn't figure out what they were doing; they were just jumping up on top of it and running around." They also made good targets for the troopers in 16 who promptly cleaned off the roof of 15 with M-16 fire.

Farrington noticed that because Bunker 17 was offset behind the perimeter road, the men of the artillery battery manning a berm a little further behind the road were hitting 17 when they tried to bring their rifle and machine-gun fire to bear on the enemy. So Farrington evacuated 17 and used its men to reinforce Bunker 18. The determined defense of the men in the bunkers and the artillery troops had temporarily stabilized the situation. There were still enemy soldiers inside the perimeter, but at the moment they weren't going anywhere.

Enter now the reaction force, under Lieutenant Hendrickson, the executive officer of Alpha Company, 1st of the 8th. He gathered up the fifteen members of the sector reaction force and started moving to assist Farrington's troops on the line. As the group was moving out, a voice from the rear was heard to say, "Man, I'm too short to be doing this shit. I only got twenty days!" Hendrickson turned around and retorted, "Shut up and get the fuck back in line; I've only got seven."

The reaction force met Blake's ad hoc armored team behind Bunker 19 and Blake decided to sweep the area southward along the bunker line, using tank-infantry tactics straight out of the book. He deployed the fifteen men out to the left of the armored vehicles, in the deep grass behind the perimeter road. It was slow and tedious, but thorough. Blake told his troopers to proceed carefully as there were probably still quite a few enemy soldiers in the deep grass. When the Sheridan tank reached a point just in front of Bunker 17, a lone NVA sapper jumped up from the grass not ten feet from the tank and cut loose with an RPG. His aim did not quite match his fortitude and the rocket whooshed over the top of the tank. Time stood still as the sapper stood there with his launcher in his hand, considering his error, and the tank crew began to react. The main gun of the tank belched fire and hit the man full in the chest with a beehive round. All they could find the next day was about two-thirds of a head and a left arm.

As the force rolled slowly down the row of bunkers, Farrington would evacuate each bunker in turn so the tank and ACAVs could have unobstructed fields of fire past the bunker and into the wire. Then, as the parade passed the bunker, Farrington would reinstall the defenders so that when the sweep was completed, the entire line was secure, even though the interior of the base was getting hammered with heavy mortars and large-caliber rockets. The NVA always aimed at the airstrip and the aircraft revetments, but rarely hit an aircraft. Tragically, on this night, one rocket hit the rearm area just as a Cobra gunship came in after flying in support of the troops on FSB SIDEWINDER. The rocket demolished the aircraft and killed its pilot.

At about 2:30 in the morning the NVA made its third and final assault on ANDY. In the southeast portion of the Green Sector, bunkers 67 and 68 received direct hits from RPGs while receiving AK-47 fire from sappers who had penetrated the wire. The NVA assault force started to attack Bunker 69 when Lieutenant Hitner and his All Glory reaction force intervened again on his own initiative. He left one CEV at Bunker 61 and moved the rest of his force down the road toward Bunker 68. "There were RPG rounds flying all over the place," he said, "and people were scurrying back and forth across the road. We couldn't tell if they were gooks or friendlies."

Some of the troopers on line were having similar problems. Specialist Four Albert Joines, who was in Bunker 71, said he was putting out fire from his bunker when he heard a voice behind him say, "Hey, Buddy! What bunker ya on?" Said Joines, "it sounded just like a GI to me, so I yelled back, '71.' I turned back around to defend my position when a B-40 hit the top of my bunker. I didn't know what the hell was going on. Then I saw this guy and his buddy drawing a bead on the bunker again. I cranked the Hog [M-60 machine gun] around and started throwing out lead. They lit out for the tall grass behind me." Joines's personal firefight with those NVA soldiers lasted for a quarter-hour, but finally an illumination flare caught the two flitting toward another firing position and Joines cut them down.

By 3:30 A.M. a platoon from Alpha Company, 5th Battalion, 7th Cavalry, part of the brigade's final reserve, arrived in the Green Sector to plug the gaps and allow the evacuation of the wounded. The defenders began to get the situation under control by 4 A.M., mopping up the occasional sapper who had survived the counterattacks. Despite the best efforts of the defenders, a half-dozen enemy sappers, who seemed to know exactly where they were headed, penetrated to within one hundred meters of the 3rd Brigade TOC where General Casey and his staff were working, but they fell to the withering fire of eight medics who demonstrated they knew how to use rifles as well as needles and bandages. By 4:30 A.M. it was over at Quon Loi and the NVA broke contact and withdrew. COSVN had committed three companies of its crack 4th Battalion, J-16 Sapper Regiment, had failed utterly in its mission, and had left fifty-five dead behind. Five of the base defenders died and fifty-one were wounded.

It could have been much worse. The defenders of Quon Loi, particularly those manning defensive positions along the Green Sector (southeast) of the base owe a debt of gratitude to the troopers of the Second Platoon of Alpha Troop of the Quarter Horse Cav. That the attack on ANDY was not more successful can be attributed to more of the bad luck that plagued the NVA that night. The careful plans of the VC 9th Divison came unraveled when a battalion of the 272nd Regiment, tagged as the major assault force on Quon Loi, were enroute to their final assembly area and ran into the night defensive position of A Troop's 2nd Platoon. The platoon had set up at the critical junction of roads 303 and 345 just two kilometers southeast of ANDY. The presence of an American armored unit in the path of the battalion's advance was a big surprise to the NVA. The platoon detected the enemy movement in the rubber toward the road junction and opened fire with machine guns and small arms; Platoon Sergeant Lawrence Noland, Jr., the acting platoon leader, elected to conserve ammunition by temporarily withholding the fire of the guns of his two tanks. The NVA battalion commander apparently felt he had no choice but to stage an ad hoc attack on the tanks and armored personnel carriers, hoping to dislodge the Americans quickly and then get on with the task of assaulting LZ ANDY. But ad hoc combat was not a strong suit of the North Vietnamese, and the Big Red One troopers, terribly outnumbered but better prepared for combat at this site, fought like tigers, never yielding an inch. Although RPGs flew through the air like a covey of quail, the Quarter Horse was fortunate that the RPG gunners were armed with high explosive rounds instead of the armor penetrating HEAT (High Explosive, Anti-Tank) rounds. Noland fought a lonely battle because a shot-off antenna took out his communication with his troop commander, Captain William J. Newell. Fortunately, at around 2:45 A.M., a passing helicopter established commo with the platoon and relayed the message to Newell that his 2nd Platoon was fighting for its life and running desperately low on ammunition. Newell promptly ordered his 1st and 3rd platoons from their night positions to the location of the firefight, and they arrived just in time to administer the coup de grace to the enemy force. A first-light sweep of the contact area revealed twenty-three NVA killed and a plethora of blood trails. A more detailed sweep of the area a day later produced fifteen more bodies for a total of thirty-eight NVA killed in the action. The contact cost the Quarter Horse Cav two killed and twelve wounded. But that firefight at a seemingly insignificant junction of two dirt roads prevented an NVA infantry battalion from being in position to assault through the gaps in the wire at LZ ANDY.

As the spot reports of contacts rolled into the division TOC at Phuoc Vinh, it became apparent that fighting had exploded across the entirety of the Cav's AO, from LZ BECKY and LZ GRANT in central and southern War Zone C to a brand-new LZ named CALDWELL at the eastern boundary of Phuoc Long Province with Quang Duc Province. In the Highway 13 corridor, the NVA tried to capture the town and garrison of Chon Thanh. The 101-D Regiment of the NVA 1st Division expended its 1st and 2nd battalions, already badly under strength, in a vain attempt to dislodge the town's defenders, the 2nd Squadron of the ARVN 1st Armored Cavalry Regiment, which was reinforced by Troop F of the 11th ACR.

The final 9th Division ground attacks of the night in Binh Long Province came at FSBs ASPEN and SIDEWINDER. The K2 Battalion of the 271st Regiment had a go at ASPEN at 2:27 A.M. but was beaten back by the firepower of elements of the 2nd Squadron, 11th ACR. Just minutes after the attack on ASPEN started, the balance of the 271st Regiment assaulted the ARVN defenders at SIDEWINDER from the east and northeast. The NVA assault breached the wire and forced a salient on the northeast side of the base. Echo Troop of the 11th ACR, in mobile reserve status in the rubber along Route 13 about two kilometers from the firebase, was directed to get to SIDEWINDER in a hurry to reinforce the defense and repel the invaders. The troop's 1st Platoon arrived first, swept north of the firebase, and fought its way through the NVA attackers from the rear. The platoon rolled through to the interior of the firebase and then wheeled around and began attacking back toward the berm, eliminating the penetration. By 4 A.M., all of E Troop's tracks were on the berm and the 271st Regiment had lost another seventy-eight soldiers.

In An Loc itself, for a brief period the VC D368 Battalion made an appearance. The city's east gate was under fire and VC agents were inside the city passing out propaganda leaflets that proclaimed a communist victory and declared An Loc as the site of the capital of the new Provisional Revolutionary Government. The announcement was premature. The ARVN 15th Armored Cavalry's overwhelming firepower turned back the desultory VC effort, and fifty VC regulars died in front of the city's gates without even coming close to accomplishing their mission.

The VC 9th Division and its VC allies were pretty well spent, but the NVA 7th Division still carried a lot of punch. At the northernmost part of the defensive line on Route 13 near Loc Ninh, the 209th Regiment of the NVA 7th Division made its presence known by staging attacks on FSBs JON and KELLY. One of the most ferocious battles was fought by C Troop of the 1st Squadron, 11th ACR, and the 1st Company of the 34th ARVN Ranger Battalion. The ARVN company commander later was awarded the Silver Star medal for killing seven of the enemy with his .45 caliber pistol, shooting six and clubbing the seventh. The actions at JON and KELLY cost the NVA thirty-nine dead.

For Binh Long Province, it had been quite a night. In less than two hours, the North Vietnamese had launched major ground attacks, involving units of three main-force divisions at six different points over the entire length of the province. It was an offensive of unusual scope and ferocity, the first time since Tet-68 that the enemy had attempted to mount a coordinated effort on such a scale. Those who believed the propaganda of COSVN resolutions purportedly foregoing major offensives were probably surprised. The allied forces in Binh Long were not, thanks to painstaking intelligence-gathering and assessment. The defense plans had used the available resources intelligently and then benefited from the ferocious fighting spirit of the allies. From the time the enemy arrived in the province he was harried, hit and terrified by B-52 strikes, chased and killed by hunter-killer teams, and pounded with hundreds of rounds of artillery whenever he was picked up by surveillance means. His mind was worked on by psychological operations which played on his fears so effectively that twenty-nine *Hoi Chanhs* fell into allied hands during the fighting. And when they attacked, the NVA soldiers found themselves pitted not only against the massed defensive fire of the ground units but also overwhelming firepower of aerial rocket artillery (758 rockets, 1,400 40-mm cannon rounds, and 22,650 rounds from the miniguns) and more than five thousand rounds of artillery of every caliber and type. On top of this the Air Force gunships, Spooky and Shadow, were on station continually during the night. Although at times it was touch and go at some places, at no time during the night was COSVN able to win its point. As a GI remarked while searching the heaps of corpses at ANDY, "Man, for Charlie, the twelfth of August was the Twelfth of Never."

Of course the enemy attacks in the 1st Cav AO were not entirely limited to Binh Long Province. Lieutenant Colonel Dick Wood, who had weathered a violent NVA storm at LZ CAROLYN a couple of months earlier and now was the division G-3, had been at his post all night, monitoring the progress of the battles and relaying orders from the Task Force Casey forward command post at Quon Loi. One situation in central War Zone C drew his worried attention. Wood's former battalion, the 2nd of the 8th Cavalry, was working out of LZ BECKY. A battalion of the 1st NVA Division's 18-B Regiment had moved in during the night and, in a bizarre note, used a truck or trucks to move mortar crews and ammunition. The base defense radar picked up the movements of a single truck that made two trips, discharging personnel at the end of each trip. The North Vietnamese pushed their luck with the second trip and an artillery concentration put an end to the truck nonsense. A next-day recon found a smashed Russian truck, camouflaged with freshly cut jungle foliage attached to a bamboo platform that was lashed to the truck frame.

Inexplicably, the NVA waited until just before dawn to stage its attack on LZ BECKY. The rockets and mortars started pouring into BECKY's perimeter around 3:40 A.M. One of the first mortar shells struck the trench where the excess powder bags from the 155-mm howitzers were tossed. The hit caused a tremendous explosion that badly damaged a howitzer and killed the battery commander. The NVA threw in more than four hundred mortar and rocket rounds, causing most of the casualties sustained on BECKY that night. When the inevitable infantry attack came, the troopers of Delta Company were ready and put out an extremely heavy volume of fire from infantry weapons augmented by artillery killer junior, aerial rocket artillery, an Air Force Shadow gunship, and a new innovation called "Night Hawk." This was a Huey helicopter equipped with night vision devices, a searchlight, and a minigun, the six-thousand-rounds-a-minute Gatling gun.

The inevitable shower of RPG rockets that accompanied the assault temporarily neutralized two perimeter bunkers, but before the NVA assault teams could exploit the momentary advantage, the defenders fired off their final protective fires of claymore mines and Fougasse, the infantryman's organic napalm strike. Fougasse was a field-expedient weapons system. It consisted of a fifty-gallon drum half-buried at an angle with the open end facing out into the protective wire. At the bottom of the drum was placed a claymore mine or quantity of high explosive, rigged with an electrical fuse. The drum was then filled with jellied gasoline and whatever chunks of metal could be found around the firebase. A piece of plastic covered the open end to keep out the rain. When the explosive was detonated, the barrel belched out a sheet of flaming napalm. The flames and the lethal swath of steel ball bearings from the claymores usually took out the initial assault wave. This was the time when it was critical for the NVA commander to have enough troops to launch subsequent assaults to pour in over the bodies of comrades to exploit that portion of the perimeter defense that had exhausted its final protective devices. But that night there was no second wave of attackers.

Over the summer, the 18-B Regiment had spent a lot of its personnel assets evading the Cavalry's web of foot patrols, night ambushes, and aerial surveillance, and squandered the balance charging into the deadly defenses of firebases in a futile attempt to loosen the interdiction forces' choke-hold on the communist lifelines. Of course, well-trained sappers, working stealthily, could sometimes neutralize the defensive devices by disarming the claymores and cutting the detonation wires to the Fougasse barrels. But it took time and a wealth of personnel assets to pull a regular infantry company out of its assigned combat role within a line battalion, place it in a secure area, and retrain it as a sapper unit. COSVN's offensive capabilities in War Zone C had been nearly exhausted, and the balance of power elsewhere in South Vietnam militated against any massive reinforcements. Sapper units were being trained up north and infiltrated south as quickly as the Hanoi training command could churn them out. COSVN's "Armor Office" had a number of these elite sapper companies and had expended three in the abortive attack on Quon Loi. But in War Zone C, the 1st and 2nd brigades had done their job and the NVA 1st Division had only a few combat-ready units for Hanoi's big August offensive.

When dawn came, it was time for the allies to switch from the defense to the offense. All of the units in Binh Long Province began executing previously prepared counterattack plans. Casey and his commanders knew that the NVA would be scrambling to get back to their Cambodian sanctuaries, so time was of the essence. Three airmobile infantry companies were air-assaulted into blocking positions approximately halfway between An Loc and the Fishhook. From the north of An Loc, a task force comprising two mechanized infantry companies of the 1st Battalion, 16th Infantry, reinforced by Delta Company, 5th Battalion, 7th Cavalry, began a sweep to the south and west from FSB AL-LONS. Just six kilometers west of Route 13, Task Force 1-16 made contact with a reserve battalion of the 272nd Regiment, which· had been pulling security for the headquarters elements of the VC 9th Division. The armored-infantry combined-arms team hammered the NVA, driving them from their bunkers, killing twenty-nine in the process.

In the Loc Ninh area, Major John "Doc" Bahnson's 1st Squadron, 11th ACR, teamed up with the 34th Rangers to sweep escape routes that would be used by the retreating North Vietnamese. The sweep netted only a small contact on August 12, but the following day the task force cornered a large element of the NVA 209th Regiment. When the NVA broke contact that afternoon and escaped into Cambodia, eighty more North Vietnamese soldiers were dead.

For a change, August 12 had decent flying weather early and the hunter-killer helicopter teams swarmed over the NVA escape routes, picking off small groups of individuals as they flitted through the rubber. Early in the morning a Pink Team from Charlie Troop, 1st of the 9th, received groundfire southeast of Quon Loi. They returned fire and killed two NVA soldiers. A 3rd Brigade radio-monitoring team, headed by Lieutenant Tom Brennan, was listening with an interpreter to the radio net of this particular enemy unit. Brennan said the NVA commander, upon hearing the choppers in the distance, passed word over the radio net to his subordinate leaders to ensure that none of the troops fired at the helicopters. He repeated it for emphasis: "Make damn sure that no one fires at those helicopters." (NVA and VC soldiers did use profanity. In this case, the ARVN interpreter translated it into the American approximation.) Somebody in the NVA unit didn't get the word and fired on the Pink Team, which was an almost certain ticket to extinction. As the Cav birds rolled in hot, one very angry NVA commander raged over the radio: "I thought I told you not to fire at those fucking helicopters! Now you've done it; we're going to have to get the hell out of here FAST!"

On FSB SIDEWINDER, after ensuring that the ARVN had the situation under control, Colonel Leach directed his 2nd Squadron commander, Lieutenant Colonel James H. Aarestad, to execute a counterattack sweep north and west out of SIDE-WINDER. Captain William Bristol's Echo Troop moved out and had no opposition on the outbound leg of the sweep. The troop turned west and then headed southeast along a rubber plantation access road back toward SIDEWINDER. Just outside the small village of Lang Nam, the troop had a minor skirmish, but contact was broken almost immediately by the enemy. A kilometer southwest of Lang Nam was a larger village, Minh Duc, which was the site of a rubber-processing plant. As the troop was moving through the rubber toward the town, its lead platoon, the 3rd, spotted some individuals running into the rubber to the right of the road.

The platoon fired from the tracks and turned to the right, which allowed the platoon to move directly south through the rubber trees. The balance of the troop moved up swiftly and all fifteen tracks of Echo Troop began moving south through the rubber. Contact with the retreating NVA soldiers stopped momentarily. For a period of perhaps two minutes there was a lull. Then E

Troop found itself in the center of a firestorm. RPG and machine-gun fire was coming from the front and the flanks. Echo troop tracks shuddered under the fusillade and tried to struggle forward. The enemy firepower was too great. Echo Troop had rolled into a huge bunker complex that sheltered a battalion of the 271st Regiment. Worse, the enemy rocket gunners were armed with RPG-7 launchers and HEAT rounds. The 82-mm warhead on these rockets contained a cone-shaped explosive charge that, when detonated against armor plate, transformed the explosive force into a white-hot, pencil-thin jet stream that could blow a hole through twelve inches of armor plate as easily as a hot knife slices through butter. The molten steel that was blown into the crew compartment usually killed or seriously wounded the occupants and set fire to the vehicle.

Within short order E Troop had lost five ACAVs and two platoon leaders. The squadron commander ordered the troop to pull back so artillery and tactical air strikes could be directed into the contact area. When the strikes were completed, Aarestad sent the tanks of H Company back in to try to recover the dead of Echo Troop who had been left in the contact area. A very truculent NVA force had stayed behind in the bunker complex, and the NVA soldiers knew how to use RPGs. Two of H Company's tanks were knocked out and the company was directed to pull back. Weather was closing in and air support had to be curtailed. It was the bloodiest fight of the day. Fifty-six members of the 271st Regiment died in the bunker complex; the cost to the armored cavalry units was four dead, thirty-six wounded, and two missing. Of the latter, more would be heard later.

The final contact on August 12 occurred on Route 12 north of Chon Thanh. Troop F of the 2nd Squadron, 11th ACR, was escorting a convoy north on the highway when the NVA sprung an ambush. The enemy, however, had unwisely chosen a site used many times before for ambushes and it took F Troop and the ARVN Forces with the convoy very little time to quash the ambush. The engagement cost the 101-D Regiment another fifty dead, which at this point in the conflict it could ill afford, particularly since the allied force sustained only a few slightly wounded and the convoy rolled on into An Loc without further incident.

This was the last large contact of the day, and it marked the end, for all intents and purposes, of the Battle of Binh Long Province. The 1st Cav and its OPCON units continued to chase and harass the enemy, killing some 230 NVA soldiers in the process of pursuit over the next three days. COSVN had rolled the dice in Binh Long and they came up snake eyes, particularly for the 460 NVA soldiers who died during the bloody thirteen-hour battle. On the other side of the ledger, twenty Americans were killed during the fighting.

A month after the battle, the division historian, Captain John Hottell, put together a meticulously researched and beautifully written history of this remarkable battle. Hottell, a West Point graduate and a Rhodes Scholar, had just finished a stint as a rifle company commander in the 1st Battalion, 8th Cavalry. He exhibited unusual sensitivity when, during the assessment portion of the history, he wrote these words about the human cost of the battle:

Twenty American men lost their lives during this fighting. For them the fact that they are the short part of a 23-to-1 kill ratio will be little solace, but history sometimes has a way of rewarding those who die in battle, and perhaps she will be especially kind to these twenty for having been the cutting edge of such a brilliant operation.

In the heat of battle one hardly has time to stop and think about how well things might be going. In a struggle for survival, valuations are reduced to a simple standard: good is alive; bad is dead or wounded. Then, too, nearly everyone was simply too busy and too involved to allow the luxury of such reflection. The only thing that was really clear was that there was a hell of a fight going on.

To the trooper who has lost a buddy, no amount of figures will be able to make it appear that the battle was a success. For all of us the carnage and wreckage of a bitterly contested battleground is not the atmosphere for exultation, even if the carnage all belongs to the other side. No matter who you are, you cannot help but see mothers and wives in the face of a dead enemy.

Hottell and his team of historians had already gathered most of the historical material on the August 12 offensive when Ho Chi Minh's formal reply to Nixon's peace offering arrived in Washington. Nixon received Ho's reply, dated August 25, on August 30. It contained no cause for jubilation. Ho maintained that the ten-point proposal by the National Liberation Front was the "logical and reasonable basis for the settlement of the Vietnamese problem." When the president finally revealed the content of the letter later in the year, a host of interpreters said that Ho, by saying "logical and reasonable," was being flexible and flogged Nixon for interpreting the letter as a rebuff.

What the interpreters did not know was that Nixon and Kissinger had already received other strong messages of the Politburo's intransigence. Kissinger had used his friend Jean Sainteny to arrange a private meeting in Paris with Xuan Thuy, the North Vietnamese delegate to the Paris peace talks. Kissinger hoped that a private discourse would lead to a breakthrough in formal negotiations. The meeting was held in Sainteny's Paris apartment on August 4. Kissinger, in his *White House Years*, recalls the lengthy harangue by Xuan Thuy, which boiled down to the fundamental and unchanging North Vietnamese position: The United States had to immediately and unilaterally withdraw its forces, force the withdrawal of those of other nations, and on the way out, dismantle the Thieu government. Kissinger noted that Hanoi's linkage of the military and political issues in Vietnam meant that even a speedy unilateral U.S. withdrawal would not end the war or secure the release of American prisoners.

But both Kissinger and Nixon considered Hanoi's real answer to Nixon's peace overtures to be the August 12 offensive. Kissinger later wrote, "The most generous interpretation could not avoid the conclusion that Hanoi did not believe in gestures, negotiation, goodwill or reciprocity."

Probably the most colorful analysis of the situation was by Lieutenant General Phillip Davidson in his book, *Vietnam at War*. He wrote: "Ho had taken the peace pipe Nixon had offered him, hit him with it, and then put the hot tobacco in Nixon's hand as well."

But all these machinations were terribly remote to the soldiers in the field in Vietnam. Some were just happy to be alive. At around 5 P.M. on August 15, a Pink Team was flying in the vicinity of the village of Minh Duc. About five kilometers south of the battle site, an ACAV was spotted and troops were inserted into the area to investigate. They found an officer, Lieutenant Hudkins, the platoon leader of the 2nd Platoon of E Troop, 11th

ACR. His vehicle had been one of the first hit by RPG fire. The unit medic did battlefield triage on the wounded officer and believed him dead or dying because of the welter of gore coming from his chest and groin. The medic said there were no signs of life and he moved on to treat other wounded personnel. Hudkins was left behind when the troop pulled back to bring in artillery and air strikes.

The lieutenant vaguely remembered the artillery and air strikes, and that he had managed to crawl back inside his ACAV and attempted to bandage his wounds. The next morning he was strong enough to start his vehicle, which, miraculously, despite the RPG hit, still was in running order, and he drove it to the location where he was found on August 15. The gutsy lieutenant, as he was being prepared for medevac, asked his rescuers not for a shot of painkiller, but for a cold Coke.

Hudkins's rescue accounted for one of the two missing men. The 11th ACR learned of the fate of the second on August 19, when an NVA-printed propaganda document was found in the rubber west of An Loc. The document purported to be a letter from the missing soldier, John Sexton, Jr. Sexton, who was in the troop commander's track when it was hit by an RPG, was also left for dead when the troop pulled back. His letter read:

DEAR FRIENDS IN E
TROOP 2ND 11TH ACR

Don't be too alarmed but this is me (John Sexton, Jr.). I am not dead like everyone probably thinks. I am alive and well in a National Liberation Front hospital.

As you know my track was destroyed and I was wounded in several places. My right arm is broken and I have shrapnel in my leg and my face. None of which is too serious because they've all been treated very well. The doctors have taken the shrapnel out and I just have a few scars. Whoever receives this letter tell everyone I said hello especially Marvin and Harper and Rossbach. This is no hoax letter. So take care of yourselves. Maybe someday you can all go home alive.

Your friend,
JOHN SEXTON, JR.

This story, too, had a happy ending. Instead of languishing for the remainder of the war in a jungle prison, Sexton was inexplicably released by the NVA, and early in 1970, was found by an 11th ACR unit walking south on Route 13 out of Cambodia.

No one in the 1st Cav, 11th ACR, or ARVN 5th Division spent much time savoring the victory of August 12. All the commanders knew that the North Vietnamese Army, for all its losses in the Cav's grinding interdiction campaign, still posed a tremendous threat. This was particularly true in northeast Binh Long Province and the entirety of Phuoc Long Province, where the NVA 7th Division and VC 5th Division were well entrenched and working like beavers to move supplies down into central III Corps, to compensate for the loss of the War Zone C infiltration corridors. The VC and NVA combat units in the areas south of War Zone C were hurting badly for supplies, especially food. Those shortages, combined with pacification action and the constant pressure brought by the U.S. 1st and 25th divisions, produced hundreds of *Hoi Chanhs* during the summer of 1969. The guerrilla forces in southwest Tay Ninh Province and Hau Nghia Province that depended on the muscle of the VC 9th Division operating out of the Angel's Wing and Parrot's Beak of Cambodia had that security blanket snatched away when Hanoi gambled on shifting the 9th Division to the An Loc area.

The diminished activity of the NVA 1st Division in War Zone C and the projected deployment of the 2nd ARVN Airborne Brigade into a *Dong Tien* arrangement with his 1st Brigade permitted General Roberts to consider moving his 2nd Brigade out into Phuoc Long Province. The move had been planned for late in August, but the increased threat of the VC 5th Division as a part of the early August NVA offensive caused the Cav to accelerate to August 11 the shift of the 2nd Brigade tactical headquarters from Lai Khe to LZ BUTTONS, located near Song Be, the capital of Phuoc Long Province. The next rounds of the interdiction battle would be fought in Binh Long and Phuoc Long provinces.

11

Extending the Noose

The fear fairly radiated from the ARVN colonel's eyes.

"He *knows*," Colonel Meyer thought.

The commander of the 1st Cav's 2nd Brigade, Colonel E. C. "Shy" Meyer, had gone to see the chief of Phuoc Long Province, a Lieutenant Colonel Luv Yem, to obtain any information the province intelligence collection operation may have picked up on enemy movements around the provincial capital of Song Be (Phuoc Binh). Meyer's own intelligence people were predicting an imminent major attack on the Cav's 2nd Brigade base camp at FSB BUTTONS, and possibly on Song Be itself. It was early in the evening of November 3, and Meyer had just flown back into BUTTONS from Quon Loi.

The Division's intelligence network had been picking up indicators that the communists were about to come out of a ten-week hiatus on offensive warfare in the III Corps area and throw some major forces at Cav bases. The division G-2, Lieutenant Colonel Robert Hannas, and his staff, believed that the target would probably again be the Cav's sprawling base at Quon Loi, a view endorsed by the assistant division commander, Brigadier General George Casey. This was briefed to the senior commanders during a meeting on December 3 at the Phuoc Vinh division headquarters. During the conference, Meyer suggested that BUTTONS was the more likely target, given the problems the NVA were having trying to break the brigade's stranglehold

160

on the infiltration trails in Phuoc Long Province. But Casey and the division commander, Major General Elvy Roberts, were adamant that the attack would be directed at ANDY, the 3rd Brigade base. So Meyer choppered up to Quon Loi to confer on the ground with his counterpart, Colonel Jack Barker, about possible reinforcements from the 2nd Brigade, if and when the attack came.

When he arrived at Quon Loi, Meyer called his headquarters and talked to his S-3, Major Joel Jones. Jones said, "Boss, there's some things happening over here that you need to know about and you should get over here as soon as you can." A fifteen-minute flight put Meyer back at his command post at LZ BUTTONS, or Fire Support Base BUTTONS, as it was now known by edict of Lieutenant General Julian Ewell, the II Field Force commander. There, Jones and the brigade intelligence officer, Major Burton Patrick, briefed Meyer on some new intelligence that had just came in. Patrick had directed B Troop of the Cavalry Squadron to insert a four-man team from Company H, 75th Rangers (Long-Range Reconnaissance Patrol, "LRRP") into an area about ten kilometers northwest of the 2nd Brigade base.

Sitting in his tactical operations center listening to his two young majors earnestly argue that his bosses were wrong about Quon Loi being the target of the next NVA strike, Meyer mused about his situation at BUTTONS. If he had had a choice of brigade bases, Meyer happily would have gone almost anywhere else. BUTTONS, besides being in the shadow of the second-highest mountain in Military Region III, Nui Ba Ra, was a lot like LZ ANDY at Quon Loi: it had started out as a small base and gradually been built on and around until it fairly sprawled with an almost indefensible perimeter. But only BUTTONS was readily available when the 2nd Brigade was hurriedly deployed in strength into Phuoc Long Province on August 11 to counter the threat of the VC 5th Division. The consistent logistical buildup prevented a change in location for the brigade base, so Meyer, who took command of the 2nd Brigade in early October, grudgingly settled in and tried to make the best of a bad situation, knowing that inevitably he would be the target of a major NVA attack. BUTTONS was located on Provincial Route 310, about six kilometers west of the provincial headquarters town of Song

Be City, and only four kilometers from the base of the 743-meter-high Nui Ba Ra. The communists knew that it was the head-quarters of the Cavalry unit that was causing them so much misery on the infiltration trails in Phuoc Long Province and that the continued presence of American units in rural Phuoc Long was causing major defections among the population base that the Viet Cong had exploited for years. Besides, COSVN reasoned, BUTTONS was the only real defense for Song Be City, the provincial capital. Take out BUTTONS and Song Be City would fall to the communists like a ripe apple.

Standing in front of his boss, Major Patrick recounted the series of events and intelligence indicators that had persuaded the brigade staff that an attack was imminent. The latest intelligence nugget had been delivered just a couple hours earlier by the Ranger team. Patrick told Meyer that the team had been on the ground less than a half-hour when the team sergeant called in and reported seeing 450 NVA, heavily laden with what appeared to be large boxes of supplies or equipment. Patrick said the report puzzled him at first, particularly since the patrol said the NVA formation was headed for BUTTONS. Patrick recalls that he turned to the young captain who was his intelligence specialist and asked him, "What do you make of this? Why don't you check with your people and get back to me right away." Patrick said that the captain disappeared into the tent that housed the intelligence section and was back within minutes, and "his eyes were like two big saucers." The captain said, "Major Pat, we have concluded that those are not equipment boxes those people are carrying; they more than likely are very, very large satchel charges."

"Bingo," thought Patrick. "Sappers!" And, as he reviewed the intelligence picture in his mind, he realized they probably were sappers from higher headquarters, most likely the COSVN Armor Office. Patrick had a pretty good reason to believe that the sappers were headed right for BUTTONS. Early in October, the radio-monitoring people had intercepted a mysterious transmission from the center of Song Be City. They couldn't make much of it, but it was out of the ordinary, and Patrick marked it on the intelligence indicators board in the TOC. Throughout the early part of October, there were radio intercepts from unidentifiable units north, northwest, and northeast of BUTTONS. Then, in mid-October, the Cavalry scouts spotted a dozen or so NVA on the side of Nui Ba Ra taking a hard look at BUTTONS, and the scouts took them under fire. When the infantry was landed to check the bodies, documents on some of the dead enemy soldiers indicated that they were members of an elite reconnaissance unit working directly for COSVN. So Patrick knew BUTTONS had been thoroughly scouted by the NVA; what he didn't know was how many members of the enemy recon patrol escaped the deadly fire of the Cavalry Cobras. And the radio intercepts from the mysterious units continued through late October, all the while getting closer to BUTTONS and Song Be City.

Shy Meyer knew all this, of course, which is why he argued with General Casey about the division staff's contention that Quon Loi would be the target of the next communist offensive.

But until the Ranger team reported seeing 450 NVA sappers only a few kilometers from BUTTONS, all the intelligence information had been circumstantial. Meyer decided to make a quick check with the province chief. When he got to province headquarters and looked at Colonel Yem, he didn't have to ask any questions. "It was one of the few times in my life when I looked into a man's eyes and saw someone absolutely scared to death; where you knew that something was going to happen. I don't know how he knew, but he knew."

Yem obviously had been playing footsie with the local-force VC, either paying them off for protection or playing the old "if you don't bother me, I won't bother you" game. But the local-force boys didn't have anything to do with the coming attack. COSVN was sending in the first team. Yem knew that if they overran BUTTONS and walked into Song Be City, his head would decorate the city gate.

After the encounter, Meyer hustled back to BUTTONS and called his staff together. He said, "Troops, our LURPs are right. After looking in Yem's eyes, I'm damn sure were going to be hit tonight." The brigade staff put the base on a hundred percent alert. The message went out to the other two Cav battalions working in Phuoc Long Province to go on alert, particularly FSB ELLEN, which was only six kilometers west of BUTTONS. Meyer was fortunate in having a troop from the 11th ACR on the base, and he spread the tanks and ACAVs around to maximize his defensive firepower, because there were still some parts of BUTTONS that did not have a decent defensive berm. Additionally, all available men from the infantry and artillery unit headquarters that were based on BUTTONS were given a heavy ammo load and sent to positions on the perimeter.

The NVA sappers did not get a clean shot on their approach march. Once the Ranger team was safe from compromise, tube artillery, gunships from B Troop of the 9th Cav, and B Battery of the aerial rocket artillery battalion punished the columns of NVA. Pilots were able to count forty-one bodies before nightfall cast a protective blanket over the North Vietnamese. It took the NVA about four hours after dark to get in position for their assault. At fifteen minutes after one o'clock on November 4, the ground at BUTTONS shuddered under a heavy hammering of 107-mm rockets and 120-mm and 82-mm mortars. The indirect fire was followed by assault fire from NVA base-of-fire cells. The attackers poured toward the firebase defenses, breaching the wire in several places, then fanning out to place the satchel charges where they could do the most damage. A half-dozen of Hanoi's finest were heading for the command bunker when they were intercepted by a one-man army named Master Sergeant William R. Ikner, a newly arrived operations sergeant in the brigade operations section. Ikner gunned down a couple of sappers and, when one threw a grenade into Bunker 19, Ikner covered it with his chest to protect two wounded GIs in the bunker. But, miracle of miracles, the grenade was a dud, so Ikner continued on his mop-up of the sappers who had penetrated the wire, killing six. Other defenders cut down sappers within feet of Colonel Meyer's command bunker.

Over on FSB ELLEN, the men of Charlie and Echo Companies of the 1st Battalion, 8th Cavalry, had ten minutes to contemplate the NVA's plans for them. "We were watching the light show at BUTTONS and wondering when we were going to get hit," said Captain Rocco Alexander, commander of Company E. "Ten minutes later, we got our answer." At ELLEN it was the same attack pattern: rockets, mortars, RPGs, heavy small arms, and then sappers. But at ELLEN, which had a tight perimeter and a couple of tough infantry companies defending it, the sappers were stopped short of the third band of wire. At both BUTTONS and ELLEN, the defenders on the ground were supported by the overwhelming firepower pouring from Air Force gunships and the Blue Max Cobras of the 2nd Battalion, 20th Aerial Rocket Artillery (ARA).

At BUTTONS, the enemy broke contact at 5:30 A.M., leaving sixty-three dead behind. Two Americans died in the attack and twenty-six more were wounded. But it could have been a disaster. Patrick, now a retired lieutenant general, recently noted that the battle was touch and go for a while, and had not the base been ready, the Army would very likely have lost a future chief of staff that night. It was that close. The NVA losses at ELLEN were thirty-five, and no Americans were killed, although fourteen were wounded.

The NVA commander had badly miscalculated both his capabilities and the Cav's ability to defend a base. Had he not split his formidable force to attack ELLEN, a rather insignificant target in the overall scheme of things, the NVA likely would have completely overrun BUTTONS and Shy Meyer still could have been lost. But as it was, the NVA had shot its wad in those attacks and broke contact without ever threatening Song Be City. It was the high-water mark for the NVA in Phuoc Long Province. An examination of papers taken from the bodies revealed the sappers were not retrained infantrymen from NVA line regiments; these were from elite units that worked directly for the COSVN J-16 Armor Office. An infantry battalion from the 141st Regiment of the NVA 7th Division also participated in the attacks.

Oddly enough, the 3rd Brigade base at Quon Loi, which division G-2 Robert Hannas had convinced General Casey would be the target that night, never heard a shot fired in anger. George Casey was wrong, but the young general didn't miss many calls. He had made a brilliant career of being right. Casey was a classic Irishman with a ruddy complexion, quick smile, and merry blue eyes. He was gifted with a unique combination of soldierly talent, intellect, courage, and a charismatic leadership style that had marked him for greatness in the Army. Casey was born in Boston and attended Harvard for a year before entering the U.S. Military Academy, from which he graduated in 1945. He served with the 11th Airborne Division in Japan, and during the Korean War was a company commander with the 31st Infantry Regiment of the 7th Infantry Division, winning a Silver Star in the hard fighting at Heartbreak Ridge. After Korea he had a succession of challenging command and staff assignments and completed all of the Army's good schools. He also picked up a master's degree in international relations from Georgetown University and later got an MBA from George Washington University. His last assignment before returning to the 1st Cav was commanding general of the U.S. Army Combat Development Command's Combat Arms Group at Fort Leavenworth, Kansas. Best of all he was a "Cav Sandwich," a term given to those Skytroopers who returned to the division for a second tour. The term derived from the practice of wearing a 1st Cavalry Division shoulder patch on both the left and right shoulders, denoting more than one combat tour with the division. Casey's first tour with the airmobile division was as the commander of the 2nd Brigade from October 1966 to April 1967 and then as chief of staff of the division until October 1967. Casey had worked for and learned from two of airmobility's finest advocates, Generals Jack Norton and Jack Tolson, and thus had more than a clue as to what made an airmobile division work best.

George Casey was not often wrong, but on November 3, as he ruefully admitted later, he had misread the indicators. No harm was done, though. Quon Loi was spared.

But further to the east, in War Zone C, the VC 9th Division, which had taken over from the badly bruised NVA 1st Division the mission of battling the allied interdicting forces, set out to learn for itself the painful lessons absorbed by its predecessor. The 1st Brigade, now commanded by Colonel Joseph E. Collins, had picked up some valuable reinforcements to help strangle the NVA lifelines. After brief joint training sessions to pick up airmobile tactics and techniques, the 2nd Brigade of the ARVN Airborne Division, working as part of the Cav's *Dong Tien* program, had set up their own firebases on the infiltration routes in War Zone C.

The bases were sited to be mutually supporting with Cav firebases. This meant that ARVN artillery would be firing in close support of American soldiers. For those who had watched the ARVN play with artillery in the earlier part of the war or in other parts of the country in late 1969, the thought was a bit scary. But the doughty little paratroopers were fine soldiers, and before long the Skytroopers had full confidence in the ability of the ARVN Airborne to provide key close support. The NVA commanders probably also remembered the bumbling of other ARVN outfits and contemptuously underestimated the abilities of the airborne units.

This was another fatal North Vietnamese miscalculation. Throughout the early morning hours of November 4, there were rocket and mortar attacks at most of the allied bases in War Zone C. But the NVA had picked FSB IKE as its special target. The NVA first threw suppressive fire at FSB VICKY, on which was located the ARVN artillery battery supporting the 9th ARVN Airborne Battalion. This was the firebase IKE would depend on for indirect artillery fire support. Then, shortly after midnight, the NVA unleashed a rocket and mortar attack on IKE, which was followed by a ground assault with the 2nd Battalion, 271st Regiment of the VC 9th Division, supported by the 95th Sapper Company. IKE was defended by the 2nd Battalion, 5th Cavalry. The sappers breached the wire and overran one bunker, but as so often happened during firebase defense, the fighting spirit of noninfantrymen provided the key to victory. A mess sergeant gunned down a sapper as he ran through the sergeant's kitchen, avenging a personal affront, then ran toward the embattled bunker and poured in more than two hundred rounds from his M-16 to stop the NVA advance in its tracks.

Again, as in all such battles, key fire support came from the air. Cascading red waterfalls of tracers outlined the path of leaden showers of death from the miniguns of the gunships. But the crucial close-in fire support came from the 105-mm artillery battery on VICKY. "I've got to give the ARVNs at VICKY credit," recalled Lieutenant Colonel Stephen Woods, Jr., commander of the 2nd Battalion, 5th Cavalry. "They were giving us plenty of artillery support while taking incoming at the same time." A great deal of the credit for the ARVN's fine performance obviously had to go to the U.S. advisory team on the firebase, but the advisors didn't load and fire the tubes. The NVA lost sixty-three men in the attack, and the concept of *Dong Tien* won a small victory.

Additionally, the 2nd Battalion of the NVA 271st Regiment

was about to discover why War Zone C was a tougher theater than the cozy confines of the Angel's Wing to the south and east. FSB IKE was twenty-five kilometers from the nearest Cambodian sanctuary, so the attacking force had to head for bunker complexes along the infiltration trail that IKE had been interdicting. But at daybreak came the Cavalry helicopters. Alpha Troop of the 9th Cavalry put three Pink Teams on the trail of the retreating NVA. "Man, it was just like a turkey shoot," said Warrant Officer William McIntosh, scout bird pilot. The pilot of the overwatching gunship, First Lieutenant Steve Justus, harrassed the retreating enemy battalion as it withdrew to the north of IKE. The NVA soon discovered that the Cobra struck with rocket and minigun fangs and there was no remedy for its bite. "We caught the first group in a trench line about 300 meters north of IKE," said Justus. "Then we just followed the trails to the north and kept picking them off." Justus said he used all the ammo from his Cobra six times during the day, and other scout-gunship teams reported likewise. "As they [enemy soldiers] got farther away from the firebase, they started grouping together and heading for several small bunker complexes. Only one group fired at us; the rest appeared to be taken by surprise." said Mr. McIntosh. When the shooting stopped by nightfall of November 4, another seventy or so NVA soldiers had perished.

This all happened just hours before President Nixon was scheduled to make a major speech on Vietnam. That was probably coincidental, as were the attacks made later in the week by the NVA and VC on other American and ARVN bases in Vietnam, including a mild attack on Saigon. Nixon had not even contemplated a speech when the painstaking NVA preparations for the attack on BUTTONS had gotten underway. Nixon was discouraged by the utter lack of response to his peace feelers from the North Vietnamese Politburo. Even the death of Ho Chi Minh on September 3 did nothing to soften Hanoi's rigid position: that the United States immediately withdraw unilaterally and dismantle the South Vietnamese government on the way out.

Every peace proposal or withdrawal announcement whetted the appetites of the militant antiwar activists. The president wanted the speech to help stop what he felt was a gradual erosion of the initial support he had felt he had in the Congress and with the people. As he wrote in 1985, "No president has a limitless amount of time to invest in any policy. Because my predecessors had exhausted the patience of the American people with the Vietnam War, I was acutely aware that I was living on borrowed time. If I was to have enough time for my policies to succeed, my first priority had to be to gather as much political support as possible for the war from the American people." From this position came the speech that Nixon considered to be the most effective of his presidency . . . the famous "silent majority" speech.

After outlining the history of the conflict and the steps the administration was taking or planning to take to end the war, Nixon came to his concluding paragraph, which he said he had spent hours writing. In it, he said "I sought to go over the heads of the antiwar opinion-makers in the media and to appeal directly to the American people for unity." Looking straight into the camera and speaking with typical Nixon earnestness, the president said, "And so tonight—to you, the great silent majority of my fellow Americans—I ask for your support. . . . The more divided we are at home, the least likely the enemy is to negotiate in Paris. Let us be united for peace. Let us also be united against defeat. Because let us understand: North Vietnam cannot defeat or humiliate the United States. Only Americans can do that." Although phrased as an appeal, the last sentence was chillingly prescient; Americans did deliver South Vietnam into the hands of Hanoi.

In Vietnam, the death of Ho Chi Minh was greeted by the North Vietnamese and Viet Cong with a three-day cease-fire, which the allies generally observed. In the Cav's area of operations, the death of North Vietnam's leader was indirectly responsible for one of the few major media flaps the Cav had endured since it had arrived in country in 1965. In fact, this was about the time the Cav's press relations in general began to deteriorate; when the division's senior officers began to believe that reporters were no longer really interested in what the division was doing, but simply wanted to interview soldiers to obtain their opinions concerning whatever antiwar cause was gaining headlines in the United States. Thus the welcome mat, which had always been out for the media, was selectively rolled up and tucked out of sight. But there were still reporters and media organizations that the Cav knew and generally trusted, so it was somewhat receptive when the Associated Press pitched a story idea that involved comparing a day with a combat unit with a typical day at the Paris peace talks. General Elvy Roberts was skeptical of the whole idea, believing that probably nothing good would come of it, but his information officer persuaded him that everything would be okay, primarily because the Vietnam side of the story would be done by two old and trusted Vietnam hands, Peter Arnett and Horst Faas. Just as they arrived at the Cav's headquarters at Phuoc Vinh to do the "day" with the Cav, the news of Ho's death came, and since the Paris talks were to be recessed, the original story idea came unglued. But it had been a while since Arnett and Faas had been in the Cav's AO. "So," said Arnett, "as long as we're here, we might as well go on out to a firebase."

With the concurrence of the division chief of staff, Col. Bob Shoemaker, the pair was sent, unescorted, as was the long-standing custom of the Cav, to LZ IKE in War Zone C. IKE, at that time, was the home of the 2nd Battalion, 8th Cavalry, one of the truly tough, battle-tested battalions in the Cav. Its commander was Lieutenant Colonel Fred Lindsay, who during part of his former tour had run a press camp at Nha Trang. It seemed a natural fit. Lindsay, who knew Arnett and Faas, gave them a complete and candid background briefing on a firebase preparing for an anticipated attack by an NVA unit. When the battle came in the early morning hours, an assault by a battalion of the 95-C Regiment, it was beaten back by C and E companies of the 2/8 Cav fairly handily. However, the story that Arnett filed had little to do with the bravery of the men defending the firebase. Instead, it rambled on for some thirty paragraphs, telling about two soldiers allegedly strung out on dope (They weren't. They had been at battalion rear, but had been brought to the firebase for a battalion commander's administrative punishment.); about four others who didn't want to fight (They didn't, but the news was three weeks old when Arnett got it from Lindsay, who used it to illustrate the leadership problems being faced by commanders at that time.); and about a barking dog that purportedly alerted the garrison of the attack (The dog did indeed bark, but the account and an accompanying picture showing the dog barking at the firebase gate, and in broad daylight at that, was made ludicrous by an earlier portion of Arnett's yarn telling of classified radio intercepts and radar alerting the firebase, and of course, the fact that the attack took place just after midnight.).

When the story broke in Vietnam via the *Stars and Stripes*, it created a terrible flap. The MACV chief of information, Colonel Gordon Hill, labeled it one of the three worst in Vietnam that year. The *Stars and Stripes* ran the picture on page one, with a caption that implied that an important American firebase had to depend on a mongrel dog to keep it from being surprised by the tricky Cong. Shortly afterward, Colonel James Campbell, the information officer for U.S. Army, Vietnam, touched off a firestorm by calling the *Stripes* the "Hanoi Herald." But the most serious criticism leveled against the division concerned the portion of Arnett's story dealing with classified radio intercepts. All of this came rushing down the chain of command to rest on Roberts's shoulders, and the tall Kentuckian was furious. The 2nd of the 8th, which had been in steady and heavy contact in War Zone C for months, was brought back to Camp Gorvad for a much-needed quiet stint as palace guard, and soon the battalion had a new commander, Lieutenant Colonel Michael Conrad. The division IO almost got himself fired in the process, and the press welcome mat disappeared entirely.

The abortive attack on BUTTONS on November 4 was followed up by a major thrust by the NVA 7th Division's 141st Regiment against the Special Forces camp of Bu Dop, and the district headquarters town of Bo Duc, located in the extreme northeast corner of Phuoc Long Province, just seven kilometers from the Cambodian border. The Cav had brought law and order to the area following the August high point, in the process creating an artillery firebase named JERRI just south of the population center. When the enemy retreated across the border, the CIDG element at the Special Forces camp and the small ARVN garrison at Bo Duc were sufficient to defend the area. So the Cav closed JERRI and moved the infantry battalion over to the Song Be River to help shut down the Serges Jungle Highway infiltration routes.

Then came the November enemy offensive and the district

headquarters and the Special Forces camp came under heavy seige by the 141st Regiment and were in grave danger of being overrun. II Field Force and III Corps Headquarters ordered a massive reinforcement of the area. Unlike other attacks in the Cav AO, this one was less concerned with shaking loose the division's choke-hold on the infiltration routes than with forcing the allies to reinforce with units that had been used for population security. This had been the pattern in the dry-season attacks on the Special Forces camps at Ben Het and Bu Prang in II Corps. But there was a special urgency in III Corps because the pacification of the densely populated rice-growing regions had denied the Viet Cong fighting units the opportunity to recruit replacements and, more importantly, to obtain food. Combined with the Cav's interdiction of supply routes, cutting off food supplies had caused acute hunger among many of the small Viet Cong units still lurking in the jungles around the population centers.

On November 7, Charlie Company of the 1st Battalion, 5th Cavalry, air-assaulted into JERRI to reopen the firebase. They promptly made contact with an NVA force. General Casey was monitoring the battle from his chopper. When it needed refueling, rather than leave the scene of the fight, he opted to stay in touch with Charlie Company's clearing action by having the chopper land him on a part of JERRI that had been swept by the Skytroopers. Casey, who had an absolute disregard for his personal safety, wandered about the abandoned firebase, oblivious to the slugs that whizzed by from the nearby firefight. In tight tow with a radio on which Casey monitored the course of the battle was a lieutenant, a former platoon leader, who had been dragooned into the job of temporary aide de camp. The instinct of the lieutenant, along with some other straphangers who had disembarked the chopper with Casey, was to seek cover. They were, however, faced with the unhappy dilemma of standing semierect and acting brave when Casey had his eye on them and cowering among some convenient teak logs when he didn't.

Charlie Company quickly subdued the NVA unit and began reconstructing the firebase to handle a battery of 105-mm howitzers. Meanwhile, two ARVN battalions were deployed from areas not critical to population defense into the Bo Duc area, followed by a couple of troops of the 11th Armored Cav. For three days, the enemy vented his fury on JERRI with heavy mortar and rocket attacks and occasional ground probes. A CBS-TV news team rode one of the troop-carrying C-130s into the airstrip serving the Bu Dop–Bo Duc complex and then hitched a ride on a resupply helicopter into JERRI. CBS assumed that the Bu Dop –Bo Duc fight was but a rerun of the earlier battles at Ben Het and Bu Prang in II Corps, and never bothered to ask anyone in authority if there was a difference. (Or whoever they asked didn't know. Unfortunately, Saigon staff officers did not universally understand what was happening along the Cambodian border in III Corps.)

Therefore, the object of the reportorial exercise was not to report on the significance of the enemy's November offensive and how it was being defended against without disturbing the pacification effort. Instead, CBS used the Cav's reopening of JERRI as evidence that the ARVN couldn't defend themselves, that this part of the war had been re-Americanized. This was the report the American people saw on the evening of November 10, despite the fact that reporter Gary Shepard and his team had to wade through a Bo Duc airstrip fairly awash with ARVN Rangers being shuttled into the battle. And, of course, neither he or any other reporter stuck around long enough to see the deployment into the Bo Duc area of the 2nd Battalion, 3rd Mobile Strike (MIKE) Force, a Green Beret–run indigenous force, which was commanded by Major Ola L. "Lee" Mize, or to see the 9th ARVN Regiment establish a command post in the Bo Duc area and the 5th Cavalry again be redeployed back to the interdiction campaign on the Song Be River.

During the firefights that swirled around Bu Dop, the Special Forces camp commander steadfastly refused to permit the press to enter the compound. Some of this was pure cussedness; most commanders simply didn't want anything to do with the media. But a more cogent reason was that many of the top secret cross-border intelligence missions, either through the Green Berets' Project GAMMA or by operatives of MACV SOG (Special Operations Group), were launched from Bu Dop, and there were things inside the compound that no one wanted the press, or anyone without clearances, to see.

Visiting the Cav's headquarters at Phuoc Vinh at the time was an NBC-TV reporter, Liz Trotta, who already was very unhappy with the Cav because the information officer wouldn't stage a phoney air assault into a defoliated area for the benefit of NBC's cameras. (Defoliation had just become one of the media's hot buttons.) But her pique turned to white-hot anger when the IO told her that the Special Forces commander had banned reporters in general and television crews in particular, and especially didn't want a female TV reporter in his compound. Even though he was only the messenger, the IO took the brunt of the lady's anger and frustration. Ms. Trotta scolded the major about the rights of women (the feminist revolution had just really gotten underway in the United States) and finally capped her tirade with the assertion: "Anything a man can do, I can do better."

Whereupon, the major wearily pointed to the field urinal (more commonly known simply as a "piss tube") a few yards away in an open field and said, "Okay, why don't you go out there and give that a shot."

"Well," Ms. Trotta raged, "you're certainly no gentleman!"

"Madam," replied the major, "that was not the issue in question here. And you still can't get into Bu Dop."

The weight of allied firepower in the Bo Duc and Bu Dop area finally forced the 141st Regiment back into its Cambodian sanctuaries, and the American units returned to the grinding job of interdiction. It was a tough job, one that demanded the utmost in skill and professionalism by commanders and staff members. Casey had spent his first four months on the job quietly taking stock of the division. When he first came back he was not happy about how entrenched the battalions had become. But he also recognized that the enemy, mission, and terrain were substantially different than the Cav had faced on his first tour. He also was well aware that the division belonged to Elvy Roberts and Casey was loyal to his boss, even though he disagreed with some of Roberts's decisions and tactics. So he bided his time and began formulating a tactical approach that would maximize the advantage helicopters gave the Cav. He also continued assembling a team of key leaders and staff officers that made the division an even more formidable opponent for the NVA.

What Joe Kingston was to the 1st Brigade in War Zone C earlier in the year, Shy Meyer and Colonel Robert Kingston (no

Skytroopers of the 1st Air Cavalry Division, carrying their "Cav Country" sign, board a C-130 at Camp Evans for a flight to their new area of operations along the Cambodian border in northern III Corps. *(U.S. Army photo—John Talbott collection)*

Below, at the site of a Cav firebase near Cambodia, General Creighton Abrams, commander, Military Assistance Command, Vietnam, gets a briefing from Major General George I. Forsythe, commander of the 1st Air Cav (right), and one of the division's unit commanders. *(U.S. Army photo—Author's collection)*

Under Abrams's concept of interdiction, the Cav was immediately set to work rooting out the enemy's system. The division's units scoured the jungle looking for NVA or VC base areas that contained living and storage bunkers like this one. (*U.S. Army photo—John Talbott collection*)

NVA or VC base areas were always guarded by numerous fighting bunkers like this one being searched by a Skytrooper. The bamboo logs held two to three feet of earthen overhead cover. It often took direct hits from artillery projectiles to knock out one of these bunkers. (*U.S. Army photo by Jim McCabe—John Talbott collection*)

The Cav originated the "high bird–low bird" teams, which it called Pink Teams and other outfits called hunter-killer teams. The enforcer for the team was the Huey Cobra, seen here from the pilot's seat of the scout bird. *(U.S. Army photo by Dean Sharp—Dean Sharp collection)*

The "low bird" in the team was the light observation helicopter, popularly called a "loach." These birds, manned by the bravest of the brave, flew right in among the treetops. They usually flew in tight right-hand turns; the pilot and the gunner, called a "torque," could spot trails, bunkers, and enemy soldiers dumb enough to be caught in the open. *(U.S. Army photo—Author's collection)*

Once the enemy was located, the Cav did a combat assault often called a "Charlie Alpha." As a general rule, in the tangled jungles of War Zones C and D the Charlie Alpha took place on small one- or two-ship landing zones. Here Skytroopers of the 1st Battalion, 8th Cavalry, are delivered by a lift ship from B Company, 227th Assault Helicopter Battalion to a tiny hole in the War Zone D jungle. (*U.S. Army photo by Terry Moon—Author's collection*)

The occasional exceptions to the use of small LZs took place when a large clearing could be used to deliver a larger body of troops in a single lift. Here, Bravo Company, 2nd Battalion, 5th Cavalry, is dropped into a dry lake bed in War Zone C. (*U.S. Army photo by Bob Borchester—John Talbott collection*)

After all the machines had done their work, what remained on the ground were the grunts. Such terribly young men, so very brave. Here are pictures of three Cav Skytroopers. The unidentified soldier above typifies the youth of the average grunt in Vietnam in 1969. (*U.S. Army photo—Author's collection*)

From the dawn of time, warriors have had a special look. The face of PFC Richard Coleman could have been seen at the Little Big Horn, on Luzon, or at the Yalu River. (*U.S. Army photo—Author's collection*)

Because they spent weeks on end in the bush, the grunts tended to be a scruffy lot, which offended the sensibilities of the polished-and-shined rear-echelon types. But they had a special sort of discipline, marked not by clean-shaven chins, short hair, and salutes, but by proficiency, dependability, and automatic habits of survival learned the hard way. This is Mike Hoffman of Delta Company, 2nd Battalion, 12th Cavalry. (*U.S. Army photo by Bill Ahrbeck— John Talbott collection*)

One unique aspect of the Cav's airmobility was its ability to transport the bunker-busting 155-mm howitzer to the depths of the jungle, miles from any road. Here, a Flying Crane hook operator keeps a wary eye on his cargo as the rubber country of Binh Long Province passes underneath. *(U.S. Army photo by Len Fallscheer —John Talbott collection)*

One of the most effective methods of defending a firebase under attack was to fire howitzer rounds with fuses set to detonate the projectiles just after they cleared the berm. In the 25th Division, where C Battery, 2nd Battalion, 77th Artillery, demonstrates the technique using white phosphorus shells, the method was known as a "firecracker." In the Cav, it was called "killer Junior." *(U.S. Army photo by Joseph T. Primeau—Author's collection)*

The Air Cav invented aerial rocket artillery. By 1969, its ARA battalion was known as the "Blue Max." Its Cobras struck with rocket fangs, and there was no remedy for their bites. "Blue Max is inbound" were the most comforting words a unit in contact could hear. With two birds always on strip alert, a section of Blue Max could be firing support for infantry units in contact within minutes of the call for help. All this fire support is why the Cav could establish firebases deep within the forbidding depths of War Zone C and maintain them there indefinitely. *(U.S. Army photo—Author's collection)*

A Cav firebase in the process of being fully hardened. When banked with sandbags, the half-culverts made reasonably safe sleeping quarters. They also were reasonably snug and comfortable during the dry season, but during the monsoons, the air mattresses had a tendency to float away. The firebase was ringed by bands of concertina wire and bristled with trip flares and claymore mines. *(U.S. Army photo—John Talbott collection)*

Caked with red clay and clad only in shorts, the sapper inched his way through three rows of concertina and razor wire. In the process he quickly and silently disconnected two claymore mines and tied off two trip flares. Once through, he picked up his AK-47 and TNT charges and trotted upright into Quon Loi. It was the second time that Sergeant Nguyen Van Phenh had penetrated the defenses of Quon Loi. The first was on August 12, when he was the sole surviver of a group of elite sappers who made it inside the wire. As a *Hoi Chanh* he volunteered to demonstrate his skills for a division training program. The observers discovered that NVA sappers were not superhuman; they could not walk on air, nor were their skins impervious to cuts. But they did see that sappers were skilled and patient. Their allies were darkness, confusion, and unwary defenders. *(U.S. Army photo by Paul Sgroi—John Talbott collection)*

The author forms part of a receiving line of the division staff during welcoming ceremonies for Brigadier General George Casey. Major General Elvy Roberts, the division commander, accompanies Casey through the receiving line. *(U.S. Army photo—Author's collection)*

This was the final face-off in the jungle that is described in Chapter Four. Major Jean Sauvageot interprets for Lieutenant Colonel John V. Gibney (far right), the senior American negotiator on the ground. The cold-eyed dude in the center is the interpreter for the Viet Cong boss, the man with the lump on his jaw, apparently caused by an infected tooth. Shortly after this picture was taken, the VC released the three American prisoners to American control. (*U.S. Army photo—Author's collection*)

Lieutenant Colonel Dick Wood, commander of the 2nd Battalion, 8th Cavalry, is interviewed by CBS TV newsman Don Webster. The interview took place within hours after Wood's firebase, LZ CAROLYN, beat back a determined attack by the NVA 95-C Regiment. (*U.S. Army photo—Dick Wood collection*)

Wet down, soap up, rinse off. And do it with one bucket of water. That was the routine for a shower on a firebase, where water had to be choppered in and was a precious commodity. A shower doesn't seem like much, but when you've been in the bush for three weeks without one, even a single bucket of water is a luxury. (*U.S. Army photo—John Talbott collection*)

Sergeant Bill Ellis, who had been a grunt in the 1st Battalion, 5th Cavalry, until he was pulled back to division to tour the firebases with songs about soldiers. Here, on LZ GRANT, Ellis entertains his fellow grunts. Besides singing currently popular songs, Ellis also wrote and sang songs about the life of a grunt. Two of those songs were titled "Firefight" and "Grunt," but one of the Skytroopers' favorites was "Freedom Bird," a haunting refrain about the moment every soldier in Vietnam dreamed about—the day he boarded the Freedom Bird to "go back to the world." *(U.S. Army photo—Bill Ellis collection)*

Nothing beat getting on the Freedom Bird, or going on a real R and R. But the consolation prize was in-country R and R. Here battle-weary grunts from Delta and Echo Companies, 2nd Battalion, 8th Cavalry, unload at Bien Hoa for a three-day stand-down that will be marked with hours of untroubled sleep, showers with gallons and gallons of hot water, clean clothes, and a new OD towel to slip under the straps of the rucksack. *(U.S. Army photo by Len Fallscheer—John Talbott collection)*

relation to Joe) provided for the 2nd and 3rd brigades by December. Both were hard-driving commanders who demanded and received top performance from subordinate leaders, but they also had strong feelings for the welfare of soldiers. Neither suffered fools gladly, and they were ruthless about rooting out subordinate commanders and staff officers who did dumb things that unnecessarily risked soldiers' lives. They came along at precisely the right time. Race and marijuana problems had begun manifesting themselves in rear areas of the division, despite the efforts of the morale and esprit builders. General Roberts remained the principal cheerleader and through the fall and winter of 1969 refused to believe that any of his Skytroopers would do dope.

Colonel Meyer was one of the Cav Sandwiches, having served as 3rd Brigade deputy commander during the Ia Drang campaign in 1965 and later as commander of the 2nd Battalion, 5th Cavalry. A West Pointer from the class of 1951, Meyer had been among the first in his class to reach the grades of major, lieutenant colonel, and colonel. He would go on to four stars and culminate his career as chief of staff of the U.S. Army. Bob Kingston, on the other hand, started his career as an infantry OCS graduate and won a reputation as a tough commander in Korea, where he picked up the sobriquet "Barbed-Wire Bob." Nothing had occurred in the intervening years to mellow his bristly command persona. He, too, eventually went on to four-star rank in the Army. At about the same period, the division artillery got a new commander, Colonel Morris J. Brady, who commanded the 2nd Battalion, 20th Artillery, in the Cav on his first tour. Brady was also a hardnose who demanded near-perfection from the officers and NCOs charged with delivering life-preserving fire support to troops in contact.

Casey complemented these commanders with a smart senior staff. By early December the crucial G-2 and G-3 slots had also been filled by Cav Sandwiches. Lieutenant Colonel John Galvin returned to the division to be the G-2. A 1954 West Point graduate, he was a scholarly man, and had already published two books on military history, including one on the theory and tactics of air assault. He was the perfect partner for the G-3, a tough wiry lieutenant colonel named George Stotser, who came down from six months command of the 1st Battalion, 12th Cavalry, in War Zone C. Stotser's troops, working out of FSB GRANT, had virtually sanitized the NVA and VC redoubts in old Base Area 355.

Galvin and Stotser had worked together in the division operations shop in 1966 and 1967. Back together again in late 1969, they formed what Chief of Staff Joe Kingston considered to be the finest G-2–G-3 team in Vietnam. They knew what it took to run an airmobile division in combat, and they were completely in synch with Casey's concept of operations. They also served up impressive briefings for senior officers. After delivering a briefing to Julian Ewell in early December, one of the first in which the three-star general did not engage in his favorite exercise of Cav bashing, Joe Kingston smiled and told Galvin and Stotser, whom he thereafter dubbed the "Gold-dust Twins," "Boys, I think we're finally out of the doghouse." With airmobile veteran Bob Shoemaker, now wearing a brigadier general's star, handling logistics and maintenance for the division, General Roberts had plenty of time to play his cheerleader role.

By late November the division, the 11th ACR and the ARVN Airborne units, had pretty much put immovable stoppers in the NVA lifelines that lay within the 1st Cav's general area of operations. But there still were trouble spots along the Cambodian border in Binh Long and Phuoc Long provinces. The 7th NVA Division never fully reconciled itself to losing control of the area around the Bo Duc district headquarters and the Bu Dop Special Forces camp and made continual forays against the ARVN and MIKE Force defenders. The area had to be resupplied by air because National Highway 14A linking Loc Ninh with Bo Duc was regularly interdicted by the NVA. The ARVN 9th Regiment under Lieutenant Colonel Ma Son Nhon had a command post at Bo Duc but had not been particularly aggressive in either opening the road or defending the area, basically disregarding the suggestions of Colonel Barker, the 3rd Brigade commander.

The division also appeared to have trouble getting Lee Mize's MIKE Force to do what it thought should be done in the area. The Mobile Strike Force commands were a Special Forces innovation. The original purpose was to provide a reaction force to come to the aid of the isolated Special Forces camps when they came under attack. The forces comprised Montagnard tribesmen and other ethnic minorities equipped by the Green Berets and organized into tough, hard-hitting combat units. Unlike the ARVN forces, in which Americans functioned only as advisors, the Mobile Strike Forces were commanded by American Green Berets. However, General Abrams, a conventional soldier who disliked and distrusted Special Forces, was gradually moving the MIKE Force out from under Special Forces control and into a conventional alignment with Vietnamese Rangers. But in December 1969, the transition still was incomplete.

Three days after he assumed command of the 3rd Brigade on December 1, Colonel Bob Kingston flew to Bo Duc and visited Mize, whom he had known for a long time. Kingston remembered Mize as a nineteen-year-old master sergeant who had won the Medal of Honor in Korea. Mize, a veteran Special Forces operative, tended to be a bit hard-headed. Kingston, who had left command of a Special Forces Group at Fort Bragg to come to the Cav and who had been in MACV SOG on a previous tour in Vietnam, wasted little time getting his message across to Mize.

"Look," Kingston said to Mize, "You're screwing around with the Cav."

"What do you mean?" Mize responded.

"You're not obeying orders," Kingston said.

Mize then indicated that the accusation was "bullshit," as were most of the orders he received.

So Kingston laid it on the line: "Look, you little fucker. You're in my AO and you work for me. If you get orders from anyone else in the Cav, you let me know and I'll take care of it. But if you get orders from me and you don't obey those orders, I'll throw your ass out of the country."

Mize rogered the message, and promptly became a productive member of the allied team in the Bo Duc area. Kingston stayed the night with Mize. And then he flew back in the next night to stay there again. Finally, Ma Son Nhon could stand it no longer. He came to see Kingston and wanted to know why the American commander was spending his nights at Bo Duc. Kingston explained that one of his missions was to make sure that Bo Duc and Bu Dop remained secure. He intimated that if the road to Loc Ninh was opened and secured, it would be easier to get

American and ARVN armored units into the area to restore the balance of power there. And he would probably be able to sleep more safely when he spent the night.

Kingston said he never actually ordered Ma Son Nhon to open the road. But the ARVN commander had lost face through Kingston's actions, and he quickly went on the offensive. He moved a battalion into positions where it could patrol and keep the road open, and then he built a big bunker at Bo Duc for Kingston's use. But once Kingston got everyone's attention, he never went back to spend the night. Kingston also solved some problems the division had been having with the Bu Dop Special Forces camp and effective intelligence-gathering and -sharing. He did it in typical Barbed-Wire Bob fashion: brutal, profane, and to the point.

In the period between the August NVA offensive and early December, the 2nd and 3rd Brigades had been particularly effective at choking off the flow of communist supplies down the Serges Jungle Highway and the Adams Road complexes, and the 1st Brigade under Colonel Joe Collins was holding its own in War Zone C. Nevertheless, intelligence reports indicated that substantial quantities of arms, ammunition, rice, and salt were still getting through into War Zone D. Other intelligence assets such as aerial reconnaissance, electronic sensors, and agent reports also began pointing to some mysterious west-to-east movement along the northern boundary of Phuoc Long Province. It was all very puzzling. Not only was there heavy foot traffic, but the ubiquitous scouts of the 9th Cavalry Squadron spotted and destroyed a number of Russian trucks, all heavily camouflaged with fresh-cut jungle greenery. The movement appeared to originate in both major base areas along the Cambodian border, 350 and 351, and terminate somewhere near Bu Gia Map in extreme northeast Phuoc Long Province.

It was time for Colonel Shy Meyer to cast his net further to the east.

12

Wrapping Up
Phuoc Long

Early in December a Ranger LRRP team was inserted almost on top of the political boundary between Military Regions II and III. The team members eased their way through the jungle toward the east. Then, slipping through a heavy underbrush screen, the five Rangers found themselves on a well-traveled and superbly camouflaged trail. They pushed a bit farther and found another, and then another. They were in the middle of the biggest trail complex they had ever seen. The team pulled back out, found protective cover, and the team sergeant, his voice betraying his excitement, radioed his controlling element, Bravo Troop of the 9th Cavalry. The news caused B Troop to throb with anticipation. Major Charles Jolley, the troop commander, quickly cranked up his assets, which he had laagered at Duc Phong on Route 14, about twenty kilometers from the boundary line. The troop's rifle platoon, the Bravo Blues, had been lolling in the shade of their choppers. The platoon leader came running out of the meeting with Jolley. "Saddle up, Blue," he shouted over the distinctive whine of starting Huey turbine engines.

Within minutes the Bravo Blues, personally led by Major Jolley, were on the ground and making their way toward the Ranger team, which had come out to guide the platoon back to the trail. With his Pink Teams overhead for protection, Jolley and his Blues followed the Rangers back down to the trail. When they broke through the undergrowth screen the Skytroopers couldn't

179

help standing around and gawking. It was unbelievable! This was bigger than anything found on the Serges Jungle Highway or the Adams Road. To call this NVA engineering marvel a simple trail was to call the Santa Monica Freeway just another road. This jungle superhighway was a very wide, intertwined complex of roadways, some narrow, some wide enough for trucks. Some trails were hard-packed earth for dry-season transit; others had a bamboo mat surface, a Southeast Asia variation on the old corduroy road of American Colonial times.

After their shock wore off, the Blues scurried about investigating the trail complex. It had way stations and well-sited bunker complexes. It was almost completely covered by jungle growth, which had been trained and woven into a cover, creating natural tunnels through which the road wound its way south. In the days that followed, as B Troop Blues explored the complex, they discovered many bridges. One, about twenty kilometers southeast of Duc Phong, was constructed of logs and was six feet wide and one hundred feet long, camouflaged with bamboo matting on top. Although the North Vietnamese engineers had made it possible for trucks to move as far south as the point where National Highway 14 crossed into Quang Duc Province, it was obvious that the cargo bicycle was the principal means of transporting rice and ammunition south from Cambodia. Where the system turned up or down hill, steps were cut alongside the trail to make it easier for the men to push the bicycles with their four-hundred-pound loads.

The reconnaissance elements also found that the complex hugged the boundary between II Corps and III Corps. The North Vietnamese and Viet Cong knew that the ARVN had trouble coordinating the two ARVN administrative sectors and therefore did not generally even try. The trail's location thus virtually guaranteed that it would not be discovered. Another factor besides its location on the political boundary was that this part of Vietnam long had been conceded to the communist insurgents. As the search of the trail continued south into the maze of tributaries of the Dong Nai River, hundreds of sampan docking points were discovered.

When news of Jolley's discovery reached higher headquarters, it suddenly became clear how the VC units in War Zone D were getting their supplies. The discovery also explained to intelligence analysts how the VC 5th Division had managed to outflank the Cav's first interdiction efforts a year earlier. Closer inspection of the infiltration route, which the division named "the Jolley Trail," revealed that it had been in use for many years, albeit in a more modest manner. But the squeeze on the Serges and Adams routes and the desperate straits of the Viet Cong in Long Khanh and Bien Hoa provinces had forced the NVA engineers to markedly upgrade the Jolley complex.

Now the question was: what would the Cav do about it? The *Dong Tien* program came to the rescue. The arrival of the ARVN Airborne's 1st Brigade into Phuoc Long Province permitted Colonel Shy Meyer, the 2nd Brigade Commander, to reposition some of his cavalry battalions from the infiltration routes in central Phuoc Long and begin aggressively interdicting the Jolley Trail. Another factor was Casey's determination to get the 1st Cav airmobile again. He had been itching for weeks to get the 1st Brigade to shut down GRANT and reposition the 1st Battalion, 12th Cavalry, now commanded by Lieutenant Colonel Rodriquez "Ric" Ordway.

In December, with the diminished activity in War Zone C and the excellent performance of the ARVN Airborne brigade, Casey saw an opening and pounced. He talked Roberts into staging a massive movement of the 1st of the 12th. Ordway's battalion was moved first to JERRI, more as an exercise in training the battalion in how to make a move than as a tactical necessity. At the time, it was the longest redeployment of a battalion totally within the Cav's AO, a distance of some ninety kilometers. Casey gave Ordway's troops a chance to catch their breath and then turned them over to Meyer, who on December 13 sent the battalion another fifty kilometers to the east into FSB LEE near Duc Phong and targeted it against the Jolley Trail.

Now that GRANT was empty, Casey would not permit its regarrisoning, so the 1st Brigade reluctantly came in and tore it down. It was a big job. In the twenty-two months of its existance, GRANT had grown from a small LZ into a fair-sized urban establishment. For several days Chinooks and Flying Cranes back-hauled ammunition, Conex containers, bunker culverts, and anything else the NVA or VC could reclaim and use. The protective wire that had tangled the feet of hundreds of NVA attackers was reclaimed, and finally bulldozers leveled the berm. GRANT was fini.

On the Jolley Trail, Meyer neatly solved the boundary coordination problem by getting division headquarters to negotiate an administrative action that, in effect, moved the boundary some five kilometers back into II Corps territory. Now, no matter which side of the boundary the road wandered, the Cavalry units had the ability to shut it down through their interdiction actions without going through cumbersome coordination efforts.

Concurrently, Meyer used the ARVN Airborne battalions to continue choking off the central Phuoc Long Province infiltration routes. To Meyer's west, Kingston was driving against the NVA 7th Division, using the 11th ACR units to hold open Route 13 by providing security to Rome Plow units, and to continue interdiction of the Serges Jungle Highway.

By now, the 1st Cavalry had made interdiction a refined science. Day after day, the infantry companies from battalion firebases would move through the jungle, looking for trails, bunker complexes, and supply caches. In the war rooms of the brigades, the division, and II Field Force, these patrol routes were marked by squiggly lines drawn by operations specialists with grease pencils on the acetate-covered maps. And particularly at II Field Force, woe to the commander of the unit that Julian Ewell discovered had not moved what he considered an appropriate distance. A lot of operations types of all ranks spent an inordinate amount of time relaying grid locations of every unit so the three-star commander could micromanage the actions of infantry platoons.

In the bush, those grease-pencil lines translated into columns of grunts, young backs bent under the weight of sixty-pound rucksacks with only the green GI towel to relieve the bite of the shoulder straps, clawing and sweating their way through the jungle in search of trails being used by an enemy desperately trying to move supplies south from Cambodia to NVA and VC units operating closer to the population centers surrounding Saigon. In the earlier days of the war, the enemy chose to remain elusive and searching units could go for days without finding an enemy soldier, but now the areas on the infiltration routes near the Cambodian border proved to be a target-rich environment.

As long as the Cavalry unit was working a known infiltration route, searches were short and contacts were frequent—too frequent, as far as the grunts were concerned. For most of these searching units, making their serpentine way through the jungle, contact with the NVA usually came when the grunts discovered a cache site. Frequently the supply areas were guarded by a complex of defensive bunkers occupied by NVA soldiers, who would make the Cav unit pay a price for the discovery. The overwhelming firepower available to an infantry company commander generally ended enemy resistance quickly and led to American ownership of the arms, ammunition, or rice stashed in the caches. But it was hot, dirty, dangerous work because the North Vietnamese soldier was a tough, determined, and resolute foe.

Sometimes the columns of Skytroopers met NVA security forces for porterage units while everyone was out in the open, and it would be an even-up hipshoot. But more often daylight meeting engagements were the result of aggressive NVA countersweep operations to prevent the Cav patrols from ferreting out their trail systems and jungle warehouses. The NVA often had the advantage in those encounters because the jungle around the major trail areas was honeycombed with extensive bunker complexes, giving the communist soldiers readily available fighting positions. But the NVA also had to pay a price for daylight operations. Their soldiers had to move into positions in the daylight, and overhead, the Cavalry squadron's gunships would pounce on the slightest hint of a movement in the jungle. The Cav's Pink Teams were accomplished and efficient killers. By early 1970, the 9th Cavalry Squadron owned more than one-quarter of the division's reported kills of enemy soldiers.

Additionally, the Cav, through the efforts of Casey, had begun to use its airmobility more effectively. The division had instituted a program of prepositioning one- and two-ship landing zones by blowing holes in the jungle with the "Daisy Cutter" and "Commando Vault" bombs. The Daisy Cutter was a 750-pound bomb with fuse extender that blew down enough trees to make a single-ship landing zone. The Commando Vault was a 10,000-pound bomb that blew down even more trees and thus made an even larger LZ. These LZs were scattered about and permitted the Cav units to use their choppers to hopscotch around the AO.

The NVA had long before learned that the Allied ground forces tended to stay within the artillery fans from the firebases, so when possible, it tried to keep its trail security base areas and cargo bike repair shops well away from the permanent firebases. Once Casey made the move with the 1st of the 12th, there was no stopping him. He gave missions to the brigades that couldn't be accomplished without moving some infantry outside the range of the firebase artillery. So the Cav reached back into its history book and pulled out some stunts that had worked well in 1966 and 1967. By deploying three tubes of artillery into a temporary firebase and projecting a couple of companies of infantry into the area around that base, the Cav could surprise the NVA, stage some lightning strikes, and then take the "skinny battery" back to the main base before the NVA could get a fix on the location of the temporary firing positions. This was merely following the old Harry Kinnard dictum that if you move your artillery base every three days, "they'll never lay a glove on you."

So in daylight, it was the Cav's mobility against the North Vietnamese with their hundreds of prepared bunker complexes. The NVA could stage a determined fight, but once the battle was joined, the overwhelming firepower available to the company commander ultimately made it an uneven contest.

Nights were a different story. For years, the media had trumpeted that "the night belonged to the Viet Cong." That was quite true in parts of Vietnam and during the earlier days of the war, and was automatically assumed to be true of the North Vietnamese as well. But in late 1969 and early 1970 along the Cambodian border in III Corps, the night was totally owned by the allies. There were several reasons for this startling turnaround.

The first was that by late 1969 the division had perfected a new weapon system that soon surpassed even the B-52 strikes as a weapon of terror. Earlier, in War Zone C, Colonel Joe Kingston had always believed that intelligence and the 155-mm howitzers were the keys to shutting down the NVA infiltration, and they certainly were during his tenure as 1st Brigade commander. Late in the year, however, the new weapon, probably more accurately described as a tactic, was introduced—the automatic ambush, which came to rule the jungle. Good, solid combat intelligence still was the key to finding base camps and trail systems. And the 155-mm howitzer still was smashing bunker complexes. But the automatic ambush terrorized enemy soldiers not known for their timidity.

The automatic ambush was simplicity itself, and the wonder is that no one thought of it before late 1969, when it began being used in earnest on the infiltration trails in III Corps. The heart of the system was the M-18A1 antipersonnel mine, more commonly called the claymore. The claymore had always been one of the deadlier items in the infantryman's inventory of killing devices. Five inches high and ten inches wide, it looks like a little olive drab "keep off the grass" sign when it is staked to the ground. A charge of high explosive molded against a curved metal backing sends seven hundred steel ball bearings through a thin plastic front shield in a sixty-degree swath of death. Lethal out to fifty meters, the mine most commonly was used as a command-detonated, close-in defense weapon. Since the earliest days of the war, detonaton devices that could be rigged to a trip wire or other enemy-actuated device had been available. But until some bright soldier figured out how to string a number of the claymores together into a system, the mine remained essentially a single-shot weapon. The deadly features of the claymore were multiplied when a cluster of claymores were placcd along a trail with their electrical detonators wired to a battery and a device that simply closed the common circuit when an attached trip wire was jerked. When a column of NVA came down the trail, a thunderous simultaneous detonation of the claymores sent thousands of steel balls humming into the kill zone.

There were many advantages to the automatic ambush, besides almost always killing anyone in its zone. Because it was un-manned, no personnel in the immediate area could compromise its location. The enemy's automatic response to an ambush with counterambush fire was negated because there were no friendlies in the area. When used with a conventional ambush, the au-tomatic ambush was ideal to punish any surviving enemy soldiers attempting to elude the initial ambush. It was also used as a "stay-behind" measure to persuade the NVA that it was not healthy to trail U.S. units too closely.

David Hackworth, in his book *About Face*, acknowledges that the automatic ambush was a fine concept but contends that the NVA wised up in three or four days and stopped using the trails. It is true that the NVA could simply have quit using the trails that led from the Cambodian base areas to the transshipment bases along the fringes of War Zones C and D. But the NVA mission transcended simple combat with the allied forces. Daily, allied intelligence intercepted anguished messages from Viet Cong and NVA combat units in central Military Region III, begging for resupply of food, medicines, and ammunition. The credibility of the masterminds of the communist insurgency was at stake. The ruthless senior commanders did not let the slaughter of their soldiers stand in the way of trying to move the vital supplies. And as long as they had to move supplies south in large quantities, mostly using cargo bicycles, there were no counter-measures the NVA commanders could take and still accomplish their resupply mission. The infantry escorts sometimes pushed livestock down the trail ahead of the carrying party in an attempt to trigger ambushes, or used the livestock to trigger the ambushes and then tried to push the cargo bikes down a parallel route. Or they tried to switch trails, but there were simply not many alternates within a major infiltration route that could handle the cargo bike. This was a major NVA weakness. Cutting new trails invited rockets and minigun fire from Cavalry Cobras. So to move large quantities of supplies rapidly, the enemy transportation battalions had to continue blindly following the existing trail systems.

This is where good combat intelligence-gathering came into play and why the Cav's infantry companies worked the jungles during the day, looking for alternate trails and way-station caches. Then, as they were located and plotted on maps for future reference, there would be the inevitable series of ambushes, both automatic and manned.

The allied units involved in strangling the communist lifelines all had policies of aggressive night ambushing. Platoon-sized ambushes were the most common, although in certain circumstances, the companies were split in half, with the company commander running one half and the next senior officer operating the other. Not surprisingly, opinions differed on what kind of manned ambush was best. The commanders preferred the platoon and smaller ambushes because there was less chance of breaches of noise and light discipline. The grunts favored the larger ambushes simply because in numbers there was security.

But it was unquestionably the automatic ambush that made it possible for the allies to shut down the infiltration routes south from the Cambodian border. The beauty of the automatic ambush was that if it were not triggered on one occasion, sooner or later some hapless NVA carrying party would feel the bite of the steel ball bearings. Colonel Meyer, along with Colonel Donn Starry, who now commanded the 11th ACR, both recalled that period as essentially "running the trap line." Meyer said that it was almost like putting traps on a game trail to a water hole; the game never stopped coming.

The poor souls who had to push their bikes into the ambushes were initially VC recruits press-ganged out of the villages to the south. When this supply was used up, NVA regulars began pushing bicycles; many of these regulars were luckless teenage draftees just down from the north. On occasion they would succeed and break through the primary choke points. But the transportation battalions in lower War Zone C had a long way to travel to find sanctuary. The old transshipment area at the northern edge of the Michelin Plantation, Base Area 355, had been eradicated by Rome Plows and the determined patrolling of the 25th Infantry Division and its *Dong Tien* partners. The previously inviolate bases south of the Michelin, the Trapezoid and Iron Triangle, no longer offered unqualified sanctuary. In fact, due to the gains from pacification and increasingly aggressive ARVN actions in the area between Saigon and Tay Ninh, many NVA and VC combat elements migrated to the east into War Zone D's Base Area 359, also known as the Hat Dich Base.

In the northern sector of this base area, located right on the Phuoc Long–Long Khanh Province boundary, was the town of Rang Rang. Once the Jolley Trail was discovered, it seemed obvious to the Cav's G-2, Lieutenant Colonel Galvin, that a major NVA transshipment area had to exist near the northern edge of War Zone D. Before he transferred to the 1st Cav in 1966, Galvin had served briefly at Phuoc Vinh, and he knew that Rang Rang was an almost legendary center of Viet Cong activity and a supply base at that time. He reasoned that its utility could only have increased in the intervening years, particularly since there had been no major allied incursions into the base area. Galvin continually pestered General Roberts to ask General Ewell to extend the eastern boundary of the Cav's area of operations about thirty kilometers east of Phuoc Vinh to include the Rang Rang area so the Cav could go in and tear up the supply dumps Galvin was convinced were there. Roberts demurred, either because he felt the Cav's platter was already overflowing or because he didn't really believe Galvin's premise.

Finally Galvin wrote an intelligence summary entitled "All Trails Lead to Rang Rang," in which he presented good evidence that the termination points of all the trails in Binh Long and Phuoc Long provinces were in the Rang Rang area. He sent the treatise to his counterpart at II Field Force. Someone down at Bien Hoa took it seriously, because shortly thereafter the entire Third Mobile Strike Force was sent into the Rang Rang area and some of the largest supply caches ever found in Vietnam were turned over by the strikers. Ewell was delighted but Roberts was pissed. He groused at Galvin, "Why didn't you tell me about this?"

"But I did tell you, General," Galvin protested, "lots of times; you told me you didn't want anything to do with Rang Rang."

Roberts told Galvin he didn't remember being told about Rang Rang and finally grumped, "You sent all that information down there and all those other guys got into it."

It didn't make much difference to the communists who got the credit; the main point was that tons of rice were captured along with arms, ammunition, and medicines. The investment of Rang Rang was not a happy occasion for COSVN, because it dried up the last source of supply for communist combat forces operating in the midsection of Military Region III. Meanwhile, with the Jolley Trail blockaded, the NVA river of supplies that had been flowing down the trail began backing up in temporary base areas in northeast Phuoc Long Province near the town of Bu Gia Map.

The NVA rear service group responsible for the flow of logistics made a painful decision. The seemingly inexorable flow of supplies to the south had been stopped, and in the interests of preserving its storehouses, the river was going to have to run backwards. An emergency evacuation of the caches was ordered. As soon as 2nd Brigade intelligence picked up the northern movement of supplies, Colonel Meyer decided it was time to go to Bu Gia Map. Located on Provincial Highway 301 about ten kilometers from the province border, Bu Gia Map was the site of a Special Forces border-surveillance camp abandoned in 1964. It had a big airstrip, last used in 1966, when the 101st Airborne Division had operated in the area. But from 1967 on, Bu Gia Map and the surrounding area had been considered to be far too deep in dangerous territory for allied units to operate. Knowing the Cav's propensity for using airstrips for airheads, the 174th Regiment of the VC 5th Division created an impressive defensive system around the Bu Gia Map airstrip and waited. And waited some more, confident that the Cav would soon fly into the airstrip and become sitting ducks for the NVA defensive fire.

But the Cav did not come to the airstrip, at least not on the 174th's timetable. Colonel Meyer resisted the temptation to stage a quick strike into the Bu Gia Map strip, and instead, using two Air Cav battalions and three ARVN Airborne battalions, began a systematic drive from Highway 14 north and east toward the objective. While the drive was systematic, it was by no means slow. Meyer had the five battalions making lightning thrusts using highly mobile, temporary firebases for fire support. By the time the NVA realized what the allies were up to, American and ARVN combat units were operating right in the middle of the temporary base areas. In some cases the marauding 2nd Brigade units raided NVA base camps as the porters were loading up for a trip to Cambodia!

Extensive use of air strikes and heavy artillery was one key to success in the operation. The air strikes, both tactical air and B-52 strikes, opened up the triple canopy jungle so that the Cavalry scouts could see the trail and bunker systems. Meyer moved 175-mm and 8-inch guns far forward and could mass up to thirty-six artillery tubes of all calibers for targets that were extremely lucrative. Finally, satisfied that most NVA combat forces had fled to Cambodian sanctuaries, the 2nd Brigade moved in and seized the Bu Gia Map airstrip.

When the smoke finally cleared on the campaign, Bu Gia Map was secured and returned to GVN control. Besides killing 492 enemy soldiers, Meyer's troops had captured supply caches, netting 433,421 small-caliber rounds, 2,650 large-caliber rounds (both rockets and mortars), and 151 tons of rice. The major combat elements of the VC 5th Division had been driven from Vietnam. The battle for Phuoc Long Province had ended in victory for the *Dong Tien* partners.

But no one in the 1st Cavalry heaved a sigh of relief, because things had been heating up to the west, in War Zone C. Even further west, in Cambodia itself, events were occurring that would dramatically affect the interdicting forces along the border.

13

Strangulation

At the center of the group of senior 1st Cav officers gathered in the division's tactical operations center, the division G-2, Lieutenant Colonel John Galvin, was illustrating his "waterfall" theory on a map of III Corps. He pointed out on the map that the boundary between Vietnam and Cambodia in the III Corps area vaguely resembled a series of stair steps, with the highest in the extreme eastern part of the zone and the lowest in the west.

Galvin argued that just as gravity would pull water down these steps in cascades, so the exigencies of the tactical situation would pull the NVA combat and service units to the point on the border where the distance was the shortest between the Cambodian sanctuaries and Saigon. He predicted that the next major NVA push would be in War Zone C, particularly the northwestern sector, which in early 1970 was part of the 25th Division's AO. The reasoning was that with all known infiltration trails in Phuoc Long and Binh Long provinces blockaded, it made good tactical sense for the North Vietnamese to forge new trails at a point where the distances were considerably shorter.

The extreme northwestern part of the border formed an oddly shaped "elbow" as the border bent back sharply to the east before plunging south to the deep enclave called the Parrot's Beak. The outline of the elbow in northwest Tay Ninh Province resembled the head of a dog, and was known as the Dog's Head. At the part of the head where one might expect to find the ears, the

NVA had established a sanctuary the allies had labeled Base Area 707. This base area had been the starting point for the X-Cache Trail, which thrived as the major infiltration route through War Zone C until the 1st Cav cut it off during the summer of 1969. Within the confines of Base Area 707 was the Cambodian town of Krek. It was located on the crossroads between the end of Vietnamese National Route 22 and Cambodian National Route 7, which to the west and south ultimately linked the border region with the port of Sihanoukville and to the north and east paralleled the border enroute to the rubber-plantation town of Snoul.

Until late March 1970, the North Vietnamese did not actually occupy Krek or any other major town adjacent to the border, such as Memot or Snuol. This permitted both the North Vietnamese and Viet Cong to indulge themselves in the fiction that the Cambodians actually controlled the border provinces. There were small Cambodian Army outposts in these border towns, and although as good Khmers they may have resented the presence of the Vietnamese on Cambodian soil, their purpose was as much to be traffic controllers for the convoys from Sihanoukville as to provide security to the Cambodian residents. Starting at the throat of the dog and following the border about thirty kilometers south was Base Area 354, a huge base area that straddled the border and extended some ten kilometers into both Vietnam and Cambodia. The southern terminus of the base area was at the beginning of the populated zones of Tay Ninh Province almost due west of Tay Ninh City. Base Area 354 had been serving more as a rest and retraining sanctuary than as a supply base. But the acute needs of the guerrilla bands to the south had forced COSVN to rethink its purpose.

The cutting of the infiltration routes in War Zone C had backed up an enormous amount of supplies in Base Area 353, sprawled across the top of the zone, as well as Base Area 707. The narrow neck of the Dog's Head was tempting to the NVA logisticians since the straight-line distance between 707 and 354 was fifteen kilometers. By improving the existing infrastructure of trails in that remote part of Tay Ninh Province, the transportation battalions could avoid the lengthy detour all the way around the Dog's Head, a distance of about forty kilometers. Since the B-52s were striking on both sides of the border anyway and the allies had not heavily patrolled the ground for several months, developing a new system of supply trails across the neck of the Dog's Head seemed logical. COSVN planners knew that the U.S. 25th Division, in whose AO this part of War Zone C lay, was shifting its forces south and east to cover for the redeployment of the U.S. 1st Infantry Division. The Big Red One, as its commander, Major General A. E. Milloy, said when the White House announced the Increment III withdrawals, "had worked itself out of a job." It was slated to be totally out of Vietnam by April 15, but in mid-February, many of its combat units had already begun the tedious job of standing down and turning equipment over to the ARVN. So the North Vietnamese, sensing a vacuum in northwestern War Zone C, moved rapidly to exploit it.

However, COSVN still had the same mission of getting food, arms, and ammunition into the hands of combat units near the populated areas outside Saigon, so its actions were entirely predictable. Moreover, General Tran Van Tra, the senior communist general in the south, again underestimated the capabilities of the Americans' airmobile division and the willingness of General Abrams to unleash it.

Until February 1970, generals Roberts and Casey had permitted the 1st Brigade to maintain the string of firebases across central War Zone C. The location of the bases some twenty kilometers below the border was deliberate: the experience of the Cav in late 1968 had revealed the folly of maintaining permanent firebases within rocket and mortar range of the Cambodian sanctuaries. So the firebase line in central Tay Ninh Province kept the noose tight around the infiltration routes and made the enemy move its artillery units long distances to strike against a base. Conversely, the location of the firebases could do little to prevent the enemy from making an end run to the west. But because during most of 1969, the NVA had ample existing supply routes in Binh Long and Phuoc Long provinces, there was no need to try to create new ones in extreme western Tay Ninh Province. In early 1970, however, COSVN found a great, pressing need to do so.

Beginning in February, acting on intelligence that the NVA units were moving west, Casey turned up the heat. He gave the

1st Brigade commander, Colonel Joseph E. Collins, and his successor on February 15, Colonel William V. Ochs, Jr., raiding missions that forced the brigade to deploy into temporary firebases into northern War Zone C to begin tearing up some NVA bases—rest and retraining areas as well as supply dumps. A supplementary mission was to interdict any east-to-west movement below the Cambodian border.

One of the first thrusts was by the 2nd Battalion, 7th Cavalry, now commanded by Lieutenant Colonel Robert Hannas, the former division G-2. The battalion was rooted out of the comfortable confines of FSB JAMIE and sent into a landing zone some sixteen kilometers north of JAMIE, smack into the middle of an area intelligence believed was occupied by the 95-C Regiment. When the lead company for the combat assault arrived, a heavy pall of dust from a just-completed B-52 strike hung in the air. The temporary firebase, named TINA, was secured by Delta and Echo companies. The other three companies started searching for NVA bunker complexes in the heavily jungled areas adjacent to Provincial Route 246, a dirt track that more or less connected Katum in north-central Tay Ninh Province with the rubber plantations at An Loc. The companies made only sporadic contacts during the first two days after their insertion; the NVA simply did not want to be found. On the third day, elements of the Ninety-Five-Charlie did let their presence be known, attacking a night defensive position of Alpha Company and making a brushing contact with Charlie Company. Just before dawn on the fourth day, two companies of the NVA regiment attacked TINA with rockets, mortars, and small arms. The attack was driven off as the Cav mustered all its aerial firepower and the artillerymen on the base leveled the muzzles of their 105s and fired at the attacking infantry. Contact appeared to break at dawn, but a couple of hours later, a platoon from Delta beginning a sweep of the tree line found that the NVA had left a stay-behind force that had pulled into positions just inside the tree line all around TINA. The NVA sniped at Skytroopers on TINA all morning until all of Delta Company got on line and assaulted the NVA positions one by one. The final tally was forty-four NVA killed, with four Americans killed and nine wounded.

In this action, the Ninety-Five-Charlie had sent a couple of messages to the Cav: don't leave your firebases in place too long or they'll get hit, and don't assume that every NVA combat unit in War Zone C has the mission of moving supplies. The 95-C Regiment's actions were typical of a NVA unit acting within an overall COSVN directive to conserve manpower while still inflicting casualties on the Americans. At the same time, other NVA regular units had the mission of moving supplies regardless of cost, and these were easy prey to the automatic ambushes. The duality of NVA unit missions made combat in War Zone C a dicey affair, and unfortunately, this was not well understood by all commanders.

To give the Cav running room to the northwest, II Field Force readjusted the boundaries in Tay Ninh Province and gave the Cav responsibility for most of the province north of Tay Ninh City. This put the Dog's Head in the Cav's AO. To provide the 1st Brigade with more punch, Casey detached Lieutenant Colonel Mike Conrad's battle-hardened and airmobile-wise 2nd Battalion, 8th Cavalry, from Meyer's 2nd Brigade and returned the battalion to its old battlefields of War Zone C.

The changing tactical situation and the extension of the Cav's AO also permitted General Roberts to make some internal boundary adjustments early in 1970. Both of the ARVN airborne brigades, now fully capable airmobile outfits, were given their own AOs. The 2nd Airborne Brigade was assigned the Song Be River infiltration route (Serges Jungle Highway), and the 3rd Airborne Brigade took over responsibility for the central slice of War Zone C. The tactical proficiency of the 9th ARVN Regiment of the 5th ARVN Division had progressed to the point that, when reinforced by ARVN Armored Cavalry units, it could assume control of the Route 13 corridor in Binh Long Province. These moves allowed Roberts to shift Kingston's 3rd Brigade into eastern War Zone C to continue choking off the Saigon River infiltration routes, while Meyer's 2nd Brigade maintained its firm control of central and eastern Phuoc Long Province. The 11th Armored Cavalry Regiment's Colonel Starry, weary of having his regiment constantly parcelled out, had been lobbying unceasingly for an area of operations of his own. He finally was given a slice of northeastern War Zone C, basically Provincial Route 246, which Roberts wanted cleared and "Rome Plowed." Starry assigned his

2nd Squadron, commanded by Lieutenant Colonel Grail Brookshire, to the task. The ACR's 1st Squadron was detailed to provide security to the land-clearing company (Rome Plow) that was carving a two-hundred-meter swath straddling Provincial Route 4, which connected Tay Ninh City with Katum in north-central Tay Ninh Province.

During early February, Casey assigned the 1st Brigade only limited missions and allowed the brigade to reoccupy the old, permanent bases when the mission was completed. This was essentially a warm-up drill to get the battalions accustomed to Casey's brand of airmobility. But late in February, he began assigning missions that could be accomplished only by having the 1st Brigade battalions permanently close their old, comfortable firebases and constantly move north and west. It was essentially the same kind of airmobility that Meyer and Kingston had been executing to perfection in December and January. This airmobility involved not only infantry battalions, but also artillery batteries, and it was combined with an incredibily sophisticated system of fire control.

Colonel Bob Shoemaker, as chief of staff, had long been concerned by the Cav's inability to orchestrate defensive fire to permit concurrent use of airspace by artillery projectiles and aircraft. Previously, DivArty commanders had just never gotten the hang of it, but when Colonel Morris Brady returned to the Cav, he brought with him the accumulated knowledge of the early days of airmobility in Vietnam. He agreed with Shoemaker and Casey that the artillery should not have to stop firing its cannons to permit use of close air support, so he quickly started bearing down on commanders and staff officers, working with each artillery battalion according to battle priorities; this meant that 2nd and 3rd brigades got priority in January and February. Therefore, the last battalion to get the instruction and practice was the 2nd Battalion, 19th Artillery, supporting the 1st Brigade. Officers and men carefully studied the pamphlet published by DivArty, entitled *Fire Support Coordination*, and then put the principles to work, first in live fire exercises and subsequently in direct support of the infantry companies in contact. The objective was to permit continuous cannon fire while maintaining safe zones for aerial rocket artillery, other helicopter gunships, and the Air Force's tactical warbirds, plus flight corridors for medical evacuation.

Besides fine-tuned artillerymen, this sophisticated fire support plan required superb aviators in both the Army and the Air Force. The Cav was blessed with two first-rate commanders of the aviation group, Colonel Leo Soucek and his replacement, second-tour Cav man Colonel Kenneth Mertel. The Air Force forward air controllers (FACs) from the 19th Tactical Air Support Squadron flew OV-10 Broncos and were intimately familiar with the Cav's concept of fire support.

All in all, with but one exception, the Cav had assembled a team that even an airmobile purist like George Casey felt satisfied with. Casey was never really happy with the 1st Brigade's progress in relearning airmobile lessons and complained that its commander had a tendency toward dithering over tactical decisions. In Casey's scheme for War Zone C in March and April 1970, there was no room for dithering. With Roberts's acquiescence (and the tacit approval of the chain of command up through Creighton Abrams), Casey planned nothing short of complete victory over the North Vietnamese by driving the last vestiges of enemy units from Vietnam's III Corps into the Cambodian sanctuaries.

Even though the battles in War Zone C were conducted under the aegis of Operation *Toan Thang* (Certain Victory), victory was a word that had long since disappeared from the vocabularies of the bureaucrats in the departments of State and Defense. Certainly victory by American forces was the last thing in the mind of Secretary of Defense Mel Laird. He paid another visit to Vietnam in early February and returned to Washington with the news that Vietnamization was progressing at a reasonable pace; "not as fast as he hoped," he said, "but there was no reason for outright gloom." He also preempted Henry Kissinger and the president by announcing that the situation in Vietnam justified the withdrawals of 150,000 U.S. troops on an accelerated schedule. Kissinger had wanted to use the announcement of withdrawals and the rate of withdrawals as political capital for President Nixon. But going into the second year of the Nixon administration, Kissinger was well aware that Laird marched to the beat of a different political drummer. Some observers have made the point that Laird was to Nixon what Clark Clifford was to Lyndon Johnson.

During March and April 1970, some momentous events were occurring in the other parts of the old French Indochina empire. First it was Laos and a severe crisis that taxed the Nixon administration, and then the deposition of Prince Norodom Sihanouk in Cambodia, which created a military and political situation that the North Vietnamese hastened to exploit. Even as this was happening, however, COSVN was pursuing its responsibilities in Vietnam. Although attempts for a Tet-70 high point fizzled, Hanoi was determined to stage a countrywide high point to hammer home its view that it still held the initiative in Vietnam. The offensive was slated for early April. But before it happened, the 1st Cav, usually the big winner in confrontrations with the NVA, gift-wrapped a couple of light firebases for the communists to attack.

During March the three battalions of the 1st Brigade had hopscotched their way into the extreme northwest corner of Tay Ninh Province. On the first of March, the 2nd Battalion, 8th Cavalry, struck it rich in a enormous rice cache less than five kilometers from the Cambodian border, evacuating nearly 135 tons over a two-day period. But the NVA were reteaching this generation of Cav warriors the cost of operating within spitting distance of the Cambodian border. The North Vietnamese regulars could strike quickly and then ghost back into the sanctuaries before the Cav's gunships could catch them in the open. The NVA also could direct mortar and rocket fire at the Skytroopers' positions, and although the Cav had the right to fire into Cambodia when fired upon, effective counterbattery fire was tricky even when there was solid air surveillance.

Of the three battalions engaged, the 2/8 in particular, had fought some vicious battles during mid-March. One of the casualties had been a tough young grunt named John Illingworth. So when the 2/8 popped out of FSB DRUM on March 17 after a four-day stay, the battalion's skipper, Lieutenant Colonel Mike Conrad, named the next temporary base ILLINGWORTH. It was located right in the middle of the neck of the Dog's Head, directly astride the main trail system leading to Base Area 354.

The following day, March 18, the 2nd Battalion, 7th Cavalry, air-assaulted into an area just six kilometers south of ILLING-WORTH and established a temporary firebase that its commander, Lieutenant Colonel Robert Hannas, named JAY.

The NVA took umbrage at the thought of the Americans sitting on top of their last infiltration route and tried to make the Cav pay dearly for the intrusion. Life on this unnamed trail through the Dog's Head was not the turkey shoot it had been further east and south along the middle of the X-Cache and Mustang trails. Contacts were numerous and murderous as the NVA fought hard to protect their porterage units. One of the toughest fights occurred on March 26, when the 8th Cav's Charlie Company, searching an area just five kilometers north and east of ILLING-WORTH, stumbled into a major bunker complex containing the 2nd Battalion, 272nd Regiment.

The first contact seemed to be with only an NVA platoon, but the battalion commander, sensing an opportunity to kill Americans, reinforced quickly into previously empty bunkers on the left and right flanks of the Skytrooper company. Soon Charlie Company was fully engaged and pinned down in a small, tight perimeter, its company commander among those seriously wounded. At the time, Mike Conrad had operational control of Alpha Troop, 1st Squadron, 11th ACR. Conrad had the troop return to ILLINGWORTH from the previous night's laager position, where it too had been hit, drop off disabled vehicles, pick up Alpha 2/8 from base defense duty, and move to the relief of Charlie Company. Alpha Troop's Sheridan tanks and ACAVs broke brush on the way in to the beleaguered rifle company, and soon three American units in a tight but exposed perimeter were trading fire with the heavily bunkered NVA.

In other battles throughout War Zone C, the NVA always broke contact and evaded to fight another day. On this day they hung tough in their bunkers, taking the best shots that the artillerymen on JAY and ILLINGWORTH could throw at them. Late in the afternoon, the Cavalry perimeter reported shortages of ammunition, so General Casey flew to Tay Ninh, loaded up machine-gun ammo for the infantry and armor weapons, and flew back to the perimeter to dump it out. Since the volume of enemy fire was such that the medevac birds couldn't make it in, what Casey was doing bordered on the foolhardy. His pilot hovered the command chopper over the perimeter while the crew chief and Casey's aide, Lieutenant Stephen Grubb, kicked out the cases of ammo. The NVA responded with a fusillade of AK-47 fire, puncturing the thin skin of the Huey repeatedly and wounding Grubb. It was a "million dollar wound," but that was academic to the young aide, a veteran platoon leader from the 1st Battalion, 5th Cavalry, who had only a few days until his normal DEROS (rotation date).

At nightfall the NVA had still not broken contact, so Conrad had to make a choice. He could stay in contact and try to air-assault his last rifle company into a position to the rear of the bunker complex. The danger was that, as close as the fight was to the border and given the enemy's inclination to stay and fight, the NVA might also reinforce and attack a relatively undefended ILLINGWORTH or defeat his infantry units in detail. Moreover, Charlie Company, which had been in almost continual contact for a period of many days, was almost spent.

So Conrad opted for a night withdrawal of all three companies to a less exposed position. The tracked vehicles loaded up the dead and wounded and backed out of the contact area, leaving the NVA battalion in possession of a bunker complex that would soon be the target of a B-52 strike. Amazingly, given the intensity and duration of the firefight, only three Americans had died, while twenty-two were wounded. An ACAV and a Sheridan tank were lost to enemy RPG fire. Enemy soldiers captured later identified the unit in contact and said that eighty-eight of their comrades had died during the fight, mostly from the incredible pounding by artillery and tactical air strikes. After a night medevac of the wounded and a quiet night at the temporary perimeter, Charlie Company was lifted back to ILLINGWORTH to assume responsibility for base defense. The object of the exercise was to give the company some respite from the constant contact units were getting from aggressive NVA units. It would have four days before its real agony began.

When Charlie Company began working to improve the fighting positions on its share of the ILLINGWORTH perimeter, that firebase had been in position for eleven days, one day more than JAY. Conrad had been accustomed to moving every three or four days, and under Casey's tutelage had even begun picking out firebase sites two moves in advance. Hannas's battalion also had been moving rapidly.

Then, suddenly, there was no movement. Conrad was growing exceedingly apprehensive about being in the same place for so long, particularly since ILLINGWORTH was a temporary firebase with virtually no hardening. The perimeter was made by a bulldozer scraping up some earth for a berm; the grunts dug fighting positions in the berm. Only a single roll of concertina wire surrounded the firebase. The battalion command center consisted of a deep hole scooped out by a bulldozer; some reinforcing timbers were placed over the hole and covered first with pierced steel planking and then with multiple layers of sandbags. Conrad's TOC differed from JAY's in that Hannas used a half-buried steel "conex" cargo container with sandbagged sides and roof. The same construction was used for the battalion aid stations at both firebases. The artillery's howitzers were protected only by a small earthen berm. It was a far cry from the hardened bases the Cav had used in central War Zone C.

Conrad said that he repeatedly asked his brigade commander, Colonel Ochs, to let him move. He also pleaded with General Casey. But they told him that General Roberts felt that the presence of the firebase was causing too much disruption of NVA logistics traffic to displace quite yet. The same situation held for Hannas at JAY, except that JAY was even more vulnerable due to its size and closeness to the surrounding jungle. If Roberts and Casey were looking for a fight, they had come to the right place and provided the NVA with a lucrative target.

At 4:20 A.M. on March 29, the interior of FSB JAY erupted in explosions as an undetermined number of mixed-caliber rockets and mortars detonated inside the perimeter. One of the first big rockets hurled a timber at the conex housing the 2/7 TOC. Lieutenant Colonel Hannas, who habitually slept on a cot on top of the sandbagged bunker to beat the suffocating heat, paid for his folly when the flying timber sheared off both legs. Major Gordon Frank, the S-3, although wounded himself, led the firebase defense in a manner that General Roberts later described as "brilliant." Another enemy round that hit the command bunker swept away all the antennas, cutting off communications with higher headquarters. Because the distance between JAY and IL-LINGWORTH was modest, radio contact was maintained with a small tactical radio using a normal antenna. The artillery liaison officer on ILLINGWORTH notified the headquarters of the artillery battalion at Tay Ninh of the attack on JAY; they promptly activated all the preplanned defensive fire from ILLINGWORTH and nearby FSB CAMP HAZARD. The ubiquitous gunships from Blue Max were soon oribiting the firebase, pouring rocket fire at the source of the NVA green tracers that were zipping over JAY. The battalion commo guys got some emergency antennas rigged and soon the battalion was able to adjust supporting artillery fire.

The enemy indirect fire was followed by an attack from the south and west by the 3rd Battalion of the 95-C Regiment. The bulk of the NVA infantry attack barely reached the berm before being beaten back, although a couple of squads armed with RPGs penetrated toward the 105-mm howitzer positions before being driven into a trash dump by a fusillade of small-arms fire from Redlegs turned infantrymen. Holing up in the trash dump was a fatal mistake by the NVA soldiers—Bravo Battery (2/19) artillerymen turned three of their howitzers on the trash dump and obliterated the enemy threat.

Despite the brief penetration of the berm by the infantrymen of the Ninety-Five-Charlie Regiment, the greatest damage to the base came from the concentration of large-caliber mortar shells and rockets precisely delivered. Their accuracy was not surprising since the NVA had had enough time to virtually run an engineering survey of the base. One mortar round struck the 105-mm howitzer ammo dump and blew it; another hit a dug-in dump for some three thousand pounds of composition C-3, which was to be used for clearing trees for landing zones. The explosions were deafening, but because the dumps were well dug in, there were few casualties and little damage was done to the surrounding howitzers. Nevertheless, thirteen Americans died on JAY, and fifty-three more were wounded. The fight cost the NVA seventy-four killed and three prisoners, but COSVN likely was ecstatic at the exchange ratio.

When daylight brought relief to the base and medevacs had taken out the wounded, General Casey flew in with the division

G-2, Jack Galvin, to view the carnage. Questioning the prisoners revealed the probable location of the 95-C staging area to which the attacking battalion had retreated when it broke contact at dawn. Casey wanted to gather up the two remaining companies of the 2/7 and get after the fleeing enemy. But General Roberts said no.

Galvin remembers the argument between the two generals. Casey wanted to maintain contact at all costs, but Roberts was more cautious, telling Casey that the NVA had staged attacks on consecutive nights in other parts of the Cav's AO and he wanted JAY moved immediately. So by late afternoon, JAY was history and a new firebase for the 2/7 Cav, appropriately named HANNAS, was located a few kilometers away in a dry lake bed.

Inexplicably, Roberts did not press for the movement of ILLINGWORTH. Conrad was beside himself. Roberts told Conrad that the location of his firebase was critical to interdict enemy infiltration across the Dog's Head. Conrad's memory of the event was that Casey sided with him and concurred that ILLINGWORTH should be moved. Ochs offered no opinion and no guidance. Years later, Roberts said that if Casey and Ochs had made a strong case for moving the firebase, he would have agreed. Given the caution Roberts exhibited in quickly dismantling JAY and Casey's innate aggressiveness in trying to find and fix the enemy main force units, Roberts's recollection is probably correct. To Casey, contact was not the main thing, it was the only thing. No one will ever know for sure. Casey died in July 1970, and the memories of other witnesses are hazy. Whatever the points of view of the principals at the time, ILLINGWORTH stayed put.

In an apparent attempt to placate Conrad for being hung out as bait for a North Vietnamese regiment, someone decided to reinforce ILLINGWORTH on March 31 with two self-propelled eight-inch howitzers from the 2nd Battalion, 32nd Artillery. When these behemoths came trundling in from a corps artillery base at FSB ST. BARBARA, Conrad called Ochs, saying, "Look, don't do me any favors." He tried to explain that the howitzers were more valuable in a support role from the artillery base at ST. BARBARA than inside his perimeter at ILLINGWORTH, where they just enriched an already lucrative target for the NVA.

Neither Ochs nor anyone at division apparently understood that the threat to ILLINGWORTH was precisely plotted indirect fire. Conrad said his protests were to no avail and he had to patch the howitzers onto his perimeter, making a vulnerable bulge on the southwest quadrant. Conrad said that because the artillery battery was not placed under his operational control, he could only suggest emplacements for the guns. Then, to his horror, Chinook after Chinook flew in, bringing tons of ammunition for the big guns. There was no time remaining on March 31 to properly dig in the ammo or even put up sandbag revetments, so it was just piled up in a huge stack in the center of the battery's position.

Conrad had the engineers from the division's 8th Engineer Battalion use the airmobile bulldozer to scrape up a small earthen berm and stretched his already thin perimeter defense even more by shifting some men from his Echo Company, mostly from the recon platoon, into five fighting positions spread along the bulge. The recon platoon's positions were augmented by some fighting positions to be manned by the artillerymen from the eight-inch guns.

When it became clear that ILLINGWORTH was going to remain at the eye of the coming storm, Conrad persuaded Roberts to permit Support Command to slingload in some metal half culverts. All day on March 31, the grunts of Charlie Company and Echo-Recon worked frantically filling sandbags to cover the culverts and to improve the fighting positions on the berm by filling wooden ammo boxes with dirt.

Intelligence indicators abounded that ILLINGWORTH was going to get hit that night; in fact, there was a state of alert all over Vietnam. Agent reports had indicated to allied intelligence that this was the night for the April high point. On ILLING-WORTH, Conrad had every man up and waiting. A few minutes before midnight, the ground-surveillance radar spotted some movement at the jungle's edge. Conrad executed a preplanned defensive maneuver; artillery from nearby bases crashed into potential enemy rocket launch sites and mortar positions, and gunships raked the edge of the jungle with rockets and minigun fire. At the base itself, a "mad minute" was staged from dummy firing positions, and then the machine guns were repositioned when the drill was over. There was no more movement at the edge of the jungle, but Conrad knew more was coming, and at two hours after midnight on April 1, with the base on full alert, there was little surprise when the grunts along the berm heard the hollow cough of mortar rounds leaving the tubes. Within seconds IL-LINGWORTH was a maelstrom of explosions. As at JAY, the NVA had plotted the indirect fire with precision and hurled more than three hundred rounds of mixed-caliber rockets and mortars at the defenders. One of the primary targets was the TOC and its antenna array. A rocket burst blew it down, but it fell in the direction of Tay Ninh, which permitted rudimentary communications with brigade headquarters. The primary source of communications initially was an Air Force forward air controller, who acted as a relay station until Conrad's signalmen could get his system operational again.

This was the dry season and the incoming rounds kicked up a heavy, suffocating pall of a dust-and-smoke mixture that obscured nearly everything. Several of the enemy rounds had detonated in the eight-inch ammo dump, and tongues of flame began flickering ominously as the assault waves of the 1st Battalion, 271st Regiment, began working their way toward the southwest quadrant of the firebase, their base-of-fire cells launching scores of RPG rockets to supplement heavy machine-gun fire from the tree line.

Bob Shoemaker always maintained that the successful defense of the Cav's firebases often turned on the heroic actions of one or two individuals. On this night that hero's spotlight shone on a tough Specialist Fourth Class named Peter C. Lemon. He had originally been in the 1st Infantry Division's Ranger company, but when the Big Red redeployed, Lemon was reassigned to the 1st Cav. In the replacement depot, contemplating which outfit he would choose to join (he had a choice), he had spotted some of the hard-bitten members of the 2nd of the 8th's recon platoon and opted for the assignment that led to his personal rendezvous with destiny.

When the infantry assault started, Lemon, a big rawboned kid from Michigan, moved to a machine-gun position to assist the gunner. Just as a group of NVA sappers came into view, the machine gun jammed. The enemy, sensing the defensive weakness, immediately charged the position, throwing Chi-Com (potato masher) grenades and firing their AK-47s. Lemon used his M-16 to kill five of the enemy before his rifle jammed. He then went to a standby case of fragmentation grenades and threw them at the enemy soldiers, slowing down their advance to the berm. When the machine gunner, who was desperately trying to repair the malfunction, was wounded, Lemon moved back toward his comrade, only to have his way blocked by the fire of four NVA soldiers just outside the berm. Lemon threw a hand grenade, killing three, and now weaponless, dove over the berm and killed the remaining NVA soldier with his bare hands. He was charged by another group of enemy soldiers, so he picked up an AK-47 and emptied the clip, again slowing down the charge, but not before he was wounded in the side by shrapnel from a Chi-Com grenade. He then dove back over the berm to the machine-gun position, where he found that the gunner badly needed medical attention. He carried the man approximately 100 meters to the battalion aid station, and with the firebase still receiving withering fire was wounded a second time on his way back to the berm.

When he arrived at his old position, he found a number of enemy soldiers on top of the berm, one of them trying to operate the M-60 machine gun. Lemon immediately engaged the group with fragmentation grenades, forcing them to fall back, then charged the North Vietnamese soldier with the machine gun, killing him with his bare hands. He quickly repaired the malfunction, and taking the machine gun to the top of the berm, he proceeded to lay down heavy fire at the attackers outside the berm. While he was firing, Lemon was wounded for the third time, lapsed into unconsciousness, and was evacuated to the aid station. Lemon recovered from his wounds, and in 1972 received the Medal of Honor from President Nixon.

While Lemon was carrying on his one-man war against the NVA assault, his fellow platoon members, inspired by his actions, were making the NVA pay dearly for every foot of ground. Led by Lieutenant Gregory J. Peters and Staff Sergeant James L. Taylor, the recon platoon beat back every NVA thrust, permitting none of the attacking sappers to penetrate into the interior of ILLINGWORTH.

After repelling the enemy at the berm, the defenders thought the worst was over. But at 3:18 A.M., the tons of ammunition for the eight-inch howitzers exploded with a thunderous roar. The southwest portion of the perimeter virtually disappeared. The explosion created a twenty-foot-deep crater, demolished one of the self-propelled howitzers, and killed a number of men. The blast knocked out the fire direction center of the nearby 105-mm howitzer battalion. Conrad had just ducked back into his TOC when the explosion occurred. "I thought the end of the world had come," Conrad remembered. The concussion blew out the lights, knocked out the radios, and filled the bunker with dust and smoke so thick that it was impossible to breath. The dust cloud was so thick that the illumination flares dangling from tiny parachutes over the base were blacked out. For about ten minutes there was no movement on the southwest side of ILLING-WORTH as both friend and foe were flattened and stunned. As the combatants came to their senses, those who could gathered up their weapons and began searching through the choking gloom for targets. Occasional shots were fired, but the battle, for all intents and purposes, was over.

Dawn brought the inevitable retreat from contact by the NVA battalion and the flutter of helicopters: medevacs, resupply, and the command-and-control choppers of the brass. Every soldier on ILLINGWORTH walked around in a daze. Jack Galvin said that Mike Conrad was dust- and smoke-streaked and so hoarse from shouting during the night that he could barely talk above a whisper. Conrad was told that he had to stay on ILLING-WORTH for another night, and then his battalion would be rotated back to the relative peace and quiet of palace guard duty at Phuoc Vinh.

The cost of staying on ILLINGWORTH had been steep. Twenty-four American soldiers died, many from the stupendous ammo dump explosion, and fifty-four more were wounded. Again, COSVN won the exchange ratio numbers contest, as only sixty-five dead NVA soldiers were found around the firebase. Hanoi had also garnered heavy ink in the United States because the desperate fight on ILLINGWORTH was the headline attraction of the April high point in which one hundred towns and installations in Vietnam were attacked by coordinated shellings, sappers, or both. Sixty percent of the total number of Americans killed during the high point were killed on ILLINGWORTH.

This was not what General Abrams had been looking for when he permitted the Cav to go charging off into northwest War Zone C. The White House wanted to know what in the world was going on, and General Roberts was required to write a detailed explanation of the hows and whys of JAY and ILLINGWORTH. On April 5, Roberts wrote a six-page justification of the battles, noting correctly that COSVN was determined at any cost to move troops and supplies through the Dog's Head into Base Area 354. After explaining the rationale for locating firebases in the pathway of the NVA infiltration routes, Roberts began restating the obvious: (1) the location of the bases so close to the border made them exceptionally vulnerable to massed large-caliber rocket and mortar fire. He wrote that other than hardening the firebases, which he doubted would prevent unacceptable casualties, the best recourse was frequent moves, even though this brought about an excessive use of helicopter blade time. Roberts did not mention that this great truth was already well known in the division and that the division and brigade leaders deliberately disregarded established airmobile doctrine. (2) Ammunition and explosives must be dug in and overhead cover provided. "In particular," he wrote, "the 8-inch howitzer ammunition was not dug in deep enough at Illingworth, and there was too much of it in one place. I believe several smaller dumps dug in at different quadrants in the firebase should be the pattern." Again, this was regurgitating established doctrine. No attempt was made to fix the blame for jamming the ammunition into ILLINGWORTH.

Nothing further was ever heard about the incident, one of the many reasons cynics believed that the Army in Vietnam tended to paper over its mistakes and that it was rare indeed that a general officer suffered the consequences of mistakes in his command.

The April 5 letter was not the only written communication Roberts had to make to the COMUSMACV. Any time a B-52 strike was aborted because of a screw-up on the ground, the commander of the unit involved had to personally write General Abrams with the justification for the abort. Within days of the attack on JAY, Charlie Company, 2nd Battalion, 7th Cavalry, was unable to get sufficiently clear of an Arc Light box and the strike had to be aborted. The official reason for the abort was that there was a screw-up in establishing communication between the helicopter lift company and the gunship unit that was supporting it, which in turn caused the lift unit to burn up enough fuel to force it to a refuel point. By the time the lift birds and escort ships got together, it was too late to make the extraction and the Arc Light was aborted. All of this may have happened, but there was more to the story.

John "Jack" Laurence of CBS News had returned to Vietnam, convinced that no one in television was doing the real story of the soldier on the ground. He persuaded the 1st Cav, with whom he had spent much time during his previous tours in Vietnam, to let him and his film team spend some time in the bush with a rifle company. One of the best companies at the time was Charlie Company, 2/7, commanded by Captain Robert Jackson, a much-beloved commander. Laurence filed a piece just before JAY was attacked, entitled, "The Heart of Captain Jackson," that spelled out the love and affection shared between the captain and his men. But Jackson had a minor heart condition that curtailed his tour with Charlie Company. He was replaced by Captain Al Rice, who moved to the company from a tour with the division's Ranger unit. He was hardly a "cherry," but being five years younger than Jackson and of a different temperament, he didn't immediately mesh with the members of the veteran company.

After JAY was hit and the battalion lost its battalion commander and S-3, there was boundless confusion as the new commander, Lieutenant Colonel Edward Trobaugh, with a brand-new S-3, tried to pick up the reins of the leaderless battalion. It was not until April 3 that the 1st Brigade managed to get Trobaugh out to FSB HANNAS. He was brand-new in-country and a new guy normally got to absorb a lot of things about running a battalion by hanging around the outgoing commander for a week or so. One of those was sending in a secure radio with a log bird (logistics helicopter) so that classified traffic on movements could be given to company commanders. When Charlie Company was logged on the afternoon of April 5, the radio wasn't sent in and Captain Rice was not given the vital information that he had to move to a pickup zone the next morning to get out of an Arc Light box.

The next morning, when brigade and battalion discovered the error, Rice received a radio message to move down a trail to a pickup zone for an air movement to another location. He was ordered to make the move as quickly as possible, which meant the company had to take the trail. Because the transmission was in the clear, the real reason for the haste could not be revealed to Rice. After giving his platoon leaders the order, the platoon leader of the 2nd Platoon, which was to be the point platoon, was told by members of his platoon that they were not walking down any trail, an act they considered to be madness. This discussion and refusal took place in front of the CBS camera. When Rice came forward to get the platoon moving, the men repeated their belief that they would be walking into certain death. No amount of persuasion would budge them. Rice told them that his orders were to get to the pick-up zone and get there quickly. So he told the recalcitrant platoon that he was going to take the point and they could follow or stay behind. He started down the road, and men started to follow, but then Rice got a sudden change of orders, and he was directed by Trobaugh to move in the opposite direction to a bomb crater where a one-ship pickup zone was available. By the time the last squad of Skytroopers was lifted out, the BUFs were only minutes away, so they were diverted to an alternate target, probably in Cambodia.

When the troops were dropped off in Tay Ninh, Laurence and his crew headed for Saigon, because he had on film a real bell-ringer for the six o'clock news—a combat refusal. And it was in the proud 1st Air Cavalry Division. When he learned of the Laurence piece, the information officer arranged a meeting at Tan Son Nhut with Jack Laurence and Colonel William Ochs, the brigade commander. Laurence listened to the IO's pitch that the real story behind his filmed story was the trauma of changes of command in a volatile combat situation, coupled with the inability of the command to inform Rice of the impending B-52 strike. Jack, to his credit, listened carefully and promised to hold up the story until the CBS bureau in Washington could verify the Arc Light mission at the Pentagon. He did, they did, and CBS toned down the story considerably when the facts were verified. But the story was not the most positive that was ever run on the Cav, and Roberts, embarrassed by having to explain away the B-52 abort, wanted to strangle somebody. Ultimately, Bill Ochs would reap the whirlwind.

COSVN took another crack at a Cav firebase in an attempt to dislodge the division's choke-hold on the Dog's Head infiltration trails. It hurled a battalion of the 95-C Regiment at FSB AT-KINSON on April 15, an attack that killed seven members of the 2nd Battalion, 7th Cavalry, while wounding another twenty-five. The NVA left sixty-six bodies behind and three live prisoners. It was the final convulsive spasm of the North Vietnamese in III Corps, and as it turned out, one of the last major battles the Cav would fight on the Vietnamese side of the border region.

14

The Cambodian Domino

Even as the Cav was starting to drive through northern Tay Ninh Province of South Vietnam, two other pieces of the old French Indochina empire, Laos and Cambodia, were about to provide a distraction from the center-stage position of Vietnam. Although events in Cambodia eventually overshadowed even the war in much of Vietnam, the North Vietnamese offensive in Laos in early 1970 grabbed most of the headlines in the United States and in the Pacific *Stars and Stripes*. There was good reason for concern. If the estimated sixty thousand North Vietnamese regulars, plus North Vietnam's puppets, the Pathet Lao, defeated the fifty-thousand-man army of the royal government of Premier Souvanna Phouma, a lot of things would happen in the Indochina peninsula, none of them good for America.

The United States was running a "secret" war by supporting General Van Pao and his Meo tribesmen, who helped maintain the uneasy balance of power in Laos. North Vietnam had never observed the 1963 Geneva accords that demanded that all non-Laotian combat forces leave the country. All 666 American military personnel departed through international checkpoints, but only *forty* of the six thousand North Vietnamese troops departed. The remaining regulars quickly provided a bulwark for the Pathet Lao, and for all intents and purposes, Hanoi annexed the eastern half of southern Laos for the infiltration system that became known as the Ho Chi Minh Trail. In the mid-sixties, as the threat of North Vietnam to the neutralist government of Souvanna Phouma became explicit, covert American aid was sought and provided. In return, Souvanna Phouma gave tacit approval for the interdiction bombing of the Ho Chi Minh Trail.

So it was obvious in Washington that if the communists succeeded in overturning the Vientiane government, America's "secret" war in Laos would come to an end, and along with it, the Air Force interdiction bombing of the Ho Chi Minh Trail. Moreover, should communist forces conquer all of Laos, the vulnerable Mekong River border with Thailand would threaten American bases in that country.

It was also during this period that Kissinger held his first series of secret meetings with Le Duc Tho in Paris, meetings that Kissinger hoped would bring a resolution to the Vietnam War outside of the main negotiation arena where propaganda posturing occupied most of the time at the sessions. At those secret sessions, Kissinger was treated to extensive lectures by Xuan Thuy and Le Duc Tho about the "correctness" of Hanoi's position, which never wavered from its demands that the United States withdraw its forces unilaterally and on an accelerated schedule and dismantle the Thieu government on the way out. The only accommodation offered by Hanoi was that its soldiers would not shoot at the Americans as they were boarding their aircraft to go home. During these secret sessions, Le Duc Tho, in a remarkable bit of candor, told Kissinger after the subject of the North Vietnamese offensive in Laos was raised, that it was Vietnam's destiny to dominate Laos and Cambodia; not *North* Vietnam, just Vietnam. This was after the implacable Politburo member had ridiculed the Vietnamization program. As Kissinger wrote: "He cut to the heart of the dilemma of Vietnamization. All too acutely, he pointed out that our strategy was to withdraw enough forces to make the war bearable for the American people while simultaneously strengthening the Saigon forces so that they could stand on their own. He then asked the question that also was tormenting me: 'Before, there were over a million U.S. and puppet troops, and you failed. How can you succeed when you let the puppet troops do the fighting? Now, with only U.S. support, how can you win?' "

The Laotian crisis only passed after some B-52 strikes were

directed at North Vietnamese troop concentrations, and Thai volunteers reinforcing the royal government's troops stymied the Pathet Lao offensive. In Washington the cries of anguish and the breast-beating that went on over those actions was astonishing. It took the Nixon administration almost a month of dithering to authorize the assistance Souvanna Phouma needed to survive, and then Nixon and Kissinger were savaged by congressional and media critics for the action.

Even before the Laotian pot started boiling in earnest, Prince Norodom Sihanouk had expressed concern about Cambodia's border with Laos and the potential North Vietnamese threat. Sihanouk had been walking an exceedingly slippery tightrope, trying to hew to a "neutralist" line while allowing the North Vietnamese and Viet Cong unfettered use of border sanctuaries. Sihanouk also had cut a deal with Peking to permit the use of the port of Kompong Som, and through his wife's family, contracted with truck companies to move the supplies to the sanctuaries. It was a cozy and profitable deal for the ruling elite of Cambodia, but the ancient antipathy of the Khmer people toward the Vietnamese formed a dark undercurrent in the relations between Sihanouk and his own government. Nevertheless, despite some squabbles between Sihanouk and his cabinet ministers, he and his wife, Monique, left Cambodia on January 7, 1970, for a two-month vacation in the south of France.

He left his government in the care of the chairman of the National Assembly, Cheng Heng; Prime Minister Lon Nol; and First Deputy Prime Minister Sirik Matak. Lon Nol was one of Sihanouk's most trusted deputies so there was no hint of the trouble to come. Certainly the United States didn't have a clue. The United States had only restored diplomatic relations with Cambodia in October 1969, and had just a small mission in Phnom Penh, headed by Lloyd Rives, the chargé d'affairs. Kissinger writes that, at the insistence of Senator Mike Mansfield, no CIA personnel were assigned to the mission. Although it is difficult to imagine that the CIA was unable to have some presence in Phnom Penh, the continuing insistence of CIA analysts that all the supplies for the North Vietnamese and Viet Cong operations in South Vietnam were coming down the Ho Chi Minh Trail, while discounting the contribution of the port of

Kompong Som (Sihanoukville), indicates a total lack of competent intelligence coming out of Cambodia.

The use of the border sanctuaries by the enemy had been irritating the United States since 1965, but despite numerous requests by the military for authority to go in and clean them out, neither the Johnson administration nor, after 1969, Nixon's team, wanted to risk harming relations with Sihanouk. Although the United States was unhappy with the steadily rising use of the border sanctuaries by North Vietnam, the United States and Thieu governments believed the uneasy equilibrium maintained by Sihanouk was preferable to the alternative, which both Thieu and Kissinger believed would be a North Vietnamese–dominated Cambodian government. Sihanouk was well aware that the increasingly oppressive North Vietnamese presence in his country's border provinces was costing him popularity with the Cambodian people. He believed that he could persuade either the Soviet Union or China to intervene with North Vietnam on behalf of Cambodia. So, on February 22, as he was completing his "cure" at Grasse on the French Riviera, he announced that he would stop in Moscow and Peking to enlist the support of "those great, friendly" countries to get the North Vietnamese out of Cambodia.

But Sihanouk no longer controlled Cambodia's destiny, even though he was not yet aware of it. On March 8, 1970, several demonstrations by villagers took place in the Cambodian provinces along the border, particularly in Svay Rieng Province, which is part of the deep salient into Vietnam that ends with the Parrot's Beak. Three days later, thousands of young Cambodians went on a rampage in Phnom Penh and laid seige to the embassies of the North Vietnamese and Viet Cong, smashing windows with stones. Nearly all historians agree that the demonstrations were stage-managed by the Cambodian government. The March 11 "demonstration" was followed by a special joint session of the two houses of the Cambodian Parliament from which came a resolution to reaffirm Cambodia's neutrality and to defend the national territory. The Parliament also urged expanding and strengthening of the Cambodian army, which had been kept weak and ineffectual by Sihanouk as a hedge against possible coup attempts.

The Prince inexplicably remained in Paris instead of hurrying home, where his indisputable charisma and popularity among certain segments of the population might have restored an equilibrium to a situation that was rapidly spinning out of control. He chose instead to issue from afar shrill denunciations of those he claimed were delivering Cambodia into the "capitalist, imperialist" camp. Then, on March 13, he blundered once more, heading for Moscow instead of Phnom Penh. Sihanouk now had totally lost control.

On March 12 the Cambodian government sent Hanoi some strong messages. Cambodia renounced a trade agreement with the Viet Cong, the cover for the importation of supplies through the port of Kompong Som. General Lon Nol also asked Hanoi to withdraw all NVA and Viet Cong forces from Cambodian territory within seventy-two hours; the deadline was set for March 15. The communiques coming from Phnom Penh that day also announced a ten-thousand-man expansion of the Cambodian army, known as FANK (Forces Armees Nationale Khmeres).

Events began moving rapidly after that point. There were more demonstrations by Cambodian citizens against Vietnamese presence on Cambodian soil. On March 13 Sihanouk flew to Moscow to enlist Soviet assistance in "persuading" their Vietnamese clients to get out of Cambodia. He had badly underestimated the gravity of the situation in Phnom Penh. On March 18, the Cambodian National Assembly passed a resolution stripping Prince Sihanouk of all governmental powers. The action was not a coup in the classical sense; there was no bloodshed, just a simple legislative fiat that named Cheng Heng as chief of state, General Lon Nol as his prime minister, and Sirik Matak as deputy prime minister. The aides surrounding Sihanouk did not have the stomach to inform him of the "coup"; it remained for Soviet Premier Kosygin to break the news as they were driving to the Moscow airport. Sihanouk then flew to China, where he proclaimed himself the true government in exile, blamed the coup on the CIA, and aligned himself with the Khmer Rouge.

In the Chinese alphabet, which is shared by the Vietnamese, the symbol for *crisis* contains two elements that taken separately, mean "danger" and "opportunity." It is clear now that Hanoi regarded the changes in Cambodia as a crisis that contained more opportunity than danger. The North Vietnamese had kept their

Cambodian communist clients at minimal strength, using the military power of the Khmer Rouge in a classic guerrilla mode. The Cambodian reds spent most of their time among the peasantry, organizing, recruiting, and occasionally making quick strikes against isolated government outposts. But Hanoi's master plan called for hegemony over all of Indochina, and to prepare for the eventuality of the use of NVA regulars in Cambodia, had infiltrated the 1st NVA Division headquarters and two regiments, the 52nd and the 101st, to locations south and west of Phnom Penh. The 1st NVA, of course, had been the Cav's primary adversary in War Zone C during most of 1969, until it was relieved by the VC 9th Division and shifted south into IV Corps.

Throughout the history of modern war, the mere thought of having to fight a two-front war has dissuaded many aggressors from excessive adventures. But the North Vietnamese viewed the Indochina war as a war of syntheses. This strategic design was articulated by General Tran Van Tra in his book *Ending the Thirty Years' War*. Tra, of course, commanded COSVN from 1967 until the final North Vietnamese triumph. He saw the war as a smooth and coordinated synthesis of many types of forces, ranging from pure political action and proselytizing units, to local-force guerrillas, to regional force units, to the big main-force regiments and divisions. The North Vietnamese had been directing this consolidated warfare in Vietnam with varying degrees of success. Hanoi had always regarded the struggle in Laos and Cambodia as linked to the war in Vietnam and only sought a propitious time to overtly commit the main-force units. North Vietnam had already made a stab at defeating the neutralist government of Souvanna Phouma earlier in the year, and although it failed to subjugate all of Laos, it still maintained firm control of the part of the country through which the Ho Chi Minh Trail ran. Thus, while the Cambodian crisis did present the danger to Hanoi of having its supply line from Sihanoukville cut, the opportunity to subjugate Cambodia was exceptionally tempting.

This basic posture of Hanoi was made very clear to Kissinger in Paris during his April 4 secret meeting with Le Duc Tho. The senior Politburo member explicitly stated that Hanoi intended to overthrow the Lon Nol regime and install a government acceptable to the North Vietnamese, which would, of course, continue to permit use of the Cambodian sanctuaries. Le Duc Tho, even in the secret session, never directly affirmed that North Vietnamese troops were being used in the attacks on the Cambodian government forces, saying instead: "The whole people of Cambodia fight against the agents of the United States. They have responded to the appeal of Prince Sihanouk and the National Front of Cambodia. The Khmer people have stood up with all their strength to defend freedom and neutrality."

Kissinger responded with exquisite irony that doubtless was lost on his communist adversary: "Who has troops in Cambodia? Not the U.S. I am impressed again with the linguistic ability of the people of the Indochinese peninsula. We discovered that the Pathet Lao speak Vietnamese, and now we find the same phenomenon in Cambodia."

In further conversations during that meeting, Kissinger realized that North Vietnam had no intention of even discussing a neutral stance for Cambodia. The only discussion Hanoi would countenance was the timetable for the overthrow of the Lon Nol–Matak government and installation of a North Vietnamese puppet state. This was the situation Kissinger sadly reported to Nixon upon his return to Washington. One of the great dangers of secret negotiations is that information learned in the sessions cannot easily be revealed with credibility. Nixon and Kissinger knew with certainty from early April that nothing short of credible military force was going to force Hanoi to desist from its goal of conquest in Cambodia. Yet with the North Vietnamese propaganda machine rolling at top speed, all of the doves in and out of government were clamoring for U.S. restraint.

Obviously North Vietnam didn't take seriously Lon Nol's March 15 "get out of Cambodia" ultimatum. It took COSVN only ten days to start the counteraction. On March 25 and 26, several demonstrations occurred in the provinces where the North Vietnamese had concentrated most of the base areas. The demonstrators all purported to be crying for the return of Sihanouk. But when the Cambodian army forces arrested some of the ringleaders, no one was surprised to find that the sweeps netted some VC and NVA cadre.

Even as this was happening, COSVN was pursuing its responsibilities in Vietnam. Although attempts for a Tet-70 high point fizzled, Hanoi was determined to stage countrywide high points as distinct phases to its "X" spring-summer offensive. The mission of the "X" campaign was specifically to disrupt pacification and the Vietnamization process and to hammer home its point that it still held the initiative in Vietnam. The first phase of the offensive had been scheduled for early April, despite the distractions in Cambodia. And COSVN still had a responsibility to move supplies to the forces in Vietnam it hoped would stage the high points. This set in motion the events that led to the battles at JAY, ILLINGWORTH, and ATKINSON.

Although the 1st Air Cavalry can rightly claim that it basically drove the North Vietnamese main-force divisions from their South Vietnam base areas, the Cav had by no means attrited the strength of the NVA. The sudden quiet along the front after the April 15 attack on ATKINSON could be explained quite easily. Hanoi had given its main-force divisions missions that were much easier to accomplish than beating themselves bloody on the 1st Cav blockade. The NVA regiments simply turned their combat orientation 180 degrees and began attacking into Cambodia. The poorly equipped, trained, and led Cambodian battalions were no match for the battle-hardened veterans of the border wars with the Americans. In rapid succession, the towns of Krek, Mimot, and Snuol fell to the North Vietnamese. In short order, the small enclaves along the border had been expanded into a twenty-five-kilometer-deep zone that stretched nearly the whole length of the Cambodian border. Southwest of Phnom Penh, the 1st NVA Division's regiments were coming dangerously close to cutting the routes from the capital to the sea.

The easy success of the North Vietnamese Army triggered violence by the Khmer people against ethnic Vietnamese living in Cambodia. Many of the Vietnamese were rounded up and herded into refugee camps, but hundreds were slaughtered and thrown into the Mekong River.

Stanley Karnow wrote in his history that Lon Nol "had unleashed the furies." Perhaps no phrase better fits the situation the Cambodian leader found himself in by mid-April. He first firmly declared Cambodian neutrality, an utter waste of words. Then he asked for United Nations intervention, citing the naked aggression of the North Vietnamese, vainly hoping for a Korean War kind of intervention. Finally, in desperation, he yelled for help from the United States.

In *The White House Years*, Kissinger devotes a score of pages to an attempt to give a true picture of the bureaucratic minuet that occurred in Washington during the latter stages of the developing Cambodian crisis. Decision-making in the Nixon administration was far from decisive, and presidential decisions were rarely implemented with dispatch. The usual cast of characters played roles. William Rogers, influenced by the Foggy Bottom doves, advocated a "wait-and-see" posture. Melvin Laird, fearful that a bellicose Nixon would endanger his carefully laid plans to disengage the U.S. forces from Vietnam, recommended only RVNAF thrusts into Cambodia. General Abrams and Ambassador Bunker, sensing an opportunity to crush the border sanctuaries, recommended an arms package for the embattled Cambodian Army and a combined-forces incursion into the sanctuaries, concentrating on those bordering Military Region III.

The CIA weighed in with the intelligence estimate that, without assistance, the days of the Lon Nol government were numbered. It also predicted that unless the Nixon administration acted quickly, "a domino was going to fall." Nixon was determined that no dominoes were going to topple on his watch.

15

The Hasty Plan

On the morning of April 24, General Creighton Abrams choppered out to Plantation, the Bien Hoa headquarters of II Field Force. It was Abrams's first visit to the big American corps headquarters since the arrival nine days earlier of the new II Field Force commander, Lieutenant General Michael S. Davison. After the usual exchange of salutes and handshakes, Abrams headed for Davison's office. He was about to drop a bombshell on the newest kid on the block. "Even after twenty years," General Davison recalled recently, Abe's announcement "had the sort of dramatic impact that renders the memory indelible."

Abrams, who along with his gruff reputation had a fine sense of the dramatic, said nothing after he was seated in Davison's office. He pulled out a cigar and went through an elaborate process of unwrapping it, still never uttering a word. He bit off the end, fired up his lighter, and puffed until he got a nice glow on the end. He leaned back in the big overstuffed chair, blew a cloud of smoke at the ceiling. Then he spoke, very calmly, very casually. "Mike, I want you to go into Cambodia and clean out those sanctuaries. I want you to do it on seventy-two hours notice; let me know when you're ready."

The announcement jarred Davison to his core. Although this was his first tour in Vietnam, Davison knew as well as any senior Army officer of the sanctity of the Cambodian base areas. In an interview with *U.S News and World Report* in 1983, Davison said that he was so new in-country and to the job that he had to consciously resist looking at the map on his office wall while Abrams was talking, to orient himself on just where these sanctuaries were. Abrams's guidance was to go into the sanctuaries in the vicinity of the Fishhook, orienting on base areas 352 and 353. Because the 1st Cavalry Division was already in position to launch a strike, it made sense to give the mission to General Roberts and the 1st Cav. Davison had been given seventy-two hours to develop a plan that would satisfy Abrams and that could be sent to Washington for review by the Joint Chiefs and Kissinger's staff in the White House.

Roberts was told to limit knowledge of the planning action to no more than five people. At the time of the warning order from Davison, the Cav's senior staff was in a state of flux. Because General Casey had been nominated for a second star and command of the 1st Cav, he was home on what Shoemaker enjoyed calling Casey's "reenlistment leave" and was not scheduled to return to the division until May 5. The MACV policy of rotating commanders out of command at six months and personnel home at one year cleaned out the G-2 and G-3 slots of the division. Lieutenant Colonel George Stotser, the seasoned G-3, was due to go home April 25, to be replaced by Lieutenant Colonel Ric Ordway, who was in Hawaii on R and R after coming out of command of the 1st Battalion, 12th Cavalry. The G-2 slot was temporarily vacant because Jack Galvin was taking his R and R prior to assuming command of the 1st Battalion, 8th Cavalry. His replacement-to-be, Mike Conrad, was also in Hawaii after coming out of command of the 2nd Battalion, 8th Cavalry, and he did not assume his G-2 duties until just before the Cav was committed in Cambodia. Colonel Joe Kingston, who had been chief of staff, rotated home on April 15. The new chief of staff was Colonel Shy Meyer, fresh out of command of the 2nd Brigade. The dreaded rotational hump that afflicted most of the units in Vietnam could not have occurred at a worse time.

Davison's warning order did not exactly come as a surprise to Roberts. Earlier in April, when the situation in Cambodia showed signs of deteriorating, he had been called by Abrams on the secure telephone and told to develop a bare-bones contingency plan for a raid into the base areas around the Fishhook. Abrams, who had an uncanny ability to anticipate events in both the military and geopolitical arenas, was always about one step ahead of the national command authority. Stotser remembers Roberts calling him in, swearing him to secrecy, and telling him to develop a contingency plan. Stotser locked himself in his office and came up with a plan that envisaged a heavily airmobile effort, providing a starring role to the cavalry battalions of the division, and to a lesser extent, a couple of squadrons of the 11th ACR. But because the Cav was up to its elbows in alligators in War Zone C, and because a raid into Cambodia seemed politically impossible, nothing came of the venture and Stotser filed the plan in a very secure safe and forgot about it.

When Davison relayed the new planning mission to the 1st Cav, it was simple to regurgitate the essential elements of the plan and present it to the new II Field Force commander. Stotser remembers that the plan did not fly with Davison and his G-3, Colonel Elmer Pendleton. They insisted on more armor and mechanized forces and a greater role for the ARVN, and their wishes were granted in the final grand scheme that received the blessings of II Field Force and General Abrams. The plan called for an airmobile assault by three ARVN Airborne battalions into landing zones in Cambodia just south of Highway 7 to put them in a position to block the retreat of North Vietnamese who would presumably be flushed out of their bases by an onrushing 11th Armored Cavalry Regiment. A second wave of air assaults would feature cavalry battalions, with the armored and mechanized support furnished by a 25th Infantry Division armor battalion and a mechanized infantry battalion from the 3rd Brigade of the 9th Division. As yet, there was no authority to extend detailed planning to the brigade level, and the Cav was told that it should be prepared to execute the plan on a seventy-two-hour notice.

All of the planners were working under a severe information handicap. Washington provided no clear guidance about the real objective or duration of the incursion. For that reason, and because a multiplicity of commands was involved, it seemed logical to II Field Force to create a special task force. The 1st Cavalry Division could as easily have been named a task force of the whole, since it remained the primary planning headquarters, but the decision was made to give Bob Shoemaker, the assistant division commander for support, a crack at the history books. Ric Ordway, the incoming division G-3, remembers Shoemaker telling him before a briefing trip to II Field Force, "Don't let them name this thing 'Operation Shoemaker.'" Ordway got half a loaf; the name picked for the operation was "Rock Crusher," or, on the Vietnamese side, *Toan Thang* (Total Victory) 43. But the actual invasion force was named "Task Force Shoemaker."

Even during this flurry of planning, which was still strictly limited to a few select individuals, there was general disbelief that the United States would actually commit to crossing the border. The cynicism was justified. During discussions at the White House about what actions the United States should take concerning North Vietnamese aggression in Cambodia, the affected cabinet officers weighed in with predictable responses. Secretary of State William Rogers, reflecting the dovishness of the State Department, suggested that the United States do nothing at all. Melvin Laird recommended clandestine shipments of captured eastern bloc weapons to the Cambodian army and only limited incursions into the Parrot's Beak by ARVN forces unaccompanied by American advisors. Kissinger writes that all the principals produced a blizzard of memos to cover their backsides. Kissinger and Nixon solicited the opinions of Abrams and Ambassador Bunker, obtaining their input directly by back channel, thus avoiding routing their replies through the bureaucracy. Both favored a strong attack into the Parrot's Beak and Angel's Wing by the ARVN forces commanded by Lieutenant General Do Cao Tri, and a thrust into the Cambodian bases directly north of Saigon by a mix of U.S. and ARVN forces.

During discussions with senior officials, CIA Director Richard Helms was the most hawkish. In fact, Helms was probably closest to the real strategic truth in the entire affair when, as Kissinger reported, he told the president that the administration "would pay the same domestic political price for two operations as for one, and the strategic payoff would be incomparably greater in the two-pronged attack." If Helms had recommended a concurrent cutting of the Ho Chi Minh Trail in Laos, he would have hit the theoretical strategic jackpot.

Kissinger also recalls that Nixon himself toyed with a stronger response to Hanoi's adventure in Cambodia, musing that the

United States should attack all the sanctuaries, resume bombing North Vietnam, and mine the Haiphong harbor. In *The White House Years*, Kissinger wrote that he did not believe the president was seriously considering the extreme option. Then, in one rueful paragraph, he summed up the inherent error in American strategy: "The bane of our military actions in Vietnam was their hesitancy; we were always trying to calculate with fine precision the absolute minimum of force or of time, leaving no margin for error or confusion, encouraging our adversary to hold on until our doubts overrode our efforts."

In Vietnam, as the planning proceeded, General Davison realized that unless the brigade-level commanders were cut into the process, there was no way the command could respond positively to a seventy-two-hour "go" notice, so on April 27, Abrams authorized detailed planning with brigade commanders and shortened the notification time to forty-eight hours. When that authorization came in to Roberts, he called Shoemaker in and told him, "We really have to get serious about this. Get yourself a little task force headquarters of a handful of people and go on up to Quon Loi and get a building from Bob Kingston and really do some serious planning. If this thing goes, all you'll get is forty-eight hours notice."

Shoemaker grabbed several majors from headquarters to act as his operations, intelligence, logistics, and fire-support planners and coordinators, and a Lieutenant Colonel Vincent E. Falter, who had just arrived as Colonel Brady's DivArty executive officer, as the task-force coordinator. He commandeered Kingston's briefing room, and no one from Kingston's brigade headquarters was permitted in it; it was probably the only time in Kingston's career that something happened in his AO that he didn't directly control. The task-force staff took the approved grand scheme and began working up detailed plans. Virtually no hard intelligence was available about the enemy forces in Cambodia. Shoemaker said that after sifting through what little intelligence there was, he and his staff were unsure of the enemy threat. Having been with the Cav since May 1969, Shoemaker knew that the division had been facing up to twelve NVA regiments along the border. What he didn't know was how many were still there and what kind of antiaircraft capability the NVA had. He received no help from

II Field Force or MACV because the secrecy had cut so many intelligence operatives out of the pattern. He had a couple of other rather basic questions: "Are there any Cambodian civilians in my area? And what is my area?" He had been assigned a fairly narrow zone of about forty kilometers for initial penetration into Cambodia. But no one had given him any feel for the proposed depth or duration of the penetration. All this led him to believe that he was planning nothing more than a simple raid of the enemy base areas in the Fishhook region.

Critical to Shoemaker's scheme of maneuver was a well-developed fire-support plan. He and Brady agonized over the concept for the fire plan. To fine-tune the fire plan, Shoemaker and Brady needed up-to-date maps of Cambodia. The intelligence channels, from which maps were obtained, didn't have any, so they started drawing in artillery concentration locations on some old maps. The division chief of staff, Colonel Meyer, put in a request for aerial photos to the MACV J-2 (intelligence officer at joint-command level). It was denied summarily. Finally Roberts called Davison and asked for help. The then chief of staff of II Field Force, Brigadier General Douglas Kinnard, called the MACV J-2 and told him that, for reasons he could not disclose, aerial photographs of the Fishhook region of Cambodia were urgently needed by the 1st Cav, and the J-2 should consult with the MACV chief of staff. Colonel Meyer remembers that MACV dispatched an Air Force colonel to Quon Loi with a roll of aerial photos with instructions that they could not be out of his sight for a minute and he had to bring them all back to Saigon at the end of the day. Meyer said that as soon as he saw the photos of the ground just inside the border of Cambodia and recognized the pockmarks for what they were—B-52 bomb craters—he understood why MACV didn't want general circulation of the photographs.

The photos revealed the kind of terrain the task force would be operating in. The area within the Fishhook was identical to the terrain in Vietnam on both sides of the Florida-shaped projection into Vietnam. The heavy jungle was denuded close to the border where the B-52 strikes had hit. Further north in Cambodia, there were rolling hills. The photos showed some villages ten or so kilometers north of the border. National Route 7 traversed the area from west to east, and north of the highway the jungle thinned out and cultivated areas showed up on the photos. For the Cav it appeared that the raid into Cambodia would be more of the same War Zone C style of fighting.

The fire plan that finally evolved out of the planning sessions called for six B-52 strikes with thirty-six BUFs; because of the excessive secrecy, Shoemaker and Brady knew only that they were going in, not where, and that the strikes were to be completed by 6 A.M. on D-Day, whenever that was ordered. Next up were more than one hundred tubes of artillery, ranging from light 105s up through the eight-inch and 175-mm cannon. Because the Cav had been operating so close to the border, most of these tubes were already in position, but plans were made to sneak the rest of the batteries into position once the operation was a go. The artillery would fire for one hour, from 6 A.M. to 7 A.M. The targets were the airmobile landing zones and possible locations of antiaircraft guns. Shoemaker was very concerned about ack-ack. Sitting in front of division headquarters at Camp Gorvad was a war trophy that provided a sense of ominous reality to the planners' apprehensions. It was a radar-controlled 37-mm Russian antiaircraft gun that the Cav had captured during its campaign in the A Shau Valley in early 1968. Shoemaker reasoned that if the NVA possessed, and used, 37-mm guns in the A Shau, it was likely that COSVN had stashed some inside the Cambodian sanctuaries and would use them to protect their base areas.

The next phase of the fire plan called for tactical air strikes, to be controlled by three FACs. Priority would go to suppressing any antiaircraft fire, and then the fighter bombers could go after any target of opportunity. The last group in would be Lieutenant Colonel Clark Burnett's 1st Squadron, 9th Cavalry. To keep from tipping off the Cav's interest in the Cambodian border area, Shoemaker would not permit reconnaissance flights. However, since someone had to eyeball the terrain, Brady and Shoemaker cooked up a neat little scheme: Brady, a rated aviator, would fly a Cobra on a recon mission with a second Cobra along to make it appear that it was a Cav fire team that was lost and had wandered across the border and was zipping hither and yon at treetop level trying to find its way back home. The deception plan would not have been credible had not a respectable number of fire teams gotten "lost" over the preceding year. So the two cobras skimmed over the LZs planned for the ARVN Airborne and for the Cav's 2nd Battalion, 7th Cav, and at other locations where Brady deemed it appropriate to throw some artillery shells. When he finished the recon, he gave the target data to Major Anthony Pokorny, the DivArty operations officer, who turned it into the completed fire plan that would be distributed to all the artillery batteries and converted to actual firing data.

The ground scheme of maneuver called for the three ARVN Airborne battalions to air-assault into blocking positions just north of the Fishhook. Two squadrons of the 11th ACR would roll across the border on the underside of the Fishhook and link up with the two easternmost ARVN battalions at LZs EAST and CENTER. The other ARVN Airborne battalion would link up with an Air Cav battalion a little further to the west, roughly in the vicinity of the Mimot rubber plantation area. The plan called for the 1st ARVN Armored Cavalry Regiment, an organization with a strength just above that of an American armored cavalry squadron, to move due west from An Loc, and after leaving the rubber, start busting brush enroute to the border. It, too, was to link up with the ARVN Airborne battalions. All told, about six thousand American and three thousand ARVN troops were committed to the initial raid, and not all of them were going over the border at the same time.

Until the very end, most senior officers involved in planning didn't believe Washington would authorize the border crossing. This belief held even though III Corps ARVN units under Lieutenant General Do Cao Tri had since April 14 been making limited incursions into the Parrot's Beak and Angel's Wing, albeit without American advisors.

In the White House, Nixon was still going through the motions of soliciting the opinions of his Cabinet officers, even though he had already made up his mind about going into Cambodia. He had accepted General Abrams's recommendation that a mixed American and ARVN force go into the Fishhook but had rejected the recommendation that the announcement of the incursion be handled as a routine announcement by MACV in Saigon.

The Boston Publishing Company's *Fighting for Time* volume of its *Vietnam Experience* series correctly noted that as far as

Abrams and his senior staff were concerned, it was only a very limited incursion, covering Base Area 352 in the Fishhook and the eastern part of Base Area 353 just to the west of the Fishhook; it was merely a continuation of Abrams's tactics of getting into the enemy's system. Still, there was a curious dichotomy in the affair. More than a year's experience with the grinding interdiction campaign waged by the 1st Cavalry Division should have indicated to the senior planners that armored "blitzkriegs" were scarcely the way to "work the enemy's system."

In General Davison's oral history at the U.S. Army War College, he is explicit about COSVN: "And mind you, finding COSVN headquarters was not in my mission as given me by General Abrams. He never mentioned COSVN to me." Oddly enough, however, in all of the 1st Cav's documents, the mission for the initial stage of the Cambodian operation tended to use the term "COSVN base." Its use, though, was consistent with the Cav's system of operations for the past year, as typified by this quote from the ground forces commander's Situation Report of May 2: "TF Shoemaker continues operations to interdict and neutralize COSVN base area. . . ."

It is interesting to note that in none of the planning guidance given to the Cav by either generals Abrams or Davison was the order given to find and seize COSVN headquarters. It was always assumed in the Cav that COSVN was located somewhere across the border. Radio intercept triangulations could fix the transmitter sites with some precision, but this did not necessarily mean that General Tran Van Tra was sitting in a bunker directly under the antennas. During the planning sequence, the Cav figured it was probably headed into the general vicinity of the COSVN base, and if its assaults turned over a major headquarters, that would be icing on the cake. The pulse of infantrymen throughout Vietnam always quickened when a sweep turned up a VC or NVA headquarters area, but experienced commanders knew that overrunning regimental or higher headquarters was rare.

Nearly all intelligence analysts agreed that, based on prisoner interrogations and rallier reports, COSVN consisted of a number of separate sections deliberately kept apart geographically and operationally for security, as much to keep their own people from knowing too much as to preclude damaging air raids. Richard

Nixon has taken a strong rap from critics for his apocalyptic approach to the announcement and for declaring that capture of COSVN headquarters was at the heart of the incursion's mission. But someone had to have told Nixon about COSVN, and as he and Kissinger massaged the plan of attack, the very nature of the operation made it appear that the allied forces were, in fact, trying to snare something. The use of the term "blocking forces" and the allusion to hammer-and-anvil tactics denoted the kind of massive and basically unsuccessful, multibattalion operation so dear to the hearts of the generals in 1967. So it was not surprising that the critics noticed the similarity and anticipated the same results.

The media, which wrote the instant history of the incursion, wrote derisive and critical accounts of the operation, and had special fun ridiculing the thought of American generals searching in vain for a "Pentagon East." But in their eagerness to write articles that discounted the possibility of a large communist command headquarters and insinuated that a handful of communist military geniuses were running the war in the south from a clutch of crude huts in the jungle, they never answered some key questions. No one apparently wondered where the North Vietnamese stashed their typewriters, mimeograph machines, and printing presses. COSVN never came close to matching the United States in sheer volume of paper generated, but it produced a fair number of propaganda leaflets, unit rosters, and supply requisitions, which, when captured, were enough to keep hundreds of interpreters and analysts busy.

By late Monday, April 27, most of the forces that would be involved in the first assault wave were in position or close to it. On Tuesday morning Colonel Meyer called Shoemaker on the secure phone and told him he had to set an H-hour for Thursday. Shoemaker said he answered with 0730 without really knowing what would be happening at that H-Hour. Later, MACV was informed that the ARVN thrust into the Parrot's Beak and Angel's Wing scheduled for April 30 would go as scheduled, but that the joint American and ARVN task force headed for the Fishhook would be delayed twenty-four hours and the first actual crossing of the border would have to coincide with the president's speech to the nation at 9 P.M. Thursday, April 30. (There is a thirteen-hour difference between Washington and Saigon, so if it was 9 P.M. Thursday in Washington, it was 10 A.M. Friday in Saigon.)

At Cav headquarters at Phuoc Vinh, the air of "business as usual" had to be maintained. For several weeks, the chiefs of the various media bureaus had been clamoring for a meeting with the 1st Cav brass. The bureau chiefs were unhappy that the Cav no longer was providing ready helicopter taxi service from Saigon to wherever they wanted to go in the war zone. The bureau chiefs, particularly those from the TV networks, refused to accept the information officer's explanation that the addition of the ARVN Airborne Division's airmobile requirements and the expansion of the Cav's AO was bleeding helicopter blade time to the point that all nonessential flying was curtailed. The media bosses believed that if they could go over the head of a major and deal directly with some generals, the helicopters would magically reappear at Tan Son Nhut for their convenience. An undercurrent in the request for an audience with the Cav's commander was the sense that the media were less than welcome in the Cav AO. This was particularly true after the Jack Laurence episode in early April, and the CBS bureau chief particularly wanted to speak to General Roberts personally to get his permission to let Laurence come back to the Cav.

After the bureau chiefs made a couple of attempts, a luncheon meeting was finally held in the General's Mess at Phuoc Vinh on Wednesday, April 29. Roberts and Shy Meyer hosted the luncheon and gave a generalized briefing on the Cav's interdiction campaign and why helicopters were in terribly short supply. Roberts, feeling somewhat expansive because of the impending Cambodian operation, agreed to let Jack Laurence come back and spend some more time with Charlie Company, 2nd of the 7th. The reporters even asked if the Cav had any plans to cross the borders into Cambodia, and Roberts told them, "You guys know we can't do that." The meeting ended with Roberts promising a more hospitable division for the media. It wasn't as if the Cav had erected a big barrier. It was pointed out to the bureau chiefs that it was still easy for reporters to catch a ride out of Tan Son Nhut or Bien Hoa on an Air Force fixed-wing aircraft bound for several bases within the Cav AO, and the Cav had never objected to reporters hitchhiking on choppers going out to scenes of action. This, of course, had been what the information officer had been telling them and they had been feeling deprived; now they were authoritatively deprived and it apparently felt better.

By nightfall on April 30 in Vietnam, the mission and operations order had been disseminated down to the company level of the American units and there was no longer any doubt that this was it. For security reasons, only a few top officers in the ARVN Airborne Division were aware of the role the ARVN 3rd Airborne Brigade was to play. Similarly, the 1st ARVN Armored Cavalry Regiment was operating under the belief that its attack to the west from An Loc was just another in the long series of skirmishes with the NVA in Binh Long Province.

The night before a big operation into the unknown is the longest night for a soldier. The planners and commanders have done all they can; they spend the night worrying if they have done all the right things and have not forgotten some vital piece of the puzzle. For those who will be on the cutting edge, the emotions are more elemental: "Will I survive this son-of-a-bitch tomorrow?" It all combines to make for weak bladders and loose bowels. And that's the way it was along the Cambodian border on the night of April 30, 1970.

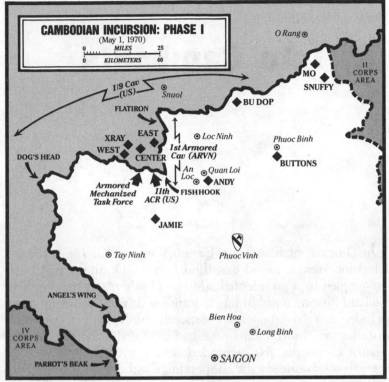

Map by John D. Talbott

This map depicts the approximate locations of the armored spearheads that rolled across the Cambodian border on the morning of May 1, 1970. Also shown are the initial landing zones for the helicopter assaults into the Fishhook.

16

Into Cambodia

On Thursday night at 9 P.M. Eastern time, millions of American television viewers found that their favorite TV shows had been pre-empted by a presidential address. On their screens they saw Richard Nixon, notes in hand, standing in front of a large map of Indochina. Nixon opened the speech mildly, correctly pointing out that the North Vietnamese had mounted a major offensive against Cambodia. He reminded Americans that he had only recently announced the impending withdrawal of another 150,000 American soldiers, and again correctly said that if Cambodia fell into North Vietnamese hands, Hanoi could use the established base areas along the Vietnamese border to endanger the lives of the remaining soldiers. Had Nixon limited his remarks to these bare facts, the reaction of his critics might not have been as strident. But he rapidly escalated his remarks to apocalyptic levels. He equated the Cambodian incursion, which he said was underway even as he was speaking, to the great battles of survival fought during the history of the republic. He also found time to stress that the main objective of the invasion was to capture COSVN. His speech has been described, with some justification, as strident, jingoistic, and divisive. He told Americans that he "had rejected all political considerations" and that he would "rather be a one-term president and do what I believe is right than to be a two-term president at the cost of seeing America become a second-rate power and to see this nation accept the first defeat in its proud one-hundred-ninety-year history."

In the 1st Cav Division's tactical operations center on the morning of May 1, Ric Ordway remembers that someone had tuned into the Armed Forces Radio broadcast of the president's speech. He said as Nixon was speaking, the various units were reporting their border crossings right on schedule. Also proceeding on schedule were student demonstrations. Within minutes after Nixon concluded his speech, there were reports of student-organized demonstrations on the campuses of two Ivy League colleges.

For Task Force Shoemaker that morning, the operation unfolded flawlessly according to plan. The thirty-six B-52 strikes thundered into the Fishhook and eastern Base Area 353. The last stick of bombs had hardly detonated when gunners pulled the lanyards of some one hundred tubes of artillery. The light and medium artillery worked over the border crossings planned for the two 11th ACR squadrons and two armored and mechanized battalions. The longer-range artillery bombarded the landing zones for the three ARVN Airborne battalions and the Cav's 2nd Battalion, 7th Cavalry. The artillery barrage lasted an hour, then three Air Force forward air controllers flying OV-10 Broncos began directing in 151 preplanned tactical air strikes. All the pilots had been briefed to be especially watchful for large-caliber antiaircraft fire and to be prepared to divert from preplanned targets to take out any flak batteries that might be operating. None were found.

When the fast movers from the Air Force cleared out of the area, Alpha and Bravo troops of the 9th Air Cav Squadron, flying at treetop level, swarmed across the border looking for juicy targets. Col. Ken Mertel, the commander of the division's aviation brigade, also flew in the lift battalion commanders along with the battalion commanders of the three ARVN Airborne battalions to do a visual recon of their landing zones. Also getting his first look at his Cambodian landing zone was Lieutenant Colonel Ed Trobaugh, commander of the 2nd Battalion, 7th Cavalry. The first of the Air Cav's LZs in Cambodia was to be named XRAY in honor of the famous battle on LZ XRAY fought by the 7th

Cavalry in the valley of the Ia Drang in November 1965. It would have been more fitting if the 1st Battalion, 7th Cavalry, had made the air-assault on XRAY. But because of the secrecy of the planning, and because the 1/7 was scattered around eastern War Zone C handling interdiction missions, the honor of being the first Cav battalion to go into Cambodia went to Trobaugh's battalion, which already was in position close to the border.

While the aerial reconnaissance was underway, the 9th Cav's Pink Teams were flitting across the Cambodian countryside looking for targets. The first good target was a truck full of troops located just south of Route 7 east of Mimot. The NVA made the usual fatal mistake of firing on the Cav's scout bird; ten North Vietnamese soldiers died for their indiscretion. Given the exceptional lethality of the Cav's Pink Teams it seemed inevitable that the first known NVA kills in Cambodia would be scored by the guys who wore the black Stetsons of the the unit they called "the real cavalry."

The ground phase of the operation kicked off on schedule and the armored units rumbled across their lines of departure into Cambodia. The 2nd Squadron of the 11th ACR had a brisk skirmish with elements of the 141st Regiment of the NVA 7th Division, killing fifty NVA soldiers while losing two Americans, the only two to die on the first day of the incursion. The mechanized infantry and armored task force, composed of two companies and the headquarters of the 2nd Battalion, 47th Infantry, reinforced by a tank company from the 2nd Battalion, 34th Armor, also had a brush with elements of the 165th Regiment of the same NVA division enroute to the task force's objective of cutting Route 7 east of Mimot.

The reason for the contacts with the NVA 7th Division so far west of the 7th's usual operational area east of the Fishhook was a manifestation of Jack Galvin's waterfall theory; the NVA attacks into Cambodia had created a vacuum along the northern Tay Ninh Province border. So the 7th had slid further to the west along the border, assuming much of the territory previously sheltering the VC 9th Division, although two battalions of the 141st Regiment had been sent north out of the 7th's old base area to assault and seize Snuol. The 9th's 271st Regiment, meanwhile, had slipped through the Cav's noose in the Dog's Head early in

April and was deep in Svay Rieng Province (Angel's Wing area), where it was fighting the incursions of the ARVN armored and mechanized columns that had kicked off their operations on April 30. The 272nd Regiment of the VC 9th Division had turned 180 degrees on its axis in mid-April and overrun the towns of Krek and Mimot, set up a major base in the Chup Plantation, and was threatening Kompong Cham, the third-largest city in Cambodia and the capital of the Cambodian province of the same name that adjoined Vietnam's Tay Ninh Province.

The airmobile plan called for the lift aircraft to pick up the troops at their scattered locations and mass enroute to target LZs, rather than tip off the enemy by premassing the forces at Quon Loi, the only American base large enough to contain them. Colonel Mertel assigned the lift of the ARVN Airborne battalions to Lieutenant Colonel David Johnson's 227th Assault Helicopter Battalion. General Shoemaker said it was a tribute to the training of the ARVN Airborne battalions that they could receive their attack missions on the run, assemble into pickup zones, and conduct effective air assaults into the Fishhook. He said that it was also a tribute to the professionalism of the lift-ship pilots, most of them young warrant officers on their first combat tour, to be able to hit all the pickup zones right on the money, lift out, and mass into the big formation almost flawlessly. Veterans of the Cav's early days said they doubted it could have been done any better in 1965 than it was in 1970. The flight path of the choppers took one huge gaggle over Quon Loi, and the GIs stood in awe as they watched forty-two Hueys and eight Cobras, roaring by at treetop level, head into Cambodia. For the troops who hadn't bothered to listen to the president's speech, it was an awesome clue that something enormous was up.

Further to the west, a heavy formation of choppers from Lieutenant Colonel Robert S. Patton's 229th Assault Helicopter Battalion thundered north across the Cambodian border, headed for a map location marked "LZ XRAY." It was similar to the countless number of combat assaults made by the members of Charlie Company, 2nd Battalion, 7th Cavalry, during their campaigning in War Zone C. This time, however, when the ships flared over the clearing, still smoking from the gunships' suppressive fire, Specialist Four Terry Hayes leaped from the skids and became, officially, the first Skytrooper to hit the ground in Cambodia. The day before, April 30, 1970, the Cav had been able to boast of being the first in Manila, Tokyo, and Pyongyang, the first U.S. division to receive the Presidential Unit Citation in Vietnam, and the only American division to have fought in all four corps tactical zones. Now, another first was recorded for the First Team—the first U.S. division to fight in Cambodia.

Bravo Company of the 2nd of the 7th followed Charlie Company into XRAY, converted it to a fire support base, and prepared to turn it over to the 2nd Battalion, 5th Cavalry, a battalion that also had historical ties to the original LZ XRAY. The 2nd of the 5th came in by Chinook and began moving east to link up with the 9th ARVN Airborne Brigade, while the 2/7 companies were later returned to the 3rd Brigade forward base at FSB BRUISER near Katum.

The first day of the great expedition into Cambodia ended quietly with all the forces in the positions plotted for them in the original plan. There had been some skirmishes but certainly no battles of the magnitude envisioned by the planners. Unfortunately, as one trooper was reported by the Boston Publishing Company's *Fighting for Time* to have said, no one had found "a guy wearing a COSVN T-shirt."

The media coverage of the incursion was moderate at first, even though the first day ended with nothing in the bag. But the mood of the press was ugly. Things had gotten off to a bad start because all the reporters felt they had been suckered into going out to cover the ARVN incursion in the Parrot's Beak. Since it had kicked off a day earlier than the Fishhook venture, Do Cao Tri's invasion was the only war in town. General Davison remembers visiting the command post of General Tri on the morning of May 1 and that it was overrun by reporters. Davison said that it was shortly before the first lift was scheduled to go into the Fishhook. "When I walked into the command post, they didn't even speak to me. They knew who I was, but they were so engrossed with General Tri's operation that they just didn't pay any attention to me at all." Davison said he hung around Tri's CP for ten or fifteen minutes, then flew on up to where the air assaults were taking place in the Fishhook.

Later in the day, after the bureau chiefs had frantically recalled their people from the ARVN operation and put them on fixed-wing birds to Quon Loi, a few of those who had visited the Cav the day before called Colonel Meyer at Cav headquarters and used some heavy-duty Anglo-Saxon words about how they had been lied to and deceived by General Roberts. Meyer did what he could to placate them and laid on a Chinook to act as a press taxi out of Quon Loi. Some of the reporters who had seen Davison earlier that morning with General Tri were still at Quon Loi when he flew in to refuel. One came up to Davison and said, "Dammit, general, you knew when you were visiting General Tri that this thing was going to happen and you saw us there and you didn't say a word to us." Davison replied, "Well, nobody asked me."

On May 1, in Washington, Nixon was visiting the Pentagon to get a firsthand briefing. In his book, *No More Vietnams*, Nixon said that as the briefers described the initial success of the operation, he noticed the map showed four areas besides the Parrot's Beak and Fishhook as occupied by communist forces. This observation probably startled his military escorts, since the map he used for his nationally televised speech the night before clearly showed several sanctuary areas other than those targeted in the initial sweep. He said he began wondering aloud whether it was possible to mount offensives against the other sanctuaries as well. He said he was told that it was possible but that the military had not offered the option because of potential negative reaction.

It was still early in the game, and the intense antiwar reaction had not yet reached Nixon's consciousness, so he projected a rough, bellicose attitude. "Let me be the judge as far as political reactions are concerned," Nixon said. "The fact is that we have already taken the political heat for this particular operation. . . . If we can substantially reduce the threat to our forces by wiping out the rest of the sanctuaries, now is the time to do it." He then issued orders to do what was necessary to knock out all the sanctuaries. Had they had the time, Thieu, Bunker, and Abrams might all have sent messages saying, "Thank you, Mr. President."

Then, having been appropriately belligerent in the war room of the Pentagon, out-toughing the generals and admirals, Nixon walked into the glare of student and congressional protest and wilted under the political heat. In short order he limited the duration of the incursion to sixty days and the limit of penetration to thirty kilometers. At this point, COSVN would have been justified in sending Nixon a cable that said, "Thank you Mr. President." Nixon had in effect provided the communists with a de facto Cambodian border thirty kilometers from the actual boundary and simultaneously told them that they did not have to worry about the methodical interdiction campaign the Cav had been waging so long and successfully in the border provinces. All the North Vietnamese had to do was play "dodge-'em" for sixty days and they would have their Cambodian playground all to themselves again.

The president's announcements about going into the other sanctuaries and about all U.S. troops having to be out of Cambodia by June 30 came as a big shock to General Shoemaker. He had stayed up in the contact area for two days, but at the end of the second day, he flew back to Quon Loi to get a hot meal. After dinner he was at his desk in the little temporary headquarters when his aide brought in a big box of administrative chores. On the top of the paper stack was a news bulletin sheet put out by the PIO, from which Shoemaker learned for the first time that he was not conducting a limited-objective, short-term raid as he originally had thought. "When we went in I believed I was running a seven-day raid," Shoemaker said. "I remembered that earlier in the day, I had run into General Davison and he had mentioned something about wanting the 11th ACR to go to Snuol. Up until that time, I had never even known that there was such a place."

Realizing that he had a rapidly widening war on his hands, Shoemaker called division headquarters on the secure phone to seek guidance. He talked first to Shy Meyer and then to Elvy Roberts. As it turned out, Roberts had some plans that had been developed by II Field Force. The raid Shoemaker thought he was leading turned out to be Phase I of a plan which was still largely "blitzkrieg" in concept. In the second phase, II Field Force wanted to have an airmobile battalion assault and seize a piece of Highway 7, then provide artillery support for the armored cavalry as it plunged northward along Route 7 to capture Snuol, a vital road junction town. Route 7 ended in Snuol, but Route 13 headed both east and north from the rubber plantation hub, and Davison figured that if the North Vietnamese intended to try to backhaul any of the materiel they had brought in from Sihanoukville or down the Ho Chi Minh Trail, their trucks would have to go through Snuol. To get the forces to accomplish this mission, Shoemaker asked Roberts to give him the 2nd Brigade so he could have a couple of battalions for his expanded mission.

The 2nd Brigade, now under the command of Colonel Carter Clarke, moved a forward CP from BUTTONS to Loc Ninh and picked up operational control of Lt. Col. James Anderson's 1st Battalion, 5th Cavalry, which had been running interdiction patterns for Kingston's 3rd Brigade in eastern War Zone C. Anderson, who had taken over the battalion in January, had been Creighton Abrams's aide before coming to the Cav and had gotten his battalion ahead of a couple of other lieutenant colonels in waiting. This placed him in a pressure-packed situation; his performance was under intense scrutiny by his peers as well as his bosses. By the time Cambodia had rolled around, Anderson had extinguished a couple of incipient racial incidents in his battalion and taken some other good leadership steps. The battalion was rock-solid when its moment came.

Late at night on May 2, Anderson huddled with Shoemaker at Quon Loi and learned that his battalion was to make an air assault into Cambodia. It was to be in the northern reaches of a place where the border ran straight as an arrow for about twenty kilometers; it was appropriately nicknamed the "Flatiron" area. This was the part of Cambodia where regiments of the NVA 7th Division would ghost into after making forays against northern Binh Long Province. An even stronger determinant for the location of Anderson's battalion was a piece of fresh intelligence just provided by one of the division's airmobile scout teams. Warrant Officer James Cyrus, a LOH driver with Bravo Troop, 1st of the 9th, spotted what appeared to be a giant supply complex. "We found the building complex almost by accident. . . . Then I spotted one hootch well camouflaged. Unless you were at treetop level, it would be almost invisible. I just followed the bamboo walks from hootch to hootch, and saw the street signs, bridges with walkways and ropes and what looked like a motor pool and lumber yard." When Shoemaker received this intelligence, he was elated. This was what the Cav was all about.

Anderson had multiple missions. One would be to provide fire support for the 11th ACR as it moved northeast on Route 7 and to block any enemy movement north and west out of the Fishhook. But his battalion's primary mission was to begin exploiting Cyrus's find. Shoemaker intended to air-assault the 1st Battalion, 12th Cavalry, now commanded by Lieutenant Colonel Norman A. Moffett, into an area just south of Anderson's position to provide mutual fire support and to aid in both the blocking action and the search patterns. Shoemaker anticipated that when the 11th ACR reached Snuol, it could use the 155-mm self-propelled howitzers of the two attacking squadrons for the necessary fire support for what he assumed could be a brisk fight to secure the airstrip.

Anderson got his air assets at 5 A.M. on May 3 so that he could retrieve his spread-out forces. After a lot of shuttle flights, he finally got all his troopers into the brigade base at Loc Ninh, fed them a hot meal, and loaded them down with three days' supplies. Then, at 10 A.M. he air-assaulted his battalion into a clearing along Route 7 that became known as LZ TERRY LYNN. Later, when the landing zone was built into a firebase, its name mysteriously became FSB NORTH. The name change didn't make any difference to the Skytroopers; they began operating just as the Cav battalion had functioned in Vietnam. Anderson set up a base defense for the artillery battery and sent two of his companies out to scour the jungle for traces of enemy that could threaten the firebase and to look for trails that could be profitable locations for ambushes. Charlie Company, commanded by Captain Kevin Corcoran, headed for the supply complex.

The 11th ACR, conditioned to moving cautiously through the jungles and mined roads and trails of War Zone C, was moving a bit too slowly for General Davison. A career tanker from the West Point class of 1939, he had learned the armored warfare business on the plains of Europe during World War II and viewed armor as a fast-moving force, a "high diddle, diddle, right up the middle" kind of movement, to ensure maximum shock action. Davison flew out to visit Starry, but the regimental commander was out visiting his troops. Davison, in reminiscing about the incident with his War College interviewer, a fellow armor officer named Dale Brudvig, noted that they had all been together in the 3rd Armored Division in Europe earlier in their careers. Davison and Brudvig had been in Combat Command A (CCA), while Starry was a tank battalion executive officer in Combat Command C. Davison left a message for Starry with the regimental executive officer that "it was high time for Starry to get his regiment moving like CCA." Said Davison, "that was exactly the needle Donn needed and the next thing I knew he had broken through to the Cambodian highway that runs east from Mimot to Snuol."

Once on the ridge line on which Route 7 was located, Starry wheeled his two squadrons (the 2nd and 3rd; his 1st Squadron was still escorting Rome Plows in War Zone C) and headed northeast toward Snuol. They moved fast, but were temporarily stymied by three blown bridges on the only road in the area. Lieutenant Colonel Scott B. Smith, the 1st Cav's division engineer and the commander of the division's 8th Engineer Battalion, had reconned the bridges with Major William Good, from the 11th ACR. They flew over and around the three small streams in a LOH and came back to Starry to inform him that two of the streams could be bridged with armored-vehicle-launched bridges (AVLBs) but the third stream was too wide. When the Cav squadrons were in a position to provide security, Smith would arrange for Flying Cranes to fly in an M4T6 bridge, which comes in sections and needs a lot of equipment, time, and hard work to assemble. Starry finally had his folks moving and was fretting about having to hold up the advance until the bridge was in.

Someone in the 11th's advance units along the stream began carefully walking the embankments and found a place upstream of the road where there would be about twelve inches of footing for the far end of the bridge when it was extended. Captain Sewell Menzell's G Troop was the first across, carefully inching the ACAVs over the tenuous span and nervously watching the narrow foothold crumble and threaten to cave in. Lieutenant Colonel Brookshire, the 2nd Squadron commander, put all of his squadron's ACAVs across first and brought the Patton tanks across last, figuring, as Starry remembered later, that if the bridge collapsed, eventually the M4T6 bridge would be in and tank retrievers could pull his tank out of the gulch. But the fragile foothold held, even for the tanks, and the squadron was across and rolling.

While the 11th ACR was on occasion rolling along Route 7 at speeds of up to sixty kilometers per hour, Charlie Company was going a bit slower. The undergrowth under the triple canopy jungle was the thickest that any of the company's veterans could remember, and progress was measured in feet per hour. The company, exhausted from beating against the jungle all afternoon, set up a night defensive position at a location that was later determined to be within one kilometer of the perimeter of the supply installation. So impenetrable was the jungle undergrowth that it took Corcoran's company the better part of the morning of May 4 to reach the perimeter. As Charlie Company approached a clearing at the edge of the base, the point squad received light AK-47 fire from two of the enemy's defensive bunkers. The skirmish cost the NVA four dead, and there were no American casualties. The door to the huge complex was wide open and Charlie Company was about to enter.

Meanwhile, the 11th ACR was moving so swiftly that Starry said he had outdistanced his artillery support. The 2nd Squadron held up outside Snuol until the 3rd Squadron caught up and the supporting artillery batteries were positioned. The 3rd Squadron had the mission of slipping around to the west of Snuol and cutting Route 13, while Brookshire's 2nd Squadron was tagged to assault and retake the town itself. In late April, the two battalions of the NVA 141st Regiment had attacked Snuol's small Cambodian army detachment and overrun the defenders after inflicting considerable damage on the town with rocket and mortar fire.

Brookshire's plan was to avoid a frontal assault on the town by refusing to use Route 7 as an axis of advance, the most direct way into the town from the south. In this way he minimized the enemy's opportunity to force the squadron's mechanized force into a costly battle in a built-up area. Instead, he had his squadron slip to the east through the rubber plantations and approach the Snuol airstrip from the south, giving stern instructions to his troopers that they were to keep their tracks off the sodded airstrip to preserve it for future use. The most controversial part of his attack order came when he said: "If you take fire, return it. If you take fire and you look like you've got prepared positions, back 'em out—shoot and back out." He said the next step would be to call in tactical air strikes and gunships to work over the NVA positions. Starry concurred in the plan, assuming that the NVA would not stick around inside a town when the Americans had the capability of surrounding and isolating the enemy fighting force.

The airstrip was the key to Snuol. Once again, as they had at Bu Gia Map, the NVA thought they had the perfect trap for the airmobile forces. The airstrip, the NVA commander believed, would be an irresistible target for the Air Cav. So the 12.7-mm antiaircraft machine guns were dug into firing pits around the airstrip; an airmobile assault force would be badly shredded before the antiaircraft defenses could be subdued. Fixed to fire into the sky, the heavy machine guns were useless in the NVA defense against the sudden onrush of the American armor. The fight at the airstrip didn't amount to much. The NVA hadn't counted on dealing with an armored cavalry squadron instead of an airmobile infantry battalion and faded away, probably to prepared positions in the center of the town. During the skirmish at the airstrip, Colonel Starry and Major Fred Franks, the 2nd Squadron operations officer, seized an opportunity to play grunt and paid a price. A defiant NVA soldier refused to be coaxed out of a bunker and punctuated his refusal with a grenade. The explosion shattered the heel of Major Franks and peppered Starry with fragments. Both were evacuated, but Starry's wounds were not serious and he was back in command of the Blackhorse Regiment by the end of the month.

After Starry was evacuated, Brookshire turned his attention to the town of Snuol. The NVA had been outwitted at the airstrip, but the enemy got even in the central marketplace of the town. It already had been heavily damaged when the NVA assaulted it in mid-April with rocket and mortar fire, and the rubble made excellent firing positions for the NVA defenders. When Brookshire's tracks moved into the central marketplace, they received a fusillade of RPG and machine-gun fire from prepared positions. The 2nd Squadron tracks, per instructions, returned fire and backed out, and tactical air was called in. The bombs and cannon fire leveled the buildings in the central marketplace, and when Brookshire's men moved back in, there was no resistance and no dead NVA, just the bodies of four civilians, including a woman and a girl. The North Vietnamese had suckered the American force into an overreaction that could be exploited as fodder for the communist propaganda machine.

Of course, the newsmen along for the ride were more than happy to oblige. The novelty of the border crossing was over, and in tune with the headlines in the United States about campus protest demonstrations, the coverage of the incursion was becoming increasingly critical. At Snuol, reporters, obviously seeking another Ben Tre kind of story ("We had to destroy the town to save it.") conveniently overlooked the damage that had been done by the NVA in its conquest of the town and reported that the American armor had leveled the town. While the central marketplace was indeed destroyed, many other commercial buildings along Route 13, the main road through the town, were intact, as was the entire residential area. So pervasive were reports about the "destruction" of Snuol that, years later, apparently using press reports for its historical research, the Boston Publishing Company would write that "American troops used a new term after that engagement—'to snuol' meant obliterate."

But the United States had set itself up for the bad press. From the outset the operation tended to the hyperbolic, from the presidential announcement to the grand scheme that made it appear that a giant net would soon rid America and South Vietnam of their North Vietnamese tormenters in Cambodia. For many reporters, when the net came up embarrassingly empty after the first two days, it was simply another example of American excess that failed. Even Jack Laurence, who had promised to be on his best behavior if allowed to return to cover Charlie Company, 2nd of the 7th, could not resist an obvious jab at American strategy with a report from Al Rice's company.* "The contact is scattered and insignificant." Laurence intoned in a voice-over. "The elaborate military trap having failed, the mission changes to a search for enemy supplies."

---

* Jack Laurence spent nearly a month with Charlie Company and out of the hundreds of yards of film shot came an hour-long report on CBS News entitled *The World of Charlie Company*. Anyone wishing to get a realistic look at the war waged by the grunts of the 1st Air Cavalry Division in April and May of 1970 shouldn't waste time with the propaganda films produced by Hollywood that masquerade as the real story. Obtain, instead, a videotape of *The World of Charlie Company*.

Map by John D. Talbott

Phase II of the incursion occurred May 4–5, when the 11th Armored Cavalry made a dash to Snuol and two battalions of the 1st Air Cavalry made combat assaults into an area where they could support the armored thrust. In the process, "the City," the first of the great cache areas, was discovered.

For Charlie Company, 1st of the 5th, that search started on the afternoon of May 4. Accompanying Charlie Company was a member of the division photo team, Sergeant Dean Sharp. It was Sharp who first recorded photographically the most incredible sight any of the Skytroopers had ever seen. The complex was three kilometers long and almost two kilometers wide. It also seemed deserted. "It was eerie and spooky at first," Sharp remembered. As Charlie Company's grunts fanned out into the complex, the hair on everybody's neck was standing on end as they expected any minute to meet fierce resistance. This was, after all, a prize of the first magnitude. The sheer size of the complex dictated its name—"the City." Then the search turned over a bunker full of old SKS rifles, always a prized souvenir because troops could legally bring an SKS home but could not come home with the fully automatic AK-47.

Then they found a bunker with *new* SKS rifles, and the great Cambodian souvenir hunt was on.

17

Cleaning Out the Caches

Even as the 1st of the 5th began exploiting "the City," General Roberts received a mission from II Field Force that would require a major realignment of his forces. The 1st Cavalry Division was going to be part of a major MACV and RVNAF offensive against all of the North Vietnamese sanctuaries in Cambodia. The 25th Infantry Division, the 3rd Brigade of the 9th Division, and a brigade of the 4th Division in II Corps would join the 1st Cav and 11th ACR as the American forces committed to the offensive. Abrams doubtless would also have liked to hurl the sizable American forces in I Corps against the Laotian sanctuaries, interdicting the Ho Chi Minh Trail in the process. Tragically, Nixon hadn't been quite that bold or prescient.

In the 1st Cav, on May 5, Roberts had four airmobile battalions committed into Cambodia under two brigade headquarters, plus two squadrons of the 11th ACR and the two borrowed battalions, the 2/47th Mech (9th Division) and 3/34th Armor (25th Division). All had been loosely confederated under the aegis of Task Force Shoemaker. But the task force had been created to handle only a limited excursion. Shoemaker had been told not to worry about the time-consuming task of rendering reports—the division staff would monitor all radio nets and make the pro forma written reports for Task Force Shoemaker, so all he had to do was run the operation from the right seat of his command chopper. Which is what he did.

But now, as the scope of the Cambodian incursion broadened, Roberts recognized it was time to fold Shoemaker's task force back into the full division. So on May 5, the major realignment of divisional forces and the dissolution of Task Force Shoemaker took place. The realignment entailed "chopping" subordinate units (changing their operational control) between larger command headquarters and redrawing major unit boundaries. Which brigade got what mission was based primarily on the location of the brigade headquarters.

The Cav's new mission called for it to continue to exploit the caches it already had discovered and also to assault into Base Area 351 in northeast Phuoc Long Province. The 2nd Brigade was the logical control headquarters for this add-on mission, so Colonel Clarke turned over his two battalions (1/5 and 1/12) in the northern Fishhook to the 3rd Brigade, closed his advance CP at Loc Ninh, and moved back to BUTTONS. To provide him with the forces necessary to do the job, Roberts gave him the 5th Battalion, 7th Cavalry, from the 1st Brigade. The 5/7 had two days previously beaten back an attack on its firebase (WOOD) by a battalion of the 95-C Regiment. WOOD was located only a few kilometers from the old locations of ILLINGWORTH and JAY in the Dog's Head, and the attack by the Ninety-Five-Charlie on an American firebase in Vietnam while the Cambodian incursion was underway was ample proof that the North Vietnamese were still around and still concerned about their Vietnam infiltration routes. Additional reinforcement for the 2nd Brigade came in the form of the 5th Battalion, 12th Infantry, a straight-leg infantry outfit out of the 199th Light Infantry Brigade from an AO near Saigon.

The 3rd Brigade headquarters, moved out of its advance CP at Katum, turned over all its battalions to the 1st Brigade and went back to Quon Loi. From there, the brigade took over the 1/5 Cav's exploitation of the City and a huge motor-pool operation discovered by the 1/12 Cav.

The 1st Brigade, whose battalions had remained in War Zone C during the initial thrust, was given operational control of the 2/7 and 2/5 Cav, the battalions that had initially gone in under 3rd Brigade control; of the two attached mechanized and armored battalions; and of the 3rd Brigade of the ARVN Airborne Division with four of its battalions. It was a sizable span of control and far exceeded the capabilities of Colonel Ochs, the 1st Brigade commander. George Casey was back in-country and had his second star, giving the 1st Cav the added distinction of having a pair of two-star generals in the AO together. Abrams wanted to wait until the Cav completed its realignment and had the situation stabilized before making a change of command, so he asked Roberts to stay in the saddle until May 12. But Casey was all too aware of the shortcomings of Ochs and told Roberts that if he didn't relieve Ochs, Casey would do so first thing when he assumed command. Roberts also got a powerful stimulus for action when General Davison told him that Ochs simply didn't have a handle on what was happening in his AO. At 6:30 A.M. on May 6, Bob Kingston got a call at his 3rd Brigade CP and was told, "Report to Tay Ninh by ten-hundred hours. You are to assume command of the 1st Brigade."

Colonel Ken Mertel, the aviation group commander, who had commanded the 1st of the 8th in 1965 during his first tour with the Cav, was detached to take temporary command of the 3rd Brigade. Eventually, the colonel originally scheduled to replace Kingston on a normal rotation, Colonel Joseph R. Franklin, arrived and Mertel went back to the aviation group in time to fly the division out of Cambodia. Mertel was able to stay with the brigade long enough to watch the loot pour out of the City. The volume was so great that it was impossible to backhaul it by helicopter, although it seemed that every chopper crew in Vietnam found an excuse to fly into the cache site to barter for souvenirs. Eventually, a crude road was carved out of the jungle to link the City with Route 13 north of Loc Ninh.

Despite the size and importance of the City and the slightly smaller supply dump and motor pool found by the 1/12 Cav about ten kilometers south of the City, the area had never been marked as a communist base area. Almost every map of the border zones sported meticulously drawn rectangles or trapezoid designs straddling the border with the number of the base area carefully labeled within. Base Area 351, the base area drawn over the Fishhook, encompassed only the tip of the projection into Vietnam. The vast area in and around the Flatiron had no base area designation, nor had it been particularly well targeted by the secret B-52 bombing. So for the sake of easy reference, everyone called the area the "upper Fishhook."

The inventory of supplies and equipment taken out of the City filled a single-spaced typewritten sheet of paper. The loot from the supply dump found by the 1st of the 12th, which was never graced with a name, took a half-page inventory sheet. Loading the supplies on choppers and trucks was backbreaking labor for the Skytroopers, but eventually ARVN labor companies were brought in to help out. The troops, who used to get excited over a cache with a dozen weapons and a few bags of rice, quickly became jaded by the surfeit of war materiel and foodstuffs.

But even the most blasé Skytrooper could not help but be impressed by the elaborate rest-and-recuperation (R and R) center they found in the heart of the City. They found a beautifully landscaped area, with wooden buildings and two elaborately furnished mess halls. Despite the communists' professions of egalitarianism, the messes were designated as "VIP and Officers' Mess" and "Enlisted Mess."

The grunts got their biggest surprise when they moved behind the main complex. There they found a spacious, well-constructed swimming pool. The sheer magnitude of the facilities led some senior officers to make the intemperate observation that the City might have contained COSVN. No evidence was found that Tran Van Tra had ever set up his headquarters here, but because of the large number of classrooms and training aides found at the City, it appeared that the Cav had ripped the training and R-and-R portion off the elusive COSVN T-shirt. And with the 1st of the 12th's discoveries, the Cav may also have gotten a fair-sized chunk of the motor transportation operation as well.

On May 6 the 2nd Brigade kicked off the Cav's next major border crossing by sending two battalions on combat assaults into locations just across the border. Now that the Cav had been across the border for a few days, it was no longer operating totally in the dark as it had been on the initial crossing. The reconnaissance squadron had Pink Teams swarming all over the landscape, and the Pink Terms had some interesting sightings just outside the magic-marker outline of Base Area 351. When Colonel Clarke picked the sites for the two new firebases in Cambodia the decision was based on some reasonably hard intelligence. The scouts had spotted some vehicular movement on trails just off Cambodian Highway 14, which was an extension of Vietnam's Route 14-A from Bu Dop and meandered north and east toward the Cambodian town of O Rang. Additionally, Major Burton Patrick, the brigade S-2, had accumulated a file of information provided by the SOG patrols about sightings of supply caches. Patrick was one of the few officers in the Cav who had faith in SOG intelligence. "When it was all over," he said, "we found their spot reports of caches and trail systems had been within 1,000 meters of being right on the money."

So Clarke sent Lieutenant Colonel Maurice Edmunds's 5th Battalion, 7th Cavalry, into an LZ named BROWN about three kilometers north of the border and two kilometers west of Route 14-A. He directed Lieutenant Colonel Francis Ianni's 2nd Battalion, 12th Cavalry, to make a combat assault into a landing zone about ten kilometers north of BROWN. Ianni named the new firebase MYRON, in honor of Major Myron Diduryk, the former operations officer of the battalion, who had been killed a month earlier. Diduryk had died when Ianni ordered the command chopper to go into an abandoned firebase to check out a North Vietnamese soldier the door gunner had just killed. The abandoned bunkers contained some other NVA who opened up when the chopper touched down, and one of the AK slugs hit Diduryk while he sat in the chopper. The incident badly corroded Ianni's relationship with the battalion. He had replaced Lieutenant Colonel Harold Iverson, a solid and compassionate commander, and Diduryk had been equally well liked by the officers and men. Ianni was the quintessential hardnose and many members of the battalion blamed Ianni for Diduryk's death, assuming that the S-3 wouldn't have flown into the old firebase. They didn't know Diduryk. Courageous beyond measure, Myron Diduryk, a native of the Ukraine who had emigrated to the United States at the age of twelve, had won the unbounded admiration of Colonel Hal Moore, the hero of the original LZ XRAY, for Diduryk's actions as a company commander in the Ia Drang in 1965.

Once on the ground at MYRON, after the companies of the battalion had scouted the terrain around the firebase thoroughly, Ianni sent Delta Company, under the command of Captain James

F. Johnson, his best company commander, to start checking out the sightings of the Pink Teams. On the morning of May 8, Delta Company made a combat assault into a clearing about four kilometers east of MYRON and started a southward trek through the heavy undergrowth. The lead element took some fire, and Johnson, leaving his trailing platoon in a tiny perimeter with the company rucksacks, fanned the remainder of his company out into a skirmish line and assaulted the NVA firing positions. The enemy resistance ended—temporarily—and Delta Company found itself at the edge of what appeared to be a modest arms and ammunition cache.

But the soldiers of the NVA rear service group that was guarding the cache didn't just fade away, and having the company mostly surrounded, poured in heavy fire while counterattacking in groups of twos and threes. Johnson formed his platoons into a tight perimeter, set up a temporary CP by a stack of ammo, and got busy calling in all the firepower available to a grunt company commander.

The firefight lasted well into the evening. Ianni got his recon platoon onto the ground at the original LZ, and by radio, Johnson guided the platoon leader, Lieutenant Jimmy Hudnall, into his perimeter. Hudnall's platoon took some casualties as he fed his men onto line to reinforce the men of Delta. The NVA finally broke contact at nightfall, but Ianni was taking no chances; he helilifted his Charlie Company into the original LZ. The reinforcing company made its way to the location of Delta's left-behind platoon and the company coiled there for the night. The two companies spent a spooky night, not quite sure what the NVA might try after sunrise.

As it turned out, only a few harmless shots were exchanged in the morning with some stay-behind forces, and the 2nd of the 12th owned an ammunition and arms cache. The cache was big; in fact, it was probably the largest communist ammunition and arms cache ever captured during any phase of the Indochina war. Some Skytrooper with a bent for irony dubbed it "Rock Island East" after the U.S. arsenal of the same name in Illinois. The cost to the battalion was seven killed and twenty wounded. Thirty-some NVA bodies were found in the contact area, but as Colonel Clarke told the newsmen who flocked to see the treasures of Rock

An important component of the 1st Air Cavalry Division's ability to maintain a chokehold on NVA supply lines across the 150-mile frontage of the northern rim of III Corps was the presence of units like the 11th Armored Cavalry Regiment. Two squadrons of the 11th ACR were under continuous operational control of the 1st Cav from early April 1969 until the Cambodian incursion was completed. Here a Blackhorse crewman, wearing a CVC helmet (armored crewman communications helmet) keeps a wary eye on the jungle. (*U.S. Army photo—John Talbott collection*)

The addition of two brigades of the ARVN Airborne Division to the interdiction forces along the Cambodian border was invaluable in throttling the NVA supply lines. But the ARVN had to be taught the techniques of airmobility. Here two Skytroopers teach an ARVN sergeant how to rig a sling load of 155-mm howitzer shells and how to guide a Flying Crane in for the pickup. (*U.S. Army photo by Len Fallscheer—Author's collection*)

The big airstrip at Quon Loi was the ideal location to mass helicopters for the air assaults into Cambodia. Hueys of the 227th Assault Helicopter Battalion wait for the word to fly out to ARVN Airborne Division firebases to pick up the forces that would make the initial assault into Cambodia. (*U.S. Army photo by Dean Sharp—Dean Sharp collection*)

Later, when the scope of the Cambodian operation broadened, the Cav's 2nd Brigade launched air assaults into target areas north of Bu Dop. Combat photographer Len Fallscheer was with the 2nd Brigade and took this dramatic shot of a lift settling into a landing zone. (*U.S. Army photo by Len Fallscheer—Author's collection*)

Another 1st Cavalry combat photographer who accompanied assault forces was Dean Sharp, who rode into Cambodia toward Mimot with an armored task force composed of elements of the 2nd Battalion, 47th Infantry, U.S. 9th Division, and the 2nd Battalion, 34th Armor, 25th Division. In the top photo, the armored personnel carriers wheel to the right and blaze away at NVA pickets in the rubber. In the bottom photo, an M-48 tank charges forward past the deployed APCs and prepares to roll into position alongside another tank already engaging the enemy. (U.S. Army photos by Dean Sharp—Dean Sharp collection)

Photographer Sharp left the armored column in time to join the 1st Battalion, 5th Cavalry, his old outfit when he was a grunt, just as Charlie Company reached the perimeter of "the City." Sharp walked in with the reinforcing unit, Echo Company. This photo illustrates the density of the jungle surrounding "the City." (*U.S. Army photo by Dean Sharp—Dean Sharp collection*)

As Charlie Company's platoons spread out to explore "the City," there was a flurry of fire. Captain Kevin Corcoran is caught in a pose familiar to all combat leaders in Vietnam—a radio telephone handset at each ear—as the commander tries to find out what's happening from subordinate units on one radio "push" (frequency) and keeps his boss informed on the other. (*U.S. Army photo by Dean Sharp—Dean Sharp collection*)

A Skytrooper from Charlie Company warily explores an arms-storage hootch. The long boxes to his rear contained 120-mm mortar tubes and the boxes to his left stored the thirty-four-pound mortar shells. *(U.S. Army photo by Dean Sharp—Dean Sharp collection)*

Major General Elvy Roberts, in one of his last visits to the field before relinquishing command of the 1st Cavalry Division to Major General George Casey, talks to a Charlie Company platoon leader near the helicopter pad where the tons of arms and ammunition were being backhauled. *(U.S. Army photo by Dean Sharp—Dean Sharp collection)*

A Skytrooper from the 1st of the 5th Cav manhandles a rocket motor for a 122-mm rocket. The origin of the rocket is easy to determine—at the base of the motor are the initials CCCP. (*U.S. Army photo by Dean Sharp—Dean Sharp collection*)

A platoon sergeant from Charlie Company holds up a brand-new SKS rifle. Even when used and worn these rifles were prime souvenirs. Dean Sharp said that once the word got out, every chopper crew in the Cav who could find an excuse to fly into "the City" did so in an attempt to dicker with the grunts for a new rifle. (*U.S. Army photo by Dean Sharp—Dean Sharp collection*)

Charlie Company, 2nd Battalion, 7th Cavalry, was the first 1st Air Cav unit to air-assault into Cambodia, but it never found the kind of loot that other units did. Here, Captain Al Rice works a radio amid a few of the NVA weapons his company found. Rice's company was the subject of CBS newsman John Laurence's hour-long documentary, "The World of Charlie Company." (*U.S. Army photo by James McCabe—John Talbott collection*)

An in-depth search of "the City" brought forth this twin-barrel 14.5-mm antiaircraft gun. It was the potential of this kind of firepower that made General Robert Shoemaker and his planners very wary during the initial plans for the incursion. Strangely, the communists never employed these powerful weapons against the allies during the incursion. (*U.S. Army photo—Ric Ordway collection*)

One of the trucks captured by the 1st Batalion, 12th Cavalry, in "the Motor Pool," a huge cache area near the battalion's firebase, FSB EVANS. Besides toting ammo and supplies, these Russian-built trucks served as prime movers for the tube and antiaircraft artillery that the communists had already started to stash along the frontier in preparation for a major conventional offensive against South Vietnam. (*U.S. Army photo—Ric Ordway collection*)

Small landing zones were blown in the jungle so choppers could get in and backhaul material out of the caches. It was hot, backbreaking labor, and the grunts despised it. They didn't mind the opportunity to grab legitimate souvenirs, but they could not understand why such an effort was made to evacuate seemingly useless arms and ammunition. The excessive secrecy of the Nixon administration kept the forces in contact from knowing that their work was helping arm the Cambodian forces for their fight against the NVA. (*U.S. Army photos—Author's collection*)

Lieutenant Colonel Frank Ianni (center, with map), commander of the 2nd Battalion, 12th Cavalry, whose Delta Company fought its way into a gigantic weapons cache known as "Rock Island East," tells visiting brass how big the cache was. At far left is Major General George Casey, commander of the 1st Air Cav. General William Rosson, the deputy commander of MACV, is to Ianni's immediate right. The tall colonel to Rosson's left is Carter Clarke, 2nd Brigade commander. The captain to his left is John Hottell, Casey's aide. *(U.S. Army photo—Author's collection)*

As Nixon's deadline for withdrawal from Cambodia neared, the Cav started the painful task of extracting from contact areas. Here, a scout team from the division's Ranger company prepares to board a helicopter while the last man pulls rear-guard security. (*U.S. Army photo—John Talbott collection*)

As Cav Pink Teams provided air cover, and artillery from nearby FSB MO stood at the ready, Skytroopers from Bravo Company, 2nd Battalion, 12th Cavalry, were the last Americans to leave Cambodia. A company NCO struggles to keep a safety line taut so the troops fording the monsoon-swollen Dak Jerman River will not be swept away by the swift current. (*U.S. Army photo by James McCabe—Author's collection*)

Under leaden skies and a persistent drizzle at Arlington National Cemetery, a caisson bearing the body of Major General George Casey moves with stately finality to his final resting place. The horse-drawn caisson is escorted by six general officers, the honorary pall-bearers. Below, these generals, five of them former commanders of the 1st Air Cavalry Division, render final honors to a departed soldier. The history of airmobility in the United States Army is represented in this picture. From right, Lieutenant Generals Harry W. O. Kinnard, John Tolson, George Forsythe, and John Norton, Major Generals Charles Gettys and Elvy Roberts. (*U.S. Army photos—Author's collection*)

Island East, the Cav wasn't into body counting. What counted, Clarke said, were the enemy's supplies.

As the exploration continued with Charlie and Delta companies sharing a perimeter defense, it was found that the cache was about one thousand meters long and some five hundred meters wide. Unlike most of the other caches found by the Cav in Cambodia, all of the stuff in Rock Island East was above ground on wooden pallets and covered with plastic sheeting. There was evidence that it had been placed there recently, and intelligence officers theorized that this may have been the hastily prepared evacuation area for the supplies threatened by the Cav's rapid advance into northeast Phuoc Long Province after cutting the Jolley Trail. That Base Area 351 had been one of the principal feeders into the Vietnam infiltration trail system, and that the Cav was the major impediment to the movement of those supplies, was confirmed by the signs at the heads of trails. Some read: "Don't use these trails." Others said, "Beware of rolling thunder and the helicopter soldiers."

As had happened at the City, engineers cut a road into the site from Route 14-A and CIDG, and local-hire stevedore units shared in the drudgery of backhauling the 326 tons of arms and ammunition. There were 787 individual weapons, including a number of rifles that were going to disappear into personal caches, along with 210 of the prized K-54 pistols. The cache also contained more than one thousand of the Soviet-type 85-mm gun rounds. These were for the Soviet 85-mm (D-44) field gun, which had not yet been seen in the southern battlefields. In other caches, Skytroopers found tank gun ammunition. These were grim warning signs that the North Vietnamese had plans to escalate the war to another level some time in the future.

The Cav's jump into Base Area 351 was just one of a number of allied thrusts into the Cambodian sanctuaries in early May as MACV worked fast to beat both the oncoming monsoon and Nixon's timetable. The 3rd Brigade of the U.S. 9th Division rolled into the extreme tip of the Parrot's Beak, which was only a short distance from the brigade's normal AO in Long An Province southwest of Saigon.

Further north in II Corps, a brigade of the 4th Infantry Division, which was in the early stages of a redeployment stand-down, was hastily reassembled, reinforced with a battalion from the 173rd Airborne Brigade, and with ARVN forces from the ARVN 22nd and 23rd divisions plus the 2nd Ranger Group and the 2nd Armored Brigade, sent west into Cambodia. The operations in II Corps were called Binh Tay I, II, and III and involved raids into the sanctuaries west of Pleiku and Ban Me Thuot. One of these was the area behind the Chu Pong Massif into which members of the NVA 325-B Division, after having been mauled by the 1st Cavalry Division in the Ia Drang, had fled for sanctuary.

The Binh Tay operations did not capture anything close to the volume of equipment and supplies netted further south in the Cambodian caches opposite III Corps. What allied forces found were scattered caches in small transshipment areas. There had been no interdiction campaign in II Corps that corresponded to the methodical rooting out of enemy supply dumps that occurred throughout 1969 in III Corps. Most of the enemy supplies were concealed in caches in the formidable Annamite mountain range separating the coastal rice-growing regions from the western plateau.

The RVNAF forces in IV Corps had launched Operation Cuu Long, which involved several limited-objective thrusts into Cambodia from Chau Doc and Kien Phong provinces and one long drive with a fairly formidable task force. This force consisted of elements of the ARVN 9th and 21st infantry divisions, five armored cavalry squadrons, and a riverine force that included both RVNAF and U.S Navy units. For the U.S. elements, the drive stopped at the thirty-kilometer limiting line, but the RVNAF forces forged westward on both sides of the Mekong River into Phnom Penh, where the river's course changed to a north-south orientation. Then, at the request of the Lon Nol government, the RVNAF task force kept on moving up the Mekong to relieve the pressure on Kompong Cham. This action was coordinated with a deep and swift thrust by General Do Cao Tri's ARVN III Corps forces through Krek and on into the Chup Plantation, to catch the NVA 9th Division in a pincers. Hanoi had never wavered in its drive to conquer Cambodia, even as the allied units began tearing up the NVA rear areas along the border. But this drive seriously disrupted the NVA and Khmer Rouge offensive and bought a substantial amount of time for the Lon Nol government.

As the Cav's 2nd Brigade was moving against Base Area 351 on May 6, Lieutenant Colonel Ma Son Nhon loaded two battalions of his 9th Regiment of the 5th ARVN Division and made combat assaults into Cambodia in the vicinity of Base Area 350. This base area, directly north of Loc Ninh, was the starting point for the Serges Jungle Highway and Adams Road infiltration routes. During the first few days contacts were light, but by May 21, after finding numerous caches, the ARVN forces, which now included the 1st Armored Cavalry Squadron, began hitting stiffer resistance from elements of the VC 5th Division. When the smoke cleared from the battlefield, the ARVN troops had captured a hospital complex capable of providing medical treatment for five hundred men. Another piece of the COSVN T-shirt got ripped away.

The U.S. 25th Division got its share of Cambodian action with a three-phase operation. At first light on May 6, the 3rd Battalion of the 22nd Infantry was combat-assaulted from its Vietnam home on FSB WOOD to a place called Taasuos Village about six kilometers inside Cambodia in Base Area 354 south of the Dog's Head. The airhead was later reinforced by two mechanized infantry battalions, the 1st of the 5th Infantry and the 2nd of the 22nd Infantry. They made sporadic contacts but didn't overrun any large arms and ammunition caches. They did uncover 270 tons of rice and ripped up acres of bunker complexes, complete with classrooms and mess halls. The incursion in Base Area 354 pretty much confirmed what intelligence had always suspected: it was used primarily for rest and retraining.

Phase II of the operation was aimed for Base Area 707, just north of the Dog's Head, and kicked off on May 9. Three battalions were helilifted into the base area and found hundreds of bunkers, tons of rice, and what appeared to be the remains of a major headquarters. The Tropic Lightning troopers found in the base camp typewriters, a mimeograph machine, and generators, as well as a hospital complex. The location of the headquarters complex made it likely that it was once used by the 1st NVA Division and later by the VC 9th Division. More than four hundred tons of rice were discovered in Base Area 707, and evacuating the two-hundred-pound bags from the caches inside the dense triple canopy jungle was an exercise in thankless labor. The troops would have preferred to break open the sacks and pour JP-4 on the rice to render it inedible for the NVA, but senior officers could not countenance destroying food when the refugee camps desperately needed every grain of rice available.

Phase III of the 25th Division incursion began on May 17 when it began operating in the western portion of Base Area 353. The eastern part had been the site of the initial assaults by the Cav and ARVN Airborne. Just west of those original LZs, the 1st Battalion, 5th Infantry, a mechanized outfit, hit some resistance. The battalion pulled back until an Arc Light was laid in, and then swept through the area, finding bunkers, classrooms, and one of the largest communications caches of the war, plus tons of documents. General Davison later declared that his troops had gotten another piece of COSVN. When General Tran Van Tra finally ended his trek from the Fishhook into the interior of Cambodia well beyond the Mekong River, all the guy with the COSVN T-shirt had left was a neck band and some tatters.

In the meantime, Maury Edmunds's battalion had been threshing around FSB BROWN essentially drilling dry holes when brigade received fresh intelligence that there might be a lucrative target to the north of Rock Island East. A scout bird had been fired at from a village, so Edmunds was directed to put in a company. This LZ was named NEIL, and it, too, was gradually transformed into a firebase. The 5th of the 7th pulled entirely out of BROWN by midday of May 12. At 2nd Brigade, Major Patrick's intelligence people got a radio intercept from an NVA unit north of BROWN. Subsequent radio intercepts indicated that the NVA knew that the firebase was now deserted, and a North Vietnamese force was ordered to move swiftly to that location during the night.

With that piece of intelligence, Colonel Clarke had to make a move. He had already committed Jack Galvin's 1st of the 8th to a supporting firebase named MO right on the Vietnam side of the border to provide artillery fire support for MYRON and NEIL. But providing security at the airstrip at Bu Gia Map was the 5th Battalion, 12th Infantry, which had been borrowed from

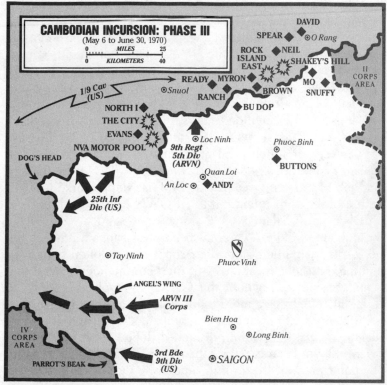

Map by John D. Talbott

This map shows the approximate locations of the major cache areas discovered in Cambodia between May 6 and June 30. It also shows the thrusts of the U.S. 25th Infantry Division into the base areas adjoining War Zone C, the armored attacks by the ARVN III Corps units in the Parrot's Beak, and the quick foray by the 3rd Brigade of the U.S. 9th Division. Off the map to the upper right is the area in II Corps where the U.S. 4th Division and ARVN units crossed the border. Also not shown on this map are the ARVN thrusts into Cambodia from the IV Corps area.

the 199th Light Brigade. Just before darkness, two companies of the 5/12 Infantry and four tubes of artillery were flown by Chinook from FSB SNUFFY at Bu Gia Map to BROWN. The action by the Cav went unnoticed by the NVA and after midnight, Patrick later said, a battalion of the 174th Regiment came ditty bopping down the trail, virtually four abreast at port arms, only to be met by a hail of fire from the firebase. The NVA scattered in all directions and the battalion leaders tried to pull their troops back together and stage some kind of attack on BROWN. But the NVA never was much good at staging ad hoc attacks and the affair fizzled out before daylight. Since the ARVN were doing a good job of providing security at Bu Gia Map, Clarke brought the rest of the 12th Infantry into BROWN to help keep the VC 5th Division off balance.

Cambodian soldiers who had been press-ganged into helping the North Vietnamese store their supplies were often helpful in pointing out cache locations. But most commanders agreed that locating caches throughout the Cav's AO involved reacting to strong enemy pressure more than getting good intelligence.

On May 23, the grunts of B Company, 5th of the 7th, were slogging their way up a rain-drenched slope known on the map as Hill 428 and started taking heavy small-arms and RPG fire. The point man hit the ground, and as he did his hand struck a piece of metal. He pulled the metal and spotted a hole in the ground. He jumped up to charge forward but a burst from an RPD cut him down. Eventually, the company, reinforced by the battalion recon platoon, took the hill and the NVA slipped away into the jungle.

The dead point man was named Chris Keffalos. His nickname was "Shakey" and the hill became known nationwide, by way of a CBS TV piece, as "Shakey's Hill." The bunker whose tin roof Keffalos had disturbed was numbered 23. It didn't take a rocket scientist to figure out that there probably were at least twenty-two other bunkers. As it turned out there were fifty-nine, all carefully buried and camouflaged and in some cases booby-trapped. It was an arms-and-ammo cache on the magnitude of the City and Rock Island East, and it was even tougher to get the stuff out because it had been carried in box by box and rifle by rifle. At the battalion and company level of operations, no one could figure out why so much effort was going into the evacuation of AK-47s and other such weapons, plus the tons of ammunition that had no utility whatsoever in South Vietnam. It would have been so much easier and considerably less risky to blow it all in place. No one ever told the people who were breaking their backs over the stuff that it was being collected in a depot near Saigon and shipped to the Cambodian Army. It made sense, since the Cambodians originally were equipped mostly with Eastern Bloc weapons, and it saved considerable tax dollars, but the penchant for secrecy that dogged every step of the Cambodian adventure prevented the troops from knowing the real value of their sweat and blood—blood, because snipers took their toll as the NVA became more aggressive.

For the 1st Cavalry Division, the operations in Cambodia from May 5 until the last unit crossed the border back into Vietnam on June 29 were merely extensions of interdiction operations in the border provinces. Except, of course, the Nixon timetable prevented more thorough searches and better mutual security between positions.

Good soldier that he was, General Davison always answered the questions of the press and visiting congressmen very positively. They would ask: "Doesn't the time and distance limitation inhibit your operations?" And he would dutifully answer, "No, not really. You see, all the major caches are well within that operations zone and, with the monsoon season almost here, the weather would have inhibited us anyway." Davison also noted that the cache discovery curve had flattened and that toward the end of the Cambodian campaign the glut of major supply depot finds had passed.

Whether the general really believed that is irrelevant. The fact is that the 1st Air Cavalry Division had not yet let a monsoon season shut down its activities, and one of the main reasons there were no major cache discoveries toward the end of June is that the Cav was preoccupied in getting its forces out of Cambodia in good order and on time. The NVA, secure in the knowledge that the Cav couldn't linger long enough to pursue them, had filtered major forces back into the border areas and made the final days in Cambodia agonizing.

To curb the VC 5th Division's aggressiveness, the 1st Brigade turned over its AO in eastern Base Area 353 to the 25th Division and moved with two battalions into the O Rang area, which was due north of the II Corps–III Corps boundary. In mid-June, the 5th sent a couple of battalions of its 174th Regiment on a mission of death directed against FSB DAVID, the command post for Bob Kingston and his 1st Brigade headquarters. For two hours the NVA had a go at DAVID, but found that a 1st Cav firebase, even in Cambodia, was too tough a nut to crack. The NVA lost twenty-eight men; the cost to the Americans was twelve wounded.

As the clock wound down on the sixty-day limit, the division began getting ready to move back across the border. One by one, the battalions leapfrogged into Vietnam, until late in the afternoon of June 29, the Skytroopers of the 2nd Battalion, 12th Cavalry, forded the rain-swollen Dak Jerman River on the border under the overwatching Pink Team and the artillery of FSB MO, to become the last 1st Cavalry troopers to leave Cambodia. The 1st of the 8th Cavalry, which had maintained MO for most of the incursion, with its rifle companies making only limited probes across the river into Cambodia, appeared to have missed the glory of the cache discoveries. Every other Cav battalion had turned over extensive caches. The preceding narrative, of neccessity, only covers some of the most highly visible operations.

But, said 1st of the 8th battalion commander Galvin, MO just happened to be sited on one of the NVA's transshipment areas just inside the South Vietnamese border. His folks had been too busy flailing about in Cambodia to pay a lot of attention to the jungle immediately surrounding MO. So, while the great Cambodian souvenir hunt had ended for most of the division because of the Nixon timetable, Galvin's troopers had plenty of time to leisurely pick the final cache as clean as a Thanksgiving turkey wishbone.

18

The Aftermath

At dawn on July 1, 1970, for the first time in nearly sixty days, all of the thirty thousand American soldiers in Vietnam awoke in Vietnam. The RVNAF were still operating inside Cambodia without U.S. advisors. President Thieu had made it clear that he would not be bound by Nixon's sixty-day and thirty-kilometer limits. General Do Cao Tri, the self-styled "Patton of the Parrot's Beak," was taking ARVN armored and mechanized task forces on skillfully conducted incursions. In Vietnam, everyone concerned was terming the operation a huge success, and as a tactical operation, indeed it was.

At home, however, the Nixon administration was under seige. Nixon and other administration spokesmen tried to put the incursion in the most favorable light, but the campuses were aflame and administration loyalists in the Congress were fighting desperate battles to keep the doves from totally gutting the war effort. The disgraceful events at Kent State exacerbated an already difficult situation. Cambodia had given America's radical Left a new rallying point, and in return for the incursion Nixon had received zilch in strategic value. A war leader in a democracy has only a limited amount of political coin and the wise leader does not squander it on incremental tactical victories.

The success of the ARVN operations led many observers to pronounce Vietnamization a success, but closer examination of the composition of the ARVN task forces revealed that Tri had cleverly assembled them to exclude the highly politicized and militarily inept division commanders and their staffs. Tri's task forces used bright, hard-charging colonels and lieutenant colonels. Although the U.S. advisors couldn't cross the border, they clung close to the boundary and helped the ARVN with their logistical and fire-support problems, which were a continuing weakness in RVNAF operations. Strangely, though no American could legally set foot in Cambodia, there was no proscription on the Air Force's flying over it and dropping bombs. Consequently, the ARVN task forces relied heavily on American air support rather than solving their own fire-support problems. They never did solve them—a fundamental weakness.

But for most of the American forces involved in the Cambodian incursion, the month of July was a time to pause, take a deep breath, relax, and count the loot. The Cav's 1st Brigade and two battalions had been redeployed into western War Zone D east of Saigon to get a handle on what remained of main-force communist troops in III Corps. The VC and NVA troops who had holed up in War Zone D had been ordered by Hanoi to disregard their lack of food and war supplies and sally forth to disrupt pacification. Kingston's brigade quickly ran the reconstituted Dong Nai Regiment to ground and scattered its battalions back into the vastness of War Zone D.

In early July, the only fighting in the border provinces was occurring around FSB MO, where the NVA stubbornly declined to give up their caches without a fight. The small firefights over the caches were so close to the firebase that Lieutenant Colonel Galvin often used his battalion mortars to support his infantry units in contact. But other than that, a great quiet settled over northern III Corps. Grunts and lifers alike in the Cav recognized that the Cambodian incursion had made their life in Vietnam infinitely easier. "You couldn't pick a fight" was the general consensus of the airmobile commanders.

The loot that was brought out of Cambodia was mind-boggling. Moreover, the packing lists on some of the materiel indicated it had come by truck from Sihanoukville, despite the CIA's continual assertions that the sole source of supply for the communist effort in the south was via the Ho Chi Minh Trail. But then, the CIA still thought the war in Vietnam was a southern insurgency. Thus it was not surprising that the CIA was disdainful of the allies' claims of casualties inflicted. The combined American and RVNAF commands claimed that 11,369 communists had been killed. The CIA called the figures "highly suspect."

The final tally for all allied forces as of June 30 was:

CASUALTIES

Killed

Enemy	11,369	
Allies	976	(338 U.S.)

Wounded

Allies	4,534	(1,525 U.S.)

Missing or Captured

Enemy (prisoners or ralliers)	2,328	
Allies	48	(13 U.S.)

MATERIEL CAPTURED

Individual weapons	22,892	
Crew-served weapons	2,509	
Small-arms ammunition	16,762,167	rounds
Antiaircraft ammunition	199,552	rounds
Mortar ammunition	68,593	rounds
Rockets, B-40 and B-41	43,160	
Recoilless rifle ammo	29,185	rounds
Hand grenades	62,022	
Explosives	83,000	pounds
Rockets, 107-mm and 122-mm	2,123	
Vehicles, all types	435	
Pharamaceutical products	110,800	pounds
Rice	14,046,000	pounds

What did these figures mean to the communist war effort in the south? The ammunition alone could have supplied all the NVA and VC soldiers in South Vietnam for at least ten months, perhaps longer, depending on the level of activity. The rice would have fed twenty-five thousand communist soldiers for a year, and the weapons were sufficient to equip seventy-four NVA infantry battalions.

Not surprisingly, the 1st Air Cavalry Division provided a disproportionate share of the booty, between 35 and 40 percent of the final totals. By itself, the Cav had killed enough enemy soldiers to form three NVA regiments. It found more than 350 caches and captured 6,100 individual and 900 crew-served weapons. The number of weapons captured would have outfitted thirty-five 250-man enemy battalions, and the rice captured by the Skytroopers would have fed those battalions for a year. The Cav also sustained the heaviest casualties of any American unit, with 123 dead, 966 wounded, and 16 missing in action.

For the Cav, the booty seized in Cambodia was much like getting an early payoff on deferred compensation. Sooner or later, the NVA would have had to try moving the rice, arms, and ammunition down to the infiltration trails. And when that happened, the Cav's interdiction program, which would have continued unabated until the division was redeployed home, would have captured it all anyway. Consider the cumulative results of the Cav's interdiction campaign from February 1969 to April 30, 1970. The division and its attached units had killed 16,143 enemy soldiers, most of them North Vietnamese. It had captured 3,240 individual weapons and 726 crew-served weapons, with 1.2 million small-caliber rounds of ammunition. It had captured more than fifteen hundred tons of rice.

When General Abrams started the interdiction campaign in Military Region III, the VC and NVA had sizable base areas within fifteen kilometers of the Saigon city limits. The units that worked the areas around Saigon eventually turned over most of those and the communists were unable to reconstitute them because of the noose the Cav had placed on the infiltration routes. As the pacification campaign began taking its toll on the Viet Cong infrastructure and the villages and hamlets became more secure, the VC's usual source of food supplies and manpower gradually dried up.

When the Cav started its campaign after beating back the North Vietnamese attacks on Saigon, the Cambodian sanctuaries were less a factor than Base Area 355 just north of the Michelin Plantation, or the supposedly impenetrable War Zone C, or the Rang Rang caches in War Zone D.

One of the great mysteries of the war is why the year 1969 and Abrams's interdiction and pacification programs disappeared from the pages of history. The Cambodian incursion simply could not have been mounted unless most of Military Region III had been cleared of enemy forces. A writer in the *New York Times Magazine* once noted that General Abrams "deserved a better war." It might also be said that he and the primary instrument of his strategy, the 1st Air Cavalry Division, deserved better from historians.

EPILOGUE

Late on the afternoon of July 6, Major General George Casey finished editing a draft of a command letter he wanted to go to every Skytrooper in the 1st Air Cavalry Division. Later that evening the general's typist returned the final copy for Casey's signature. Casey sat back in his chair and read the letter one last time.

The letter, styled in the rigid format of military correspondence, read:

1. As you know, the 1st Air Cavalry Division has been involved in operations against enemy sanctuaries in Cambodia for the past two months.

2. The results of these operations have far exceeded expectations. It has been the most successful operation in the history of the 1st Air Cavalry Division.

3. All members of the FIRST TEAM have done their part. Each one of you, doing his own job each day to the best of his ability, has contributed to the team effort—the maintenance men who kept our helicopters flying and the aviators who so gallantly flew them for more hours than they have ever flown before; the engineers who carried the massive construction load; the support personnel who worked so long and hard to keep supplies flowing to our extended front; the signalmen who accomplished near impossible feats of communication; the artillerymen who rained tons of steel on the enemy every day; the aerial scouts who sought out the enemy wherever he might try to hide; and

—most of all—the infantrymen who grappled with a tenacious enemy and searched out his hidden caches. All of you together made this success possible and deserve the accolade of the FIRST TEAM.

4. The results are impressive. You killed enough of the enemy to man three NVA Regiments; captured or destroyed enough individual and crew-served weapons to equip two NVA Divisions; and denied the enemy an entire year's supply of rice for all of his maneuver battalions in our AO. You captured more rocket, mortar and recoilless rifle rounds than the enemy fired in all of III Corps during the twelve months preceding our move into Cambodia. And, perhaps most important, by working together in an airmobile team, you disrupted the enemy's entire supply system, making chaos of his base areas and killing or driving off his rear service personnel.

5. Only time will tell how long it will take the NVA to recover, but of this you can be sure—you have set the enemy back sufficiently to permit President Nixon's redeployment plan to procede with safety while assuring that our Vietnamese allies maintain their freedom. This is your achievement. This is yet another demonstration that you of the 1st Air Cavalry Division deserve—and have earned again—the accolade of the FIRST TEAM. It is my honor to have served alongside you during this crucial and historic period.

Satisfied that the letter expressed exactly how he felt about the men he commanded, he signed the letter with a flourish. Then, in the company of Chief of Staff E. C. Meyer, he strolled the thirty yards to the building containing the general's mess. The night was going to be special, the "last night at the mess" farewell to a trusted associate of the general, Chief Warrant Officer Larry Anczjak, the aviator who had flown left seat in the general's command chopper during the months Casey had been in the division. The other Cav generals actually flew their birds and their left-seat pilots were used to monitor gauges, check in and out of artillery boxes, and generally make themselves useful in the cockpit. In Casey's bird, the left-seat pilot had to do it all. Casey had been through the Fort Rucker "instant aviator" course and obtained his wings, the necessary precondition to be a general officer in the Cav. Nevertheless, he mostly disdained the opportunity to play aviator and used the right cockpit of the aircraft as an office from which to work the battlefield.

The next day, a Tuesday, General Casey planned visits to several hospitals to talk to wounded Skytroopers before they were evacuated to Japan or the United States. Lieutenant Colonel Ric Ordway said Casey wanted it to be more than the usual Sunday morale-boosting visits traditionally engaged in by the Cav generals. Ordway's G-3 shop had put together map boards and charts, which could be used to provide an informational briefing to the Skytroopers about the success of the just-completed Cambodian incursion. Casey wanted to deliver in person the message in the letter he had just signed. Ordway said the original plan was for he and the G-2, Lieutenant Colonel Mike Conrad, to accompany Casey on the briefing trip, but Meyer at the last moment talked Casey out of taking two key members of the senior staff. Because the division weathermen forecast atrocious flying weather between Phuoc Vinh and Casey's first scheduled stop, a hospital at Cam Ranh Bay, Meyer did his best to dissuade Casey from making the trip at all.

But Meyer's protests were to no avail; Casey stubbornly insisted that the trip was important. The best Meyer could do was to lay on a chase ship to accompany the general when he left the next morning. The flight path to Cam Ranh Bay was due east, and the flight had to pass across some of the highest mountains in Vietnam. At about 10:10 A.M. the pilots of the chase ship saw Casey's Huey, now with First Lieutenant William F. Michel in the left seat, fly into a dense cloud. Casey's aircraft never emerged.

Three days later, search aircraft spotted wreckage on a mountainside. There were no survivors of the crash. When Casey perished in the crash, general officer watchers at the time said that the Army had just lost a future chief of staff. Dying with Casey and Michel was Casey's aide, Captain John A. Hottel III, West Pointer and Rhodes Scholar and author of the brilliant case study of the battle of Binh Long, who had general officer written all over his career. Command Sergeant Major Kenneth Cooper, a veteran of three wars and on his second tour with the Cav, was in the aircraft and died that day, as did three specialist fourth class troopers—William L. Christenson, the door gunner; Ronald F. Fuller, the crew chief; and Vernon K. Smolik, a stenographer. The cause of the crash was never officially determined. The best theory was that the pilot may have suffered an attack of vertigo when he entered the cloud bank, and without a copilot who had his head down and his eyes on the gauges to help him, never recovered from the initial loss of orientation and control.

When the news of Casey's death reached the United States, Frank Reynolds, then anchoring for ABC News, said of the fallen general:

General George Casey was one of those men who had soldier written all over him; a man for whom the responsibilities of high command were much more important that its privileges. He accepted all of the first, and abused none of the second. General Casey knew war and hated it. He was a splendid example of a military man who was not really militaristic. We don't give him much credit, but it is still an imperfect world, and the time will certainly come when not only will the George Caseys be *needed*, they may even be appreciated.

For its accomplishments in Cambodia, the division was recommended for its second Presidential Unit Citation. The first award was for the historic Pleiku Campaign. That the division received the first award was due as much to untiring lobbying efforts in the Pentagon by the division's former commander, Lieutenant General Harry Kinnard, and some of his close associates, as it was the division's combat record. Sadly, with Casey's death, there was no champion for the division this time around.

It is problematical, though, whether the division would have been recognized had Casey lived. The mood in Melvin Laird's Pentagon, while it didn't reflect American society in general, was nonetheless decidedly unreceptive to making a big deal out of an operation that was so controversial. The division instead settled for quietly accepting a Valorous Unit Citation—not too shabby an award, since it represented a unit equivalent of the Silver Star.

Casey went to his death convinced the 1st Cav's operations had bought the Allies valuable time. That, perhaps, was the greatest value of the incursion—it bought some time. Kissinger said the invasion bought fifteen months. Sir Robert Thompson, who defeated a communist insurgency in Malaysia and who had been very critical of the American command's conduct of the war, said his analysis of the Cambodian incursion persuaded him that the allies had set the NVA offensive timetable back "at least a year, probably eighteen months and possibly two years."

On April 1, 1972, three North Vietnamese divisions staging out of their rebuilt bases in Cambodia made an all-out assault on the northern Binh Long Province town of Loc Ninh, quickly overrunning it. Nearly all the Americans had gone home by then, and the defense of III Corps was up to the ARVN. The Cambodian incursion had bought the Thieu government twenty-three months.

That the time was squandered, and how, is another story entirely.

GLOSSARY

ACAV: Armored Cavalry Assault Vehicle. Basically an M-113 armored personnel carrier modified with armored machine-gun turrets for jungle warfare.

ACR: Armored Cavalry Regiment.

ADC: Assistant Division Commander.

AK-47: Standard NVA assault rifle.

Alpha: The letter A in the Army phonetic alphabet, used to spell out words in radio conversations. Thus A Company could also be known as Alpha Company.

AO: Area of Operations.

ARA: Aerial Rocket Artillery.

Arty: Abbreviation for Artillery.

ARVN: Army of the Republic of Vietnam; pronounced ARVIN.

AT: Antitank.

AVLB: Armored-Vehicle-Launched Bridge.

Battery: The basic building-block unit in the artillery, i.e., firing battery; also, the smallest unit in the artillery in which the commissioned leader is considered a commander.

Beehive: An artillery round containing steel dartlike flechettes.

Berm: The earthworks pushed up by bulldozers that formed the basis for defensive bunkers on firebases.

Blues: Rifle platoon of the 1st Squadron, 9th Cavalry.

Bravo: The letter B in the Army phonetic alphabet.

C-130: Air Force Hercules transport aircraft.

CA: Combat Assault; usually called a Charlie Alpha by the troops.

C *and* C: Command and control; the troops also called it a Charlie-Charlie. Aircraft in which a troop or unit commander circles a battle area to direct the conduct of the fight.

Cannister: A tank gun round; also, a round for artillery, and for the M-79 grenade launcher that fired a charge of steel ball bearings.

CG: Commanding General.

Charlie: The letter C in the phonetic alphabet; also slang for Viet Cong.

Chieu Hoi: Vietnamese for "Open arms," the name of the program for giving enemy soldiers an opportunity to rally to the cause of the government of South Vietnam.

Chinook: The official name of the CH-47 tandem rotor transport helicopter. Also known to soldiers as a "Hook."

Chopper: Helicopter.

CIDG: Civilian Irregular Defense Group. Indigenous populations recruited to serve with Special Forces units.

CINCPAC: Commander in Chief, Pacific.

Claymore: Antipersonnel mine that spews out seven hundred steel balls in a sixty-degree arc; lethal up to fifty meters.

Cobra: The nickname for the AH-1G gunship that replaced the B-model Huey gunship in 1967.

Company: The basic building-block unit for all nonartillery and noncavalry units in the Army; also, the smallest unit in which the commissioned leader is considered a commander.

COMUSMACV: Commander, U.S. Military Assistance Command, Vietnam.

CORDS: Civil Operation and Revolutionary Development Support.

COSVN: Central Office for South Vietnam. It also was known as the B-3 Front, one of four fronts the North Vietnamese Politburo maintained in the South to conduct the war.

CP: Command Post.

CS: Tear gas.

CTZ: Corps Tactical Zone, numbered I through IV north to south. The zones were as much administrative as tactical. The ARVN use of the term "corps" caused the American forces to

invent euphemisms for a corps-level command structure, e.g.,
II Field Force.

Delta: The letter D in the phonetic alphabet; also, Delta Teams
were long-range patrol teams in 5th Special Forces.

DivArty: Division Artillery, the term usually means the headquarters, but could also refer to all of the artillery in the division.

Division: The Army's major maneuver element, ranging in
strength from eighteen thousand to twenty-four thousand men,
depending on the type; commanded by a two-star general.

Dong Tien: A Vietnamese term meaning "progress together."
The name for the "buddy-up" concept used in the Vietnamization program in III Corps.

DTOC: Division Tactical Operations Center.

Echo: The letter E in the phonetic alphabet.

EM: Enlisted man (men).

FAC: Forward Air Controller; an officer of the air-control team
who directs air strikes from the ground or air.

Flare: As a noun, an illumination device; as a verb, the landing
attitude of an aircraft.

FO: Forward Observer. Usually provided by the supporting artillery batteries to the rifle companies to adjust artillery fire by
radio or other means; may also be sent from mortar platoons
to rifle platoons to direct mortar fire.

Frag: Fragmentation grenade; also, as a verb, used to denote a
fragmentary order for a unit action or movement.

FSB: Fire Support Base.

G-1: Personnel officer at division level or higher.

G-2: Intelligence officer at division level.

G-3: Operations and training officer at division level.

G-4: Logistics officer at division level.

GI: Term for American soldier, carried over from World War II.

Green Berets: Popular name for the Special Forces, taken from
the color of their distinctive headgear.

Green Line: The generic term for the outer defensive ring of
bunkers at most base camps.

Grunt: The term used throughout Vietnam for the line infantryman. Its origin is unknown, but one popular story is that it
arose from the soldier's grunting as he hoisted his heavy rucksack onto his back prior to moving out.

HE: High Explosive ammunition.

Hoi Chanh: The Vietnamese term for an enemy soldier who rallied to the cause of the government of Vietnam. See also Chieu Hoi.

HQ: Headquarters.

Huey: UH-1, the utility helicopter that was the workhorse of Vietnam. The name arose from the original designation of the aircraft—HU-1 (Helicopter, Utility). The Army's official name, Iroquois, never caught on.

JCS: Joint Chiefs of Staff

KIA: Killed In Action.

Killer Junior: The term in the 1st Cavalry for an artillery shell fired at a level trajectory with a fuse set to detonate at a point just beyond the berm.

Klick: Slang shorthand for kilometer.

Logging: Sending logistics helicopters to troop units—the airmobile equivalent of the kitchen and supply trucks of WW II and Korea.

LP: Listening Post.

LRRP: Long-Range Reconnaissance Patrol unit.

LZ: Landing Zone.

M-16: U.S. caliber 5.56-mm, the basic rifle of the infantryman.

M-60: U.S. caliber 7.62-mm, platoon and company machine gun.

M-72: Light antitank weapon, called a LAW. Fired a 66-mm projectile from a disposable launcher. Used as a bunker-buster in Vietnam.

M-79: The 40-mm grenade launcher that looked like a stubby sawed-off shotgun. It fired both HE and cannister rounds. A popular weapon for men walking point.

MACV: Military Assistance Command, Vietnam, the highest U.S. command authority in the Republic of Vietnam.

Medevac: Term used in the 1st Cavalry for aerial medical evacuation.

Medic: Medical aid man.

MR: Military Region. Both North and South used MRs to denote geographical areas.

Nam Bo: A term used interchangeably by the communists for the area usually referred to as South Vietnam.

Napalm: Jellied gasoline used in air strikes.

NCO: Noncommissioned officer, a sergeant; sometimes referred to as noncom.

Net: Short for radio network. All tactical radios operated within a defined network on a designated frequency.

NLF: National Liberation Front. The front organization created by Hanoi to make it appear that the Vietnam War was exclusively a southern civil war.

NSC: National Security Council.

NSDM: National Security Decision Memorandum.

NSSM: National Security Study Memorandum.

NVA: North Vietnam Army. Generic term for any soldier or group of soldiers from the North.

OP: Observation post.

Order of battle: Listing of units committed to a theater of operations. Obtaining a correct OB on the enemy was a major intelligence operation.

OSD: Office of the Secretary of Defense.

PF: Popular Forces. Native military forces locally recruited and employed within their home districts by district chiefs.

PIO: Public Information Officer.

Police: Military term for clean-up of an area. Implies a clean, thorough search of the battlefield.

POW: Prisoner Of War.

PRC-25: Backpack FM radio—basic communications for nearly every level of command within the division.

Prep: Short term for preparatory fire on a landing zone.

R and R: Rest and Recuperation.

Recon: Reconnaissance.

RF: Regional Forces. Native military forces recruited and employed by province chief within a province. Along with PF, popularly known as "RuffPuffs."

Rome Plow: A standard D7E tractor equipped with a heavy-duty protective cab and a special canted tree-cutting blade. It was manufactured in Rome, Georgia. Its great efficiency in knocking down tall hardwoods and cleaning out underbrush made the name "Rome Plow" synonymous with land-clearing operations in Vietnam.

RPD: Soviet (North Vietnamese) caliber 7.62-mm light machine gun.

RPG: Soviet rocket-propelled grenade that fired an 82-mm warhead. Basically an antitank weapon, the NVA used it mostly as an antipersonnel weapon.

RTO: Radio Telephone Operator.

RVN: Republic of Vietnam.

RVNAF: Republic of Vietnam Armed Forces.

S-1: Personnel officer at brigade or battalion.

S-2: Intelligence officer at brigade or battalion.

S-3: Operations and training officer at brigade or battalion.

S-4: Supply officer at brigade or battalion.

Sapper: Soldier trained to attack fortifications. Extensively used by VC and NVA after Tet-68.

Satchel Charge: Explosive package fitted with a handle for ease of handling or throwing.

Sitrep: Situation report.

SKS: Soviet carbine.

Slick: Term for the Huey troop transport, so named because it lacked the outboard weapons mounts of the early gunships. Even though the Cobra had replaced the B-model Huey gunship, the term was still used extensively in 1969.

Strikers: Slang for members of the Strike Force, a military force recruited by the American Special Forces. *See also* CIDG.

Strip Alert: State of readiness for a reaction force; generally meant they were either next to the aircraft or actually sitting in an aircraft parked along an airstrip.

TOC: Tactical Operations Center.

USAF: United States Air Force.

USARV: U.S. Army Vietnam; the Army component headquarters that controlled logistics.

VC: Viet Cong, also known as Victor Charlie.

VCI: Viet Cong Infrastructure.

Vulcan: A six-barrel 20-mm Gatling gun mounted on a modified armored personnel carrier chassis.

WIA: Wounded In Action.

XO: Executive Officer. The assistant to the commander of a unit below division level. Corresponds to the chief of staff at higher-level headquarters.

SELECTED BIBLIOGRAPHY

BOOKS

Chanoff, David, and Doan Van Toai. *Portrait of the Enemy*. New York: Random House, 1986.

Charlton, Michael, and Anthony Moncrief. *Many Reasons Why: The American Involvement in Vietnam*. New York: Hill and Wang, 1978.

Clarke, Jeffrey J. *Advise and Support: The Final Years, 1965–1973*. Washington, D.C.: United States Army Center of Military History, 1988.

Colby, William E. *Honorable Men*. New York: Simon & Schuster, 1978.

———. *Lost Victory*. Chicago: Contemporary Books, 1989.

Davidson, Lieutenant General (Ret.) Phillip B. *Vietnam at War, The History: 1946–1975*. Novato, Calif.: Presidio Press, 1988.

Garrett, Banning, Katherine Barkley, et al., editors. *Two, Three, Many Vietnams: A Radical Reader on the Wars in Southeast Asia and the Conflict at Home*. San Francisco: Canfield Press, 1971.

Gibson, James W. *The Perfect War: Technowar in Vietnam*. Boston: Atlantic Monthly Press, 1986.

Goldman, Peter, and Tony Fuller. *Charlie Company: What Vietnam Did to Us*. New York: William Morrow, 1983.

Goodman, Allan E. *The Lost Peace: America's Search for a Ne-*

gotiated Settlement of the Vietnam War. Stanford, Calif.: Hoover Institution Press, 1978.

Hackworth, Colonel (Ret.) David B., and Julie Sherman. *About Face.* New York: Simon & Schuster, 1989.

Hammond, William M. *Public Affairs: The Military and the Media, 1962–1968.* Washington, D.C.: United States Army Center of Military History, 1988.

Hannah, Norman B. *The Key to Failure: Laos and the Vietnam War.* Lanham, Md.: Madison Books, 1987.

Kalb, Marvin, and Ellie Able. *Roots of Involvement: The U.S. and Asia, 1784–1971.* New York: W.W. Norton, 1971.

Kalb, Marvin, and Bernard Kalb. *Kissinger.* Boston: Little, Brown & Co., 1974.

Karnow, Stanley. *Vietnam, A History: The First Complete Account of Vietnam at War.* New York: The Viking Press, 1983.

Kinnard, Douglas. *The War Managers.* Hanover, N.H.: University Press of New England, 1977.

Kirk, Donald. *Wider War.* New York: Praeger Publishers, 1971.

Kissinger, Henry. *The White House Years.* Boston: Little, Brown & Co., 1979.

Kolko, Gabriel. *Anatomy of a War: Vietnam, the United States, and the Modern Historical Experience.* New York: Pantheon Books, 1985.

Komer, Robert W. *Bureaucracy Does Its Thing: Institutional Constraints on U.S.-GVN Performance in Vietnam.* Santa Monica, Calif.: The Rand Corporation, 1972.

Krepinevich, Andrew F. *The Army and Vietnam.* New York: Johns Hopkins University Press, 1986.

Lipsman, Samuel, Edward Doyle, Robert Manning, et al. *The Vietnam Experience: Fighting for Time, 1969–70.* Boston: Boston Publishing Co., 1984.

Maclear, Michael. *The Ten Thousand Day War.* New York: St. Martin's Press, 1981.

Mathews, Lloyd J., and Dale E. Brown, editors. *Assessing the Vietnam War: A Collection from the Journal of the U.S. Army War College.* Washington, D.C.: Pergamon-Brassey's International Defense Publishers, 1987.

Morrison, Wilbur H. *The Elephant and the Tiger: The Full Story of the Vietnam War.* New York: Hippocrene Books, 1990.

Nixon, Richard. *No More Vietnams*. New York, Arbor House Publishing, 1985.

Nolan, Keith W. *Into Cambodia: Spring Campaign, Summer Offensive, 1970*. Novato, Calif.: Presidio Press, 1990.

Palmer, Bruce, Jr. *The Twenty-Five Year War: America's Military Role in Vietnam*. Lexington, Ky.: University of Kentucky Press, 1984.

Palmer, David Richard. *Summons of the Trumpet: U.S.-Vietnam in Perspective*. San Rafael, Calif.: Presidio Press, 1978.

Pike, Douglas. *PAVN: People's Army of Vietnam*. Novato, Calif.: Presidio Press, 1986.

Robinson, Anthony, editor. *Weapons of the Vietnam War*. New York: Gallery Books, 1983.

Scovill, Thomas W. *Reorganizing for Pacification Support*. Washington, D.C.: U.S. Army Center of Military History, 1982.

Shawcross, William. *Sideshow: Kissinger, Nixon and the Destruction of Cambodia*. New York: Simon & Schuster, 1979.

Sheehan, Neil. *A Bright Shining Lie: John Paul Vann and America in Vietnam*. New York: Random House, 1988.

Sihanouk, Norodom. *My War With the CIA*. New York: Pantheon Books, 1973.

Stanton, Shelby. *Anatomy of a Division: 1st Cav in Vietnam*. Novato, Calif.: Presidio Press, 1987.

———. *The Rise and Fall of an American Army: U.S. Ground Forces in Vietnam, 1965–1973*. Novato, Calif.: Presidio Press, 1985.

———. *U.S. Army and Allied Ground Forces in Vietnam Order of Battle*. Washington, D.C.: U.S. News Books, 1981.

Starry, Donn. *Vietnam Studies: Mounted Combat in Vietnam*. Washington, D.C.: Department of the Army, 1978.

Summers, Harry G. *On Strategy: A Critical Analysis of the Vietnam War*. Novato, Calif.: Presidio Press, 1982.

———. *Vietnam War Almanac*. New York: Facts On File Publications, 1985.

Thompson, Sir Robert. *No Exit from Vietnam*. New York: David McKay, 1969.

———. *Peace Is Not at Hand*. New York: David McKay, 1974.

Tolson, John J. *Vietnam Studies: Airmobility 1961–1971.* Washington, D.C.: Department of the Army, 1973.

Welsh, Douglas. *The History of the Vietnam War.* New York: Exeter Books, 1981.

Williams, William Appleman, Thomas McCormick, Lloyd Gardner, and Walter LaFeber, editors and commentators. *America in Vietnam: A Documentary History.* New York: Anchor Books, 1985.

Zaffiri, Samuel. *Hamburger Hill, May 11–20, 1969.* Novato, Calif., Presidio Press, 1988.

GOVERNMENT PUBLICATIONS
LIMITED DISTRIBUTION INDOCHINA MONOGRAPHS

Cao Van Vien, General, and Lieutenant General Dong Van Khuyen. *Reflections on the Vietnam War.* Washington, D.C.: U.S. Army Center of Military History, 1978.

Dong Van Khuyen, Lieutenant General. *The RVNAF.* Washington, D.C.: U.S. Army Center of Military History, 1978.

Ngoc Lung Hoang, Colonel. *The General Offensives of 1968–69.* Washington, D.C.: U.S. Army Center of Military History, 1978.

———. *Intelligence.* Washington, D.C.: U.S. Army Center of Military History, 1976.

Ngo Quang Truong, Lieutenant General. *RVNAF and U.S. Operational Cooperation and Coordination.* Washington, D.C.: U.S. Army Center of Military History, 1978.

Nguyen Duy Hinh, Major General. *Vietnamization and the Cease-Fire.* Washington, D.C.: U.S. Army Center of Military History, 1978.

Sak Sutsakhan, Lieutenant General. *The Khmer Republic at War and the Final Collapse.* Washington, D.C.: U.S. Army Center of Military History, 1978.

Tran Dinh Tho, Brigadier General. *Pacification.* Washington, D.C.: U.S. Army Center of Military History, 1977.

———. *The Cambodian Incursion.* Washington, D.C.: U.S. Army Center of Military History, 1977.

PERIODICALS, UNPUBLISHED MONOGRAPHS, MILITARY HISTORIES

Gidland, Carl A. *"The Vietnam Courier* in 1966: An Instrument of Propaganda."* Master's thesis, University of Montana, 1967.

Kalloch, Aaron E. "The American Invasion of Cambodia: May–June, 1970." Undergraduate thesis, United States Military Academy, May 1990.

Unofficial division history. *The 1st Air Cavalry Division, Vietnam, August, 1965 to December, 1969.* Information Office, 1st Air Cavalry Division, April 1970.

Unofficial division history. *The First Team, 1970–1971.* Information Office, 1st Air Cavalry Division, Fall 1971.

Unofficial history. *The First Infantry Division in Vietnam, Vol. III, 1969.*

Unofficial history, *Tropic Lightning: A History of the 25th Infantry Division.* December 1969.

14th Military History Detachment, 1st Cavalry Division. *The Shield and the Hammer: The 1st Cavalry Division (Airmobile) in War Zone C and Western III Corps,* August 1969.

14th Military History Detachment, 1st Cavalry Division. (Principal author: Captain John A. Hottell) *The Battle of Binh Long Province.* September 1969.

The Cavalair. Weekly newspaper of the 1st Cavalry Division. Issues from October 1968 through July 1970.

The First Team, quarterly magazine of the 1st Cavalry Division. Issues from October 1968 through August 1970.

Operational Reports, Lessons Learned for the 1st Cavalry Division (Airmobile). Issued quarterly. From November 1968 through July 31, 1970.

ABOUT THE AUTHOR

J. D. Coleman, a retired U.S. Army lieutenant colonel, served in Korea and Vietnam and earned a Silver Star. As a journalist he won an Associated Press Managing Editors Award. He wrote this book while the director of public affairs for the Georgia Department of Public Safety in Atlanta. He has since moved back to his original home of Kalispell, Montana, where he is employed as the public affairs officer for the Flathead National Forest. He also is the author of *Pleiku: The Dawn of Helicopter Warfare in Vietnam.*

INDEX